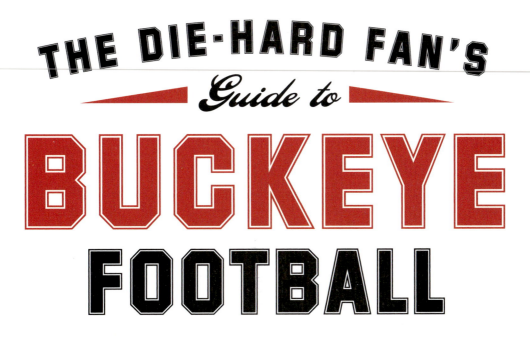

THE DIE-HARD FAN'S
Guide to
BUCKEYE
FOOTBALL

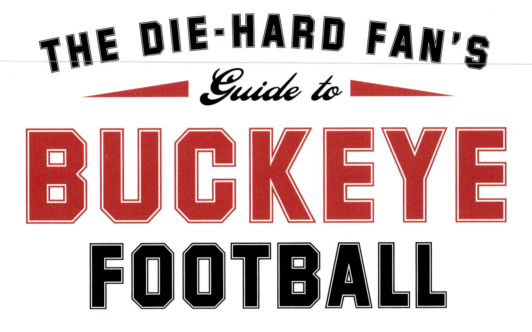

THE DIE-HARD FAN'S
Guide to
BUCKEYE
FOOTBALL

MARK REA

Since 1947
REGNERY
PUBLISHING, INC.
An Eagle Publishing Company • Washington, DC

ISBN 978-1-59698-573-5

Published in the United States by
Regnery Publishing, Inc.
One Massachusetts Avenue, NW
Washington, DC 20001
www.regnery.com

Manufactured in the United States of America

10 9 8 7 6 5 4 3 2 1

Books are available in quantity for promotional or premium use. Write to Director of Special Sales, Regnery Publishing, Inc., One Massachusetts Avenue NW, Washington, DC 20001, for information on discounts and terms or call (202) 216-0600.

Distributed to the trade by:
Perseus Distribution
387 Park Avenue South
New York, NY 10016

For Mom, Dad, Jess,
and especially Lisa,
my biggest fan.

CONTENTS

Foreword

BY REX KERN

IX

Introduction

XIII

Chapter 1

HOW BUCKEYE FOOTBALL WAS BORN

1

Chapter 2

THE EARLY YEARS

23

Chapter 3

LITTLE-KNOWN FACTS ABOUT OHIO STATE'S FOOTBALL COACHES

49

Chapter 4

WOODY COMES TO COLUMBUS

65

Chapter 5

THE HOUSE THAT HARLEY BUILT

95

Chapter 6
THE BEST OF THE BEST: HEISMANS AND NATIONAL CHAMPIONSHIPS
127

Chapter 7
TOP TEN OSU PLAYERS BY DECADE
161

Chapter 8
THE BEST DAMN FANS IN THE LAND
209

Chapter 9
OHIO STATE VS. MICHIGAN: THE GREATEST NORTH AMERICAN SPORTS RIVALRY
231

Buckeye Quiz
287

Acknowledgments
289

Index
293

Foreword

BY REX KERN,

FORMER BUCKEYE QUARTERBACK AND 1968 NATIONAL CHAMPION

The history of Ohio State's glorious football legacy is made up of wonderful stories, spanning the ranks of our coaches, players and all the football staff personnel that have been a part of more than 115 years of Buckeye Football Tradition. There are infinite stories about our storied history and it takes at least an hour to tell any one of them.

For me, it has been nearly forty years since I stepped off the Ohio Stadium field for the last time but in some respects it feels like just yesterday. My memories remain vivid of the events before my first game as a Buckeye, our season opener in 1968 at the Horseshoe against Southern Methodist.

Woody had the gameday schedule and times boldly written on **"his blackboard!"** The schedule was made out to the minute and we, the sophomores, were warned by the upperclassmen to never, ever be late! So promptly at 12:10 p.m., the quarterbacks and centers entered the field. I looked around and saw just how large the stadium was. I stood in awe of "The House Harley Built." Wow! You feel so small during a moment like that. Then when Woody entered the field, he seemed larger than life itself.

10 20 30 40 50 40 30 20 10

Just then, Jan Fetters, the captain of our great Ohio State cheerleaders, who incidentally was from my hometown of Lancaster, Ohio, came over to greet me and wish me luck. As Jan was wishing me good luck, a photographer from our hometown paper wanted a picture of Jan and me with the stadium in the background. I really believe that helped relax me for the game that day. At least I seemed to breathe a little easier from that point on. When we came out as a team, I don't remember my feet touching the ground nor being in my body. Hearing the roar of the crowd, and the playing of our great TBDBITL as it played "Across The Field" was one of my greatest experiences.

Later that year when we began our training for the Rose Bowl, on our very first day of bowl practice, the running backs were having a tackling drill. The quarterbacks were not involved in this drill, so we weren't paying much attention to it. However, everyone was pumped up, we were going to the Rose Bowl, Woody had turned the heat up in French Fieldhouse to about 98-plus degrees and he somehow decided it was a good idea to have the quarterbacks hit the tackling dummy.

Fired up and not knowing any better, we ran over to Woody and got ready to hit the tackling dummy. I was first in line, so I stepped up and flew into that thing and promptly fell down in a heap. Woody came running up in a panic as I was writhing on the ground in pain and asked me what had happened. I said, "Coach, I think I dislocated my shoulder."

He yelled a couple of things you probably wouldn't want to repeat in mixed company and then called over our longtime trainer Ernie Biggs who confirmed my initial diagnosis. Luckily, the injury was to my left shoulder.

Woody stood up, shook his head, sighed, and then in true Woody fashion said, "All right, you quarterbacks. That's enough of that for today."

I couldn't practice at all until we arrived on the West Coast, and even then I had to wear a special harness that wouldn't allow me to raise my left arm any higher than a ninety-degree angle. The harness took some time getting used to because of my new limitations but it worked almost to perfection during the game—except at the end of the third quarter when I got hit, I dislocated the shoulder again. I ran promptly to the sideline and Ernie quickly reset the shoulder for me. I didn't miss a play and we were able to beat a great Southern Cal team and win the National Championship.

Stories like these and countless others make college football such a great game and give Ohio State the rich tradition it enjoys today. College football history has been written time after time by young men proudly wearing the Scarlet and Gray—from Chic Harley, Ohio State's first true star of the gridiron, to Archie Griffin, the sport's only two-time Heisman Trophy winner, to Troy Smith, the latest Buckeye to be honored with the Heisman.

Those players are but a very, very small sampling of the names synonymous with Ohio State football. Each, and many more like them, had a defining moment during his career that elevated the athlete from the viewpoint of football historians and fans to legendary status. The only reason I am included in this book is because of my teammates. I share this place in history with them because they— my and other players' teammates even though they might not be mentioned here—are legendary.

So please enjoy *The Die-Hard Fan's Guide to Buckeye Football* which will detail the careers of such long-ago Buckeyes as Woody, Paul Brown, Bill Willis, Les Horvath, Vic Janowicz, Hopalong Cassady, and Jim Parker as well as contemporary stars like Chris Spielman, Joe Germaine, Craig Krenzel, and Eddie George. There are even a few lines about an old quarterback who was lucky to be in the right place at the right time in 1968, playing with a bunch of guys who were the greatest teammates anyone could ever ask for!

How much does Ohio State mean to me? I have been defined by The Ohio State University and I am proud to be a Buckeye. It is also a great source of pride that I was able to fulfill the hopes Woody Hayes and Fred Taylor had for me. To them, a college degree from The Ohio State University was more important than winning a National Championship. In fact, I fulfilled the hopes of Woody, Fred, and even myself with three degrees (bachelor's, master's, and doctorate).

I'm so proud of our rich football tradition that forever links my teammates and me to the men who played before us and the ones who performed long after we left campus. I am always proud to be a Buckeye! After you read the stories within these pages, it is my hope that you will feel the very same way as I do.

"How firm thy friendship … O-HI-O!"

—Rex Kern, Ole #10

Introduction

With all due apologies to Noah Webster and his dictionary, the word "fan" cannot be distilled to a simple description of "an enthusiastic devotee (as of a sport) usually as a spectator."

To truly understand the meaning of the word "fan," especially when the adjectives "die-hard" and "Buckeye" are placed before it, you have to experience the level of enthusiasm and devotion. Terms such as "off-the-charts" don't even begin to explain it.

To understand the relationship Ohio State football fans have with their team is to understand the very basic tenets of a love story. Entire generations have been weaned on Scarlet and Gray, and when it is their turn, they pass the folklore and traditions on to the next. It's nearly impossible to be anything but a die-hard fan, because there's no such thing as a casual follower of the Buckeyes. Each Saturday in the fall, millions live well when the team wins and die hard when they lose.

It was pretty much the same way in my house while I was growing up. My love for all things Scarlet and Gray came from my father, a proud 1940 graduate of The Ohio State University. It's not difficult to conjure up memories of Dad tinkering in the back yard on a football Saturday with the radio tuned to the game and the dulcet tones of Bert Charles and Marv Homan filling the crisp October air.

The first season I truly remember came in 1968—a pretty good year to cut your teeth on the Buckeyes—and following the exploits of Jack Tatum, Jim Stillwagon, Jim Otis, Ted Provost, and Rex Kern (my personal favorite) became a week-to-week obsession. My mind's eye still has a vivid picture of that Rose Bowl game against USC and the rising jubilation of a second-half Ohio State comeback after O. J. Simpson had staked the Trojans to an early 10–0 lead.

My favorite team won every game that season and were crowned national champions. I thought undefeated seasons and Rose Bowl victories were a birthright, especially when the Buckeyes won every game in 1969, too, before suffering a crushing upset in the season finale at Michigan. Four decades later, that one still stings. No wonder why OSU die-hards have no sympathy for "That School Up North."

Ohio State football has been equated to a religion, and it's hard to argue that point. Ohio Stadium is the cathedral, "Across the Field" and "Carmen Ohio" are the hymns, and the national championship continues to be the holy grail. Coaches such as Earle Bruce and Jim Tressel are viewed as disciples of the legendary Woody Hayes. The exploits of long-gone players such as Chic Harley and Wes Fesler have been reduced to ancient texts in musty corners, but their stories continue to be told and re-told through the years.

It's Brutus and Sloopy. It's the Horseshoe and The Best Damn Band in the Land. It's Gold Pants and Senior Tackle and a thousand more traditions that make Ohio State football what it is.

Most of all, it's the fans—the die-hards for whom this book was written. The tall ones and the small ones. The young and the old. Those who can buy anything they want, and those who struggle paycheck to paycheck. The ones who have season tickets, and the ones who have never laid their eyes on Ohio Stadium. The ones who were rocked to sleep in a Scarlet and Gray cradle and want to be put away in a Scarlet and Gray casket. The ones who go to the most far-flung corner of the globe and yell "O-H!" just because they know someone will answer back with a hearty "I-O!"

Within these pages, we will share stories of the glorious past—some that you have probably heard and many that hopefully will be new to you. We'll relive some of the greatest victories, revisit the championship seasons, recall the wizardry and genius of Archie and Woody, Vic the Quick, Hopalong and Eddie, and even give you some food for thought as we pare down the best of the best with top ten lists of the best Buckeye players through the decades.

Moreover, what we will share is what we share with one another every day of our lives—an affinity for the Buckeyes. Our Buckeyes.

The bond Ohio State football fans share is one that can never be broken. It's a bond that recalls with fondness cherished memories that last through the years. The images we have of favorite games or players may flicker in our minds over time, but they never leave our hearts.

As long as we draw a breath on this earth—and maybe even beyond—we will be die-hard Buckeye fans.

Chapter 1

HOW BUCKEYE FOOTBALL WAS BORN

More than 100,000 fans pack historic Ohio Stadium on a handful of Saturday afternoons in the fall, each soaking up the excitement, pomp, and pageantry that is Ohio State football.

Over the past 120 years, the Scarlet and Gray has showcased some of college football's most revered names and featured some of the game's most seminal moments. Ohio State football isn't just a game. It's a passion, an obsession, a way of life for many millions of those who pride themselves on being Buckeye fans.

It wasn't always this way, of course. Like most things that attain greatness, Ohio State football wasn't an overnight success. The Buckeyes had to strain and struggle, growing step by measured step before attaining the lofty stature they enjoy today.

When football first appeared on the national scene, it was merely a new-fangled pastime in Columbus. Ohio State's first teams played before small, informal gatherings of people who were just beginning to understand the new game called "foot ball."

Princeton and Rutgers are credited with playing the first college football game on November 6, 1869, nearly four years before the Ohio Agricultural and Mechanical College opened its doors to twenty-four students in September 1873.

Ohio's capital of Columbus was a growing city of nearly 40,000 people at that time, but the college campus was constructed on an isolated site about two miles north of downtown so that the big-city life would not intrude upon the students and their academic lives. Despite the somewhat remote location, the university quickly grew as the student body increased in size and the curriculum expanded in scope.

In 1878, the Ohio legislature changed the college's name from Ohio A&M College to The Ohio State University. That same year, orange and black were chosen as the official colors for the university. When the selection committee was informed those colors were already in use at Princeton, members instead picked Scarlet and Gray.

Baseball was the first recreational sport on campus, and several intramural teams in other sports followed in the late 1870s. As a result, an athletic association made up of faculty members was formed, and in early 1881 it created an athletic program for the university. Part of the program included annual Field Days, featuring races, jumping contests, and lawn tennis competitions held on campus each spring.

According to many accounts, some form of organized football began to be played on the OSU campus as early as 1886. Most of the footballs used in the games were crude, homemade objects—often old rags stuffed inside a round, leather pouch and then sewn shut. Sometimes, the players would pool their meager resources for a "store-bought" football, but these weren't much better than the homemade ones.

Most games in those days were played on a large athletic field located north of the "North Dorm," which was on the west side of Neil Avenue near 11th Avenue, directly across from what is now Oxley Hall. The uneven field ran lengthwise downhill toward the Olentangy River, giving the advantage to the team that held the higher ground.

By 1890, college football had taken a foothold among Eastern schools and was gaining popularity in the Midwest. The first game between Ivy League rivals Harvard and Yale was held in 1875, and Michigan fielded its first football team in 1879.

SITE OF FIRST ever Ohio State football game. OSU beat Ohio Wesleyan 20–14.

There were four stages of early competitive sports on the OSU campus, and Dr. James E. Pollard described them in *Ohio State Athletics*, a book published in 1959. Pollard wrote that sporting events were spontaneous and unorganized on campus from the late 1870s to the early 1880s, while much of the next decade saw the beginning of contests with outside teams. Some of the opponents were other college teams, but many were thrown-together squads from nearby communities. Factories, department stores, churches, synagogues—it seemed nearly everyone wanted to get in on the new game.

The 1890s were marked by three developments: the organized scheduling of games, the emergence of a group of Ohio colleges and natural rivals that became the "Big Six," and the appearance of hired seasonal coaches, particularly for football. Finally, the last and most important phase—at least as far as Ohio State was

THE FIRST Ohio State football team in 1890. George N. Cole is credited with assembling the unit. OSU was undefeated in that first spring season, winning their only game: a 20–14 victory over Ohio Wesleyan.

concerned—began in 1912 with the university's formal admission to the Western Conference (which later became the Big Ten.)

George N. Cole is credited with helping Ohio State develop its first official football team in 1890. Cole took up a collection among fellow students to purchase a "real" football and acquired a book of football rules from A.G. Spalding's sporting goods company in Chicago. The game had some remarkable differences from football today. The field was initially 110 yards long without end zones, and the scoring system awarded five points for a field goal and four for a touchdown. Touchdowns were later awarded five points, and the field goal was cut to four points in 1904. Five years later, field goals were reduced to three points, and touchdowns were increased to six.

There were no forward passes in football of the 1890s. It was strictly a ground-oriented game, and the defense played accordingly. Only five yards were needed for a first down, but there were only three downs instead of four to make it. Additionally, there was no rule requiring the number of players on the offensive line of scrimmage, and bulky linemen were often called back to lead the formation or run the football.

Cole asked one of his boyhood friends, Alexander S. Lilley, to help him teach football to other Ohio State students. Lilley, who had played the game in college at Princeton, agreed and thereby became the first head coach in program history. Cole also arranged for another former high school classmate, Knowlton Lymon "Snake" Ames, to demonstrate the proper technique for kicking the football. Like Lilley, Ames had played college football at Princeton, where he earned All-America honors as a fullback in 1889. During his four-year career with the Tigers, Ames scored 62 touchdowns and totaled 730 points; he holds the unofficial career scoring record (the NCAA didn't keep records until 1937).

Lilley was by all accounts a colorful character. He lived on East Main Street and rode an Indian pony to the campus for practice sessions. Fewer than two dozen players showed up for the first practices, and by the time Ohio State's first organized football game was played May 3, 1890, the roster had dwindled to fourteen. Nevertheless, the Scarlet and Gray won a 20–14 decision over Ohio Wesleyan, getting the program off to a winning start.

There were plans for two more games in the spring of 1890, but a return match against Ohio Wesleyan and a game against Denison never developed. The team reconvened the following fall, beginning with the program's first "home" game. It was played at Recreation Park in Columbus, now the site of a supermarket on Whittier Street in the German Village area. OSU was blown out by Wooster 64–0.

Two more losses (14–0 at Denison and 18–0 to Kenyon) followed to leave Ohio State's first official season record at one win and three losses. However, the team that played in the fall was quite a bit different from the one that beat Ohio Wesleyan in May. Several of the members who participated in that first game had graduated, causing quite a bit of roster turnover. Additionally, the team had a new coach. Lilley had decided not to rejoin the team in the fall, and Jack Ryder had taken over as coach.

Lilley returned to his duties the following fall and coached Ohio State to a 2–2 record in 1891 before Ryder took over again in 1892 as the Buckeyes posted their first winning season at 5–3.

The program continued to play its home games at Recreation Field until 1898, when the Buckeyes moved to Ohio Field, located on North High Street between Woodruff and 17th avenues. Seating capacity was approximately 5,000 until 1907, when a grandstand and bleachers were added. Another renovation in 1910 saw brick ticket booths and iron fences added, as well as a second grandstand, which boosted capacity to 14,000.

In 1916 and 1917, All-America halfback Chic Harley led the Buckeyes to their first Western Conference championships, and the team regularly played to overflow crowds at Ohio Field. Harley missed the 1918 season while serving in World War I, but when he returned in 1919, so did the crowds. Because of Harley and his popularity, university officials put forth the ambitious project of building a huge concrete stadium on the banks of the Olentangy River.

Ground was broken in August 1921 for Ohio Stadium, and the Horseshoe hosted its first game in October of the following year.

DID YOU KNOW?

Center **John Segrist** was fatally injured during the 1901 season, and there was talk of dropping the football program as a result.

Since that time, the Ohio State football program has grown by leaps and bounds. The Buckeyes captured conference titles again in 1920, 1935, and 1939, before winning the program's first national championship in 1942. That was followed two years later by the school's first Heisman Trophy winner, halfback Leslie Horvath.

In all, the Buckeyes have enjoyed more than 800 victories, 33 conference titles, seven national championships, seven Heisman winners, and 132 All-America honorees. Ohio Stadium was added to the National Register of Historic Places in 1974, and along the way has hosted countless star players and big games, welcomed more than 39.5 million fans, and become one of the most recognizable symbols in college athletics today.

It also serves as the fitting home for Ohio State football, which has grown from humble beginnings to one of the sport's towering giants.

OHIO STATE'S FIRST GAME—BUCKEYE FOOTBALL IS BORN

Nothing says Buckeye football quite like a crisp autumn afternoon in Columbus, brilliant-colored leaves falling along the banks of the Olentangy River.

While that has been the traditional setting for more than eighty-five years, the first Ohio State football game occurred some thirty miles to the north . . . in the springtime.

Only an estimated 700 people, including a handful of women who were granted special permission, were on hand for an early-morning game of "foot ball" between the fledgling programs of Ohio State and Ohio Wesleyan. Those fans gathered May 3, 1890, on a hill in Delaware, Ohio, to watch the teams play in a flat meadow below. When the game had ended, its players physically spent, Ohio State had scored a 20–14 victory, and the storied program was born.

In fact, two programs were born that day. It was also Ohio Wesleyan's first game, and the university felt its neighbor to the south was the perfect opponent. The Battling Bishops had only recently organized their football team and invited the Scarlet and Gray to contest a football game as part of Ohio Wesleyan's annual May Day festivities, which included OWU commencement ceremonies.

Alexander S. Lilley and K. L. "Snake" Ames were teammates on 1889 Princeton national championship team, and they agreed to become Ohio State's first coaching staff. Ames guided the players in the finer points of blocking, tackling, and kicking, and Lilley handled strategy—such as it was. Football was a much simpler game in those days, with power and brute strength the most important aspects.

Lilley took to wearing a black driving cap, affixed a scarlet "Block O" on top (something akin to the black ball cap Woody Hayes donned more than 60 years later), and began to take over the team's practice sessions. When Ames was called away on business, Lilley assumed control of the entire team and became known as the program's first head coach.

The game with Ohio Wesleyan was scheduled to be played in mid-April, but inclement weather forced two postponements. During that time, Ohio State lost at least three players to injury, and only fifteen suited up for the 6 a.m. ride by horse-drawn carriages and wagons to Delaware for the opening contest.

At 9:30 a.m., with the small crowd nestled on the hill above, the Buckeyes and the Bishops kicked off into history just east of what is now Ohio Wesleyan's Phillips Hall, next to a small creek called Delaware Run.

The site of the game was forgotten until a letter written in the 1940s was discovered in 2007. In the letter, Ohio Wesleyan student C. Rollins Jones, who played in the game, wrote about the game and the site.

"It was a continuous playing game, void of the present day delays," the letter read. "The huddle had not been invented. All plays were run from signals given by the captain, except when 'Old Hickory' was called, which meant a desperate drive to shove the ball over the goal line.... The players had no pads, no headgears and their heads were hard, and they had plenty of hair for protection. There was no forward passing, but the ball could be lateralled. The game was an outgrowth of British rugby and soccer with the lines facing each other and the backs behind attempting to run with the ball. A scrum took place on every play."

The rugby elements of the game were also acknowledged in a 1938 interview with George Cole, the student credited with organizing the Ohio State team and getting Lilley to coach it.

"There was none of this fancy forward passing or razzle-dazzle," Cole told the Ohio State Alumni Association magazine. "It was all power stuff and wedge work—the flying wedge, a sheer power play, was then in vogue."

Cole added that it was a tough game played by tougher men.

"Anything went but brass knuckles," he said. "It was all right to step on a man's face as long as care was taken in the performance."

In addition to the rough nature of the game, there were only eleven to thirteen players on an entire roster, and it was difficult to keep track of which player was which since no one had numbers on their uniforms. The only way a player could leave the field was if he was injured, and if he left he could not return. The game was played in two 30-minute halves with no timeouts.

> " Anything went but brass knuckles. It was all right to step on a man's face as long as care was taken in the performance. "

Even the ball was different. It was more round than a modern-day football, and players punted the ball by dropping it to the ground and kicking it on the bounce.

Joseph H. Large earned the distinction of scoring the first touchdown for Ohio State, which was worth only four points in those days. Also scoring touchdowns for the Buckeyes were Charles Morrey, Charles Foulk, and Arthur Kennedy. OSU added a pair of extra-point kicks (worth two points each) to account for the final 20–14 score.

After dispatching Ohio Wesleyan in that first game, the Ohio State team returned to Columbus amid fanfare. The squad that played the newly popular game was beginning to establish a following. As a result, the Buckeyes scheduled a game the following Saturday against Denison University. Unfortunately, bad weather canceled the contest, and the two schools could not agree on a makeup date. Later, a rematch with Ohio Wesleyan was discussed but never came to fruition.

The rest of spring came and went with only the one football game. Several members of the team, including captain Jesse Jones, either graduated or left school, while Lilley and Ames accepted job offers elsewhere.

Ohio State fielded a team again in the fall with several new faces, including Jack Ryder as head coach. That squad, however, was winless in three games and was outscored 96–0. Several of the players went on to distinguish themselves in later life, however. Paul M. Lincoln, who succeeded Jones as team captain in the fall, became a wealthy industrialist; Foulk became a chemistry professor at Ohio State; and Morrey served as the head of the OSU bacteriological department for years.

After that first game in 1890, Ohio State and Ohio Wesleyan became regular rivals on the gridiron. The schools played one another a total of twenty-nine times, and although they have not played since 1932, OWU still holds the distinction of playing Ohio State more than any other in-state school. The Bishops also helped the Buckeyes open Ohio Stadium in 1922, playing OSU tough until succumbing to a 5–0 score.

THE FIRST UNDEFEATED TEAM

The Buckeye Nation has its favorite teams, and it's no coincidence many of those favorites are undefeated squads that enjoyed championship seasons.

Memories of Ohio State's run to the 2002 national title remain fresh and vivid, as does the 1968 championship team, although many of the of fresh-faced youngsters known as the "Super Sophs" have passed or are rapidly approaching their sixtieth birthdays.

Older fans may gravitate to the 1961 team, which was denied a chance to play in the Rose Bowl, or even the 1954 squad that posted a perfect 10–0 record topped off by a 20–7 victory in Pasadena over Southern California and a consensus national championship.

Each of those teams, as well as the Buckeyes of 1916, 1917, 1944, and 1973, enjoyed undefeated seasons. None, however, enjoy the mystique of being the first team in program history to go through an entire season without a loss.

You have to go back to the turn of the century—the twentieth century—to find the team that holds that distinction.

Ohio State football was still in its infancy in 1899 when the Buckeyes ran roughshod over nearly every opponent on its schedule, finishing with a 9–0–1 record. On its way to that undefeated season, OSU scored 184 points on offense while surrendering only five on defense.

The Ohio State program kicked off its tenth anniversary season in 1899 the same way it had many of the nine previous years—by looking for a new head coach. Jack Ryder had returned in 1898 for his second stint as coach and led the team to a 3–5 season. The Buckeyes had experienced only two winning records in their previous nine years as an intercollegiate program, and the university was growing weary of losing.

Enter John B. Eckstorm, the fifth head coach in the program's decade-long history. Eckstorm had been a star player and captain at Dartmouth, and he came to the Buckeyes after one season as head coach at Kenyon. He may not have known it at the time, but Eckstorm was probably auditioning for the OSU job when his Kenyon team rolled to a 29–0 win over the Buckeyes in 1898.

Unlike his predecessors, Eckstorm took the head coaching job as a full-time enterprise. He prided himself on his organizational skills and was a proponent of his players getting themselves into tip-top physical condition. In fact, when the coach met with his new team for the first time in May 1899, he encouraged them to practice on their own during the summer and report to fall camp ready to play.

The OSU players evidently took Eckstorm's advice to heart. When they got back to campus in the fall, the turnaround was remarkable. The team that had produced only nine victories in the preceding three seasons combined embarked upon a season that remains one of the finest in school history.

Because they were able to play ball-control offense and essentially kept the ball for most of the game, the Buckeyes rolled to a 30–0 win over old foe Otterbein in the 1899 season opener. It was a performance that grabbed the attention of fans as well as sportswriters.

"It cannot be remembered when O. S. U. ever scored 30 points on an opposing team in the first game of the season and in fact it has been rather customary for the state university to lose that opening game," wrote the *Columbus Dispatch*. "But to think that those 30 points were scored against Otterbein—well, that makes it all the better for it is a well known fact that the O. S. U. boys would sooner defeat Otterbein than almost any other team in the state."

THE 1899 OSU SQUAD was the first undefeated team in school history, with a 9-0-1 record.

Photo courtesy of OSU Photo Archives

The Buckeyes had never scored more than 24 points in a season opener and had beaten Otterbein only once in four previous meetings. This time, however, the Scarlet and Gray opened with a 6–0 halftime lead and then tacked on four more second-half touchdowns to run away with the contest.

Halfback B. F. Yost, a Columbus high school product, was the offensive star for Ohio State, along with veteran quarterback Paul Hardy.

Things went much the same way the following week, as the Buckeyes settled another old score by rolling to a 28–0 victory over Wittenberg. OSU had lost three times in a row to the Tigers, including twice during the 1894 season.

In front of 1,800 spectators at Ohio Field, the Buckeyes unveiled a powerful running attack that piled up more than 300 yards against Wittenberg. Right half-back Bob Hager led the onslaught with 153 yards on 28 carries, while left half-backs John Tarbill and Yost combined for 131 yards and scored a touchdown each. Fullback James "Boss" Kittle added 52 yards and 3 TDs.

Week three of the 1899 season found OSU headed to Cleveland for its first road test of the season against the Case School of Applied Science. Again, it was an opponent the Buckeyes hadn't had much success against in previous years. Case had won three of the four previous meetings, including a 38–0 victory in 1894 in the only other time the teams had played in Cleveland.

The teams played to a scoreless halftime tie, but only because of a big defensive play by Kittle. The OSU defender made a spectacular shoestring tackle at his own 20-yard line to prevent a Case punt returner from scoring a potential touchdown.

Ohio State finally dented the scoreboard with a short touchdown run by sophomore halfback James Westwater. Unfortunately, the punt-out was knocked away by Case, and the Buckeyes were unable to try for the extra point.

Case waited until the last possible second to make up the 5–0 deficit. It forced a punt on Ohio State's final possession of the game and scored a tying touchdown with the clock ticking under a minute. The hosts then had a chance to win the game but missed the extra point kick from a tough angle, and the game ended in a 5–5 tie.

The Buckeyes rebounded the following week with a 41–0 win over Ohio University in a game that could have been much worse. Most games were played in

25-minute halves, but officials had discretion over the length of games in the event of serious injuries, inclement weather, or lopsided scoring. In this game, the gun sounded after only four minutes in the second half.

"If the second half had been played to the end," *the Dispatch* wrote, "the score would have been in the neighborhood of 75 to 0."

Kittle, Westwater, Yost, and Hager hit OU with a steady barrage of running plays, including a 66-yard touchdown bolt by Westwater.

The game also featured the first field goal in Ohio State history. Just before the first half ended, team captain D. B. "Del" Sayers dropped back for what was called a "goal from placement." With Yost holding, Sayers booted the football over the goal post crossbar from about seventeen yards away. The goal was worth five points at the time—the same total as a touchdown.

Next up was Oberlin, the toughest team on OSU's schedule that year. The Yeomen had won the Ohio state college championship six times, and the Buckeyes had never beaten them in six previous tries. The fact of the matter was the Buckeyes had not even come close in any of those six games, losing by a combined score of 204–14. The first two losses had come in 1892—a 40–4 loss at Oberlin in the season opener and a 50–0 loss in Columbus five weeks later. The legendary John W. Heisman was head coach of the Yeomen that season.

Ohio State chartered a special train to carry more than 325 students, boosters, and other fans to the game. The train left Union Station in Columbus at 6:45 a.m. Saturday morning and pulled into Oberlin a little after 11 o'clock. Headed by the OSU cadet band in uniform, a parade was formed at the station, and the hundreds of Buckeye fans marched through the streets of Oberlin on their way to the football field.

A heavy downpour soaked the area throughout the morning before the game and turned the field into a quagmire. That didn't matter to the several thousand fans in attendance who overflowed the grandstand area and stood in six-inch-deep mud around the stadium.

The contest was played mainly in the middle of the muddy field, as neither team could sustain any kind of offense. Early in the first half, though, Ohio State got a break. With the ball on Oberlin's 25-yard line, the football squibbed loose in what the *Dispatch* called "one unrecognizable mass of mud and moleskins."

Somehow, Sayers managed to scoop up the ball, fend off a pair of would-be tacklers from Oberlin, and slosh his way 25 yards for a touchdown. It marked the first touchdown scored by the Buckeyes against Oberlin in nearly three years and would be all Ohio State needed.

The defense managed to hold, forcing Oberlin to turn the ball over on downs twice late in the final minutes inside the OSU 15-yard line, and secured a 6–0 victory.

Ohio State protected its perfect record the following week with a 6–0 win at home over Western Reserve. The Buckeyes were led by halfback C. R. Wilson, who carried 23 times for 86 yards and the game's only touchdown.

Two more home games and two more shutouts followed as OSU rolled to a 17–0 win over Marietta and a 12–0 victory over Ohio Medical. Westwater did most of the damage on offense, rushing for 103 yards and a touchdown against the Pioneers and adding 71 more yards and another score against the Medics.

The Buckeyes were to have a week off in the schedule the following week, but the popularity of the team led university officials to scramble to find an additional opponent. Muskingum College obliged, but only if it could host the game. Ohio State agreed and traveled about sixty miles east to New Concord for what would turn out to be a 34–0 pounding of the Fighting Muskies.

Six different Buckeyes scored touchdowns, and Sayers added four extra point tries to account for the final tally. OSU rolled up more than 320 yards on the ground, led by left halfback James Hawk, who ran 15 times for 108 yards and a touchdown.

Sayers put the finishing touches on the undefeated season, kicking another field goal to provide all the scoring in a 5–0 win over Kenyon on Thanksgiving Day. The Lords put up an excellent defensive fight, putting up three separate goal

GAMEDAY HAUNTS

Varsity Club Located on Lane Avenue less than 500 yards from Ohio Stadium makes the VC an ideal location for pre- and post-game festivities.

line stands during the afternoon. But Sayers delighted the holiday crowd of about 6,000 on hand at Ohio Field when he booted a 25-yard field goal late in the first half.

That victory, coupled with Western Reserve's win over Case, gave Ohio State its first undisputed Ohio college championship . . . at least undisputed in most circles. A Cincinnati newspaper published a photo of the University of Cincinnati football team and labeled it "Champions of Ohio." That did not set well in Columbus.

"The ridiculousness of the claim is at once apparent," the *Dispatch* wrote the next day. "Cincinnati has played but two Ohio teams this fall—Miami and Ohio Wesleyan. Neither of those teams have done anything this season which would even place them in the first division of the Ohio elevens. Just as a matter of comparison we might point to the fact that Cincinnati defeated Miami by a score of 21 to 0. Marietta defeated Miami on Thanksgiving Day by a score of 67 to 0, and Marietta had previously been defeated by Ohio State University by a score of 17 to 0.

"There is absolutely no question about the matter. The Ohio State University football eleven are champions of Ohio, and if the Cincinnati boys are not willing to recognize this fact, they are the only ones out of the 14 or 15 college elevens in the state who do not recognize them as such."

The undefeated season, highlighted with so many triumphs and program firsts, helped transform Ohio State from also-ran to champion. It was the kind of season that inspires others to write songs in tribute, and that's exactly what OSU student Charles Gayman did. Using melodies from a trio of popular songs from *HMS Pinafore*, the Gilbert and Sullivan operetta, Gayman penned a trilogy to celebrate the success of the 1899 Buckeyes. Each of the songs was performed by the OSU Men's Glee Club and included this offering:

> *A few months ago, we were not the whole show, But now we are peaches and cream; 'Tis only of late that thru'out ev'ry state, We are known by our great football team. There's Tilton and Hager, Scott, Wharton and Sayers, Lloyd, Westwater, Kittle and Fay, And both Segrist brothers, Poole, Wilson and others, And Hardy who guides every play. The plays that beat Otterbein, Wit-*

tenberg, Athens, The Medics and Western Reserve, That killed Marietta, went Oberlin better, and gave them what they deserve. We've never been beaten and yet we have eaten Muskingum and almost ate Case, Beat, Kenyon, Thanksgiving, We're thankful for living, For O. S. U. stands in first place.

After the season, Eckstorm was rewarded by the university with an unprecedented two-year contract extension. When asked if he thought his future teams could duplicate the success of the 1899 squad, he replied, "I hope this season's record is the beginning in a long series of like victories."

It would be another seventeen seasons before the Buckeyes would enjoy an undefeated season. Eckstorm coached the 1900 and 1901 seasons before leaving to take over the program at Ohio Medical. His three-year record of 22–4–3 at Ohio State produced an .810 winning percentage, making him one of only two men in school history to coach at least 25 games and win 80 percent or more of them. The other? Jim Tressel, who entered the 2009 season with an 83–9 mark, good for an .814 winning percentage.

BOYD CHERRY—OHIO STATE'S FIRST ALL-AMERICAN

Ask Buckeye fans the name of the university's first football All-American and chances are good the reply would be Chic Harley.

That reply would be incorrect.

Harley was the first three-time All-American in Ohio State football history, winning his first honor as a sophomore in 1916. Preceding him by two years was Boyd Cherry, an outstanding offensive and defensive end who became the first Buckeye gridiron star ever bestowed with All-America honors.

Cherry earned a host of postseason awards for his play during the 1914 season as Ohio State posted a 5–2 record and finished fourth in the Western Conference standings. Cherry, a native of the Gallipolis, Ohio, area, was a rugged individual with movie star looks who played nearly every down of his senior season.

He was a multi-dimensional player, equally adept with his blocking prowess, pass-catching skills, heads-up defensive play, and kicking accuracy. As a result,

Cherry was named by *Chicago Tribune* sportswriter Walter Eckersall to the All-Western Conference first team at left end. Cherry became the first Buckeye ever chosen for the all-league roster in only the school's second season as a full-fledged member.

More accolades followed, including the ultimate honor—inclusion on Walter Camp's annual All-America list for *Collier's Weekly*. Camp, who captained the Yale football team in the late 1870s and coached at his alma mater as well as Stanford, was a renowned sportswriter who is credited with developing many of the rules of American football. Since he was based in New Haven, Connecticut, Camp typically stocked his All-America rosters with players from Ivy League powers as well as other Eastern schools.

Cherry, however, became the first Ohio State player to catch Camp's attention, and the sportswriter listed the senior end on his roster of players deserving of honorable mention. Also that year, Cherry was given second-team All-America honors by the *International News Service*, the precursor of *United Press International*.

It was the culmination of a three-year college career for Cherry, who began playing in 1912 under head coach John R. Richards. The Buckeyes enjoyed some success that season with a 6–3 record that included big wins over Otterbein, Oberlin, and Cincinnati. But Richards resigned abruptly following the season, leaving the Ohio State program in disarray.

Richards had also been the university's athletic director, and elevated to the position after his resignation was head basketball and baseball coach Lynn W. St. John. The new AD's first task was to find a new head coach, but St. John wasn't having much success. His first choice was Colorado College head coach Carl Rothgeb, who turned down the position. Former University of Chicago standout John Schommer, a disciple of Amos Alonzo Stagg, was approached, but he could not come to terms with the university. Meanwhile, several football team members, including Cherry, contemplated giving up the sport to concentrate on their studies.

St. John finally settled on a former Wisconsin football star as his new coach, and John W. Wilce began a sixteen-year stay in Columbus as head of the Buckeyes' program. Upon his arrival on campus, Wilce immediately summoned veteran players and told them his philosophy toward the game and what was expected of them. Cherry was impressed enough to return for his junior year in 1913 and help OSU post a 4–2–1 record in their first season under the new head coach.

Cherry was poised for his standout senior campaign the following year, but it nearly did not happen.

On the Saturday before the 1914 season opener against Ohio Wesleyan, Cherry was injured during a full scrimmage against the OSU freshman squad at Ohio Field. The team's medical staff at first believed the injury to be minor, but further examination revealed a fractured left cheekbone. Dr. Jack Means, the team's chief physician, estimated Cherry would be sidelined for at least three weeks.

BOYD CHERRY
plaque in Buckeye
Grove

Photo courtesy of Mark Rea

The Buckeyes pressed on and claimed a 16–2 victory in the opener against Ohio Wesleyan. But they clearly missed their star player. With Cherry in the lineup, OSU had beaten Wesleyan the previous year by a 58–0 score and by a 36–6 margin the season before that.

A much tougher opponent loomed the following week in Case, a team the Buckeyes had beaten only twice in the previous seven meetings. But thanks to some ingenuity from St. John, who was also an assistant football coach, Ohio State's chances against its in-state rival were enhanced. The athletic director spent several evenings devising a special piece of headgear for Cherry to wear that protected his cheekbone. It was a kind of primitive face shield, although face masks affixed to helmets did not become prevalent in football until the late 1940s and early 1950s.

With the protective gear, Cherry donned his No. 13 jersey for the October 10 game at Case and played a key role in helping the Buckeyes take a 7–6 victory on a muddy field. Cherry caught several passes during the contest and also played stellar defense, prompting the team's next opponent to install several special plays to try to neutralize the OSU senior.

Illinois had never lost to Ohio State in two previous meetings, and head coach Bob Zuppke wanted it to stay that way. Newspaper accounts from Champaign, Illinois reported the Illini coach "has a wholesome respect for the ability for end Cherry to gain ground by the air route. He is taken so seriously that Zuppke has developed a special defense to take care of him—if possible."

Whatever precautions Zuppke took, they seemed to work. Although Cherry drew praise for his work on defense, especially for breaking up several Illinois passing attempts, the Illini completely shut down the Ohio State offense and secured a 37–0 win. Illinois would go on to a 7–0 season in 1914, winning the Western Conference title while contending with undefeated Army and Texas teams for the national championship.

The Buckeyes fell again the following week, missing an extra point and losing 7–6 at Wisconsin. But OSU rebounded with a 13–3 win the next week at Indiana, the program's first-ever conference victory on the road. It was also the team's first out-of-state win since a 17–6 victory late in the 1908 season at Vanderbilt.

Cherry played a big role in defeating the Hoosiers as Wilce successfully employed his passing game. Cherry opened the game with a 40-yard reception from quarterback Lou Pickerel that set up Ohio State's first touchdown. Then in the fourth quarter, Cherry's 22-yard catch gave the Buckeyes the ball on the Indiana 6-yard line, and one play later, Pickerel found right end Dwight Ginn in the end zone for the clinching touchdown.

After that game, there was no stopping the Buckeyes. They cruised to a 39–0 win over Oberlin and then dispatched Northwestern by a 27–0 score in the season finale to wind up with a 5–2 overall record. They also split their four conference games to finish in a fourth-place tie behind Illinois, Minnesota, and Chicago.

Cherry played extremely well down the stretch for Ohio State. After his big game against Indiana, he had an even bigger one against Oberlin, catching a number of passes, including one for a late touchdown. He was also stellar on defense and had a hand in blocking three Crimson and Gold punts.

When the season was over, the accolades began to pour in for Cherry. First, he was named to the first team of the *Columbus Dispatch*'s All-Ohio Eleven. Joining him on that roster were four teammates—Charles Snyder at tackle, Arthur Kiefer at guard, Pickerel at quarterback, and team captain Campbell "Honus" Graf at fullback.

Of the eleven first-team members on the *Dispatch* team, only Cherry and Denison halfback N. G. Rupp were unanimous choices.

In early December, Cherry was honored again when he was named one of the first-team ends on the All-Western Conference team. A week later, Cherry was among those praised by Camp as he made his annual All-America selections. "In the line," Camp wrote, "(Charles) Coolidge of Harvard, (George) Squier and (Perry) Graves of Illinois and Cherry of Ohio State, all ends, are especially worthy of mention."

The recognition by Camp was particularly noteworthy for an Ohio State player. Eight of the first-team members that year hailed from Ivy League schools, and only five of the thirty-three players named to the first three All-America teams were from schools west of New York. Because of Cherry's trailblazing efforts, Camp began to turn his attention to more Midwestern schools, and two years later, Harley became the first Ohio State player ever to attain first-team All-America mention.

By all accounts, Cherry took his accolades in stride. By the time he had earned the school's first All-America honors in football, he had already turned his attention to another sport.

Less than a week after the end of the season, he had turned in his spikes for sneakers and was captaining Ohio State's 1914–15 basketball team. The same day he earned honorable mention All-America honors in football, Cherry contributed six points to a 30–9 basketball win over St. Mary's.

Cherry completed his college athletic career and graduated from Ohio State in 1915. He later became vice president of the Kinnear Manufacturing Co. in Columbus. He died in Fort Myers, Florida, on November 14, 1970, at the age of 77.

Chapter 2

THE EARLY YEARS

CHIC HARLEY

Take a healthy dose of Archie Griffin, mix in liberal amounts of Tom Skladany and Rex Kern, and perhaps even sprinkle in a little bit of Jack Tatum, and you would have the recipe for the quintessential Ohio State football player.

You would also have Chic Harley.

Although Harley played his last game for the Buckeyes nearly a century ago, his exploits on the football field that were captured in fading photographs, scratchy newsreel footage, and flowery prose from the football writers of the day are proof positive that he was one of the greatest—if not *the* greatest—players ever to play for Ohio State.

Illinois has Red Grange, and Michigan has Tom Harmon, players who supplemented their college careers with superlative professional careers.

Harley was a blazing star who was every bit the equal of Grange or Harmon on the gridiron, but became somewhat of an enigma following his play-

CHIC HARLEY plaque in Buckeye Grove. Harley's brilliance on the field helped launch OSU football as a force to be reckoned with.

ing days at OSU. His pro career was cut short by injury, and he returned to Columbus only a handful of times before his death in 1974. While his name is seldom mentioned anymore when discussing the greatest players ever to play for the Buckeyes, that in no way diminishes Harley's exploits.

"Keep in mind that Ohio State had just joined the Big Ten and was searching for an identity," said former longtime OSU sports information director Marv Homan. "It was searching for a player that would justify their membership because prior to that, they had been a member of the Ohio Conference. Ohio State, at that time, was a relatively small school.

"Harley was that player. He was truly the first great football player in Ohio State history. As a result, Ohio State football became big-time during the Harley era."

Long after his playing career ended, Harley returned to Columbus in the fall of 1948 after being absent for several years. He was feted with a two-day celebration that coincided with his homecoming. The festivities included a ticker tape parade for Harley attended by some 75,000, despite a chilly rain that fell throughout the weekend.

Bob Hooey, sports editor of the *Ohio State Journal*, penned an article for the occasion titled "One and Only," in which he tried to sum up what Harley meant to OSU to those who had never seen him play.

"If you never saw him run with a football, we can't describe it to you," Hooey wrote, paraphrasing famed author and Columbus native James Thurber. "It wasn't like (Jim) Thorpe or Grange or Harmon or anyone else. It was a kind of cross between music and cannon fire, and it brought your heart up under your ears.

"In the hardest-fought gridiron battles, Harley usually would get away and score the winning touchdown. With his famous side-step, his reliable toe, his dashing runs and his cool judgment, Harley paved the way for Ohio State's first two conference championships.

"His fame grew so great and spread so far that people came to look upon him as a wizard."

Two-time All-America quarterback Gaylord "Pete" Stinchcomb, who was Harley's teammate in 1919, said there wasn't anything that the OSU star halfback couldn't do on the football field.

"Chic was like a cat," Stinchcomb told former sports information director Wilbur Snypp in *The Buckeyes*. "You know how hard it is to catch a cat? It usually takes more than one person. It always took more than one player to catch Harley."

Born Charles William Harley on September 15, 1895, in Chicago, he moved with his parents, three brothers, and three sisters to Columbus when he was twelve years old. He later prepped at East High School, where he was a classmate of noted author James Thurber and painter George Bellows.

Harley quickly earned his own fame as a football star, leading the Tigers to several City League championships. In fact, he lost only one game during his high school playing days. But football wasn't his only game—he was a standout in basketball and baseball as well.

Nicknamed "Chic" by his teammates because of his Chicago roots, Harley nearly returned to the Windy City for his senior season when his father, a printer, took a job in Chicago and moved the family back there.

Soft-spoken and extremely reverential where his father was concerned, Harley was bitterly disappointed about being uprooted before his senior season of high school but had resigned himself to the move.

East principal John Harlor stepped in and asked the elder Harley if it would be possible for his son to stay in Columbus. Only when team captain John Vorys—who would later become an Ohio congressman—said that Harley could stay with his family during the school year and pleaded with Chic's father to allow him to stay in Columbus did the elder Harley finally relent.

Harley stayed at East and helped the Tigers remain unbeaten in football until the last game of his senior season, when the team was upset by North High School. It was his only loss as a high-schooler.

In 1915, when it came time to select a college, it wasn't a foregone conclusion that Harley would attend Ohio State. After all, East was accustomed to drawing more fans to football games than Ohio State.

The Buckeyes had been members of the Western Conference (the predecessor of the Big Ten) for only a couple of seasons and were taking their lumps as one of the smaller schools in the league.

> **You know how hard it is to catch a cat? It usually takes more than one person. It always took more than one player to catch Harley.**

Powerhouse programs of the day such as Illinois, Michigan, and the University of Chicago all made overtures to Harley, trying to entice the multi-sport star to join their teams and earn greater glory than he could with the Buckeyes. At the time, OSU had played those three schools a combined sixteen times—and had never won.

Additionally, the legendary coaches at those schools made it extremely difficult for Harley to resist. Bob Zuppke was at Illinois, Fielding Yost was coaching in Ann Arbor, and the legendary Amos Alonzo Stagg was patrolling the sideline at Chicago, extolling the virtues of returning home to play for the Maroons.

But Harley liked it in Columbus and had spent many Saturday afternoons with his friends sneaking into Ohio Field to watch the Buckeyes play. He admired OSU head coach John W. Wilce, who had made improvements in each of his first two seasons on the job. In addition, several of his friends pledged to the Phi Gamma Delta fraternity on campus.

So when it came time to decide which college to attend, Harley chose to become a Buckeye under considerable fanfare from the Columbus press.

Harley spent the fall of 1915 on the freshman team at Ohio State but reportedly practiced quite a bit with the varsity players. That season, the Buckeyes finished 5–1–1, their best overall record in eight seasons, and tied for third in the conference, their best finish ever.

When Harley joined the varsity team as a sophomore the following season, it was the final piece of the championship caliber program Wilce had been trying to establish.

"Every program trying to assemble itself into a consistent winner needs a cornerstone. Harley was our cornerstone," Wilce said years later.

From the moment he first set foot on Ohio Field, Harley was the featured star for the Buckeyes from his halfback position, running and throwing the ball with equal ease.

His first game as a collegiate player came in 1916 and was a 12–0 win over old Ohio Conference foe Ohio Wesleyan. The contest drew only 4,889 fans to Ohio Field, which was located near the intersection of 18th and High streets.

Ohio State rolled to victory the following week with a 128–0 pounding of Oberlin that still ranks as the highest point total ever in school history. But the third game of the season was when Harley's legend began to grow.

In their first Western Conference game of the season, the Buckeyes traveled to Illinois to take on Zuppke and the powerful Illini, a team they had never beaten in five previous tries. With Illinois clinging to a 6–0 lead in the fourth quarter, Harley broke off a 20-yard touchdown run on a sloppy field that tied the score.

Under the rules in those days, the scoring team punted the ball from the end zone to a teammate, and the extra point was attempted from the spot on the field where the punt was caught. Harley punted to teammate Fred Norton on the 22-yard line.

Then, after changing his muddy shoes to clean ones, he calmly drop-kicked the extra point to give the Buckeyes a 7–6 victory.

It was the Illini's first loss at home in four years and knocked them out of the unbeaten ranks. When reporters asked Zuppke if his team had gotten caught looking ahead to a showdown the following week with Minnesota, the coach replied, "Give Ohio credit, especially the Harley boy. They beat us, fair and square."

Later that season, Harley ran for a 27-yard touchdown, returned a punt 80 yards for another TD, and drop-kicked two extra points to account for all of his team's scoring in a 14–13 win over Wisconsin. The game was witnessed by an estimated crowd of 12,500 at Ohio Field, then the largest ever to attend a football game in the state.

"That was a huge upset at the time," said OSU football historian Jack Park. "The day Wisconsin played that game in Columbus, Illinois was playing at Minnesota, and Wisconsin's head coach—a fellow by the name of Paul Withington—went to Minnesota so he could scout those two teams. He thought they would beat Ohio State easily, so he let one of his assistants coach the team in Columbus.

"At the time, that was considered to be the biggest win in Ohio State football history."

Harley went on to gain 107 yards in the first eight minutes of a 46–7 win over Indiana, and then he closed out his first season with another remarkable per-

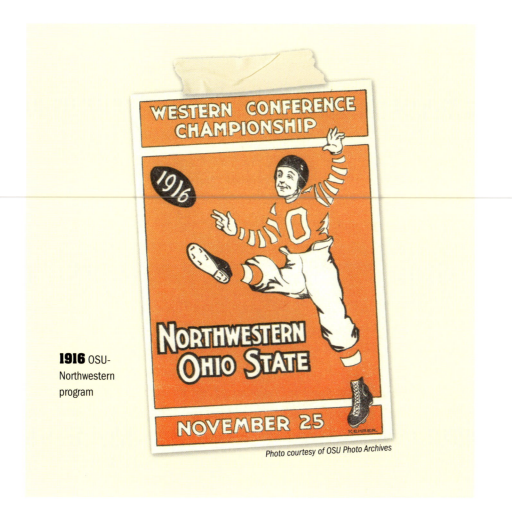

1916 OSU-Northwestern program

Photo courtesy of OSU Photo Archives

formance during a 23–3 victory over Northwestern, running for 20- and 67-yard touchdowns, setting up a third score with a 40-yard pass and booting a 34-yard field goal.

The Buckeyes rolled through the 1916 season with a perfect 7–0 record—the school's first unblemished mark in history—and won its initial Western Conference championship. For his part, Harley was named to the Walter Camp All-America team, becoming only the second Buckeye ever to be honored. Boyd Cherry was OSU's first-ever All-American honoree in 1914.

For Harley, the best was yet to come. After leading Ohio State to the championship in 1916, he didn't miss a beat when the team began fall camp for the 1917 campaign.

With Harley spearheading the attack, the Buckeyes put together one of their finest seasons in history. Joining their top star in the offensive backfield was quarterback Howard Yerges, who was beginning his third season as a starter, and Stinchcomb, who would go on to win All-America accolades twice at Ohio State and earn induction into the College Football Hall of Fame.

Along the line, the team had the services of veterans such as Charles "Shifty" Bolen at end, co-captains Harold and Howard "Hap" Courtney—the only brothers ever to serve as captains during the same season—at the tackle spots, Kelley VanDyne at center, and Robert Karch at guard.

Karch had been an All-American with Harley in 1916 and would go on to help develop the playing rules for the National Football League. He officiated NFL games for more than forty years and is enshrined in the referees section of the Pro Football Hall of Fame.

The Buckeyes began the '17 season at home on September 29, as more than 14,000 fans wedged their way into tiny Ohio Field to catch a glimpse of Harley. Unfortunately, he suffered a slight injury in the first half and spent most of the game on the sidelines.

OSU didn't need him as it demolished Case with a 49–0 shutout.

The following weekend, the fans got their wish. Harley scored three touchdowns during a 53–0 pounding of old Ohio Conference foe Ohio Wesleyan. In that game, Wesleyan recovered a fumble near midfield and drove to the OSU 2-yard line. But the Buckeyes snuffed a fourth-down quarterback sneak to preserve the shutout. It would be the closest any opponent would get to the Ohio State end zone all season.

When it came time to begin Western Conference play, the Buckeyes continued to roll. This time, Stinchcomb and Harley switched roles as the sophomore ran for three touchdowns—all of them sprung by Harley blocks—and OSU blanked Northwestern, 40–0. The game was expected to be much closer, since the Wildcats had lost only once in their previous eight games.

CHIC HARLEY. Nearly a century has passed since Harley roamed the gridiron, but his legacy as one of OSU's all-time greats lives on.

Photo courtesy of OSU Photo Archives

The Buckeyes notched their fourth straight shutout with a 67–0 pounding of Denison and then went on the road to meet Indiana. The game was vintage Harley.

He scored on touchdown runs of 40, 8, 11, and 33 yards and booted two extra points to account for all of his team's scoring in a 26–3 victory.

The following day, the *Ohio State Journal* published this account of the game: "It's going to be the talk around Indianapolis for days to come that Harley alone whipped the big, burly fellows from Bloomington."

OSU ran its record to 5–0 the following week, beating Wisconsin 16–3 at its brand-new Camp Randall Stadium. After falling behind 3–0, the Buckeyes scored a touchdown when Harley faked a punt and threw a 44-yard touchdown pass to Bolen. Later, Harley connected for 32 yards to Hap Courtney to set up the team's second score and added a 40-yard field goal for good measure.

The Buckeyes returned home on November 17 with a perfect record and a homecoming showdown against Illinois. The Illini, still smarting from a 7–6 defeat at the hands of OSU the year before, had not been scored upon all season.

Harley would change that.

After kicking an early 14-yard field goal to make it 3–0, the Ohio State star sewed things up in the fourth quarter by adding a 29-yard field goal and a 20-yard touchdown pass to Courtney. Harley also tacked on the PAT, again accounting for each of his team's points in a 13–0 victory.

With a second consecutive conference championship in hand, the Buckeyes played two more games in 1917—both were considered postseason contests for the benefit of Ohio servicemen training for action in World War I.

The team traveled to Montgomery, Alabama, on the Saturday before Thanksgiving to take on Auburn. Training at nearby Camp Sheridan were hundreds of reservists with the 37th division of the Ohio National Guard. That game ended in a 0–0 tie.

Five days later, the Buckeyes returned home to host Camp Sherman on Thanksgiving Day. Featuring a team of former college players training at the camp near Chillicothe, Ohio, they proved to be no match for OSU, losing a 28–0 verdict.

The Buckeyes finished the season with an 8–0–1 record and outscored nine opponents by an almost unbelievable 292–6 margin.

Bolen, Hap Courtney, VanDyne, and Harley would go on to win all-conference honors that season, and the quartet also earned Walter Camp All-America honors. In so doing, Harley became the first Ohio State player ever to be named All-American twice.

During the 1918 season, Harley served in the military as World War I waged in Europe. When the armistice was signed November 11, 1918, the Ohio State star was one of thousands of players who began streaming home, eager to restart their football careers.

Harley was elected team captain for the 1919 season despite the fact he hadn't played the year before. It was an homage to his past exploits and to the fact that the Buckeyes hadn't played particularly well in his absence. They finished just 3–3 during the 1918 season, but all three losses were conference defeats, including a 14–0 loss to Michigan, extending Ohio State's winless streak against the Wolverines to fifteen straight games without success.

The Buckeyes opened the 1919 season on the first weekend in October, and Harley charged from the gate with a 35-yard touchdown run on his first carry of the afternoon. It was the beginning of a 38–0 rout of Ohio Wesleyan.

Home shutouts of Cincinnati (46–0) and Kentucky (49–0) followed before Ohio State made its first road trip of the year, heading to Ann Arbor and a date with destiny.

After the Buckeyes took a 7–3 halftime lead, Harley broke things open in the third quarter with a 42-yard touchdown run around left end. It provided the final points in a 13–3 victory for the Scarlet and Gray, breaking the spell Michigan held over the Buckeyes.

The Harley Express kept going the following week when he ran 30 yards for one touchdown and passed 13 yards for another as the Buckeyes rolled to a 20–0 victory over Purdue. OSU then went to 6–0 when Harley booted a 22-yard field goal in the fourth quarter to provide all the scoring in a 3–0 win over Wisconsin.

That set up the season finale at Ohio Field against Illinois. It would be Harley's final game with the Buckeyes, and ticket demand would reach an all-time high. Nearly 20,000 fans jammed into the facility that had been built to hold about one-fourth of that crowd, and when the Buckeyes took the field, the *Ohio State Monthly* reported residents as far as a mile away could hear the roar.

Illinois was protecting a 6–0 lead in the second half when Harley changed the course of the game. He threw a 32-yard pass to teammate Clarence MacDonald to get his team to the Illini 1-yard line and then did the scoring honors himself, bolting into the end zone on the next play. His PAT kick gave the Buckeyes a 7–6 advantage heading into the fourth quarter.

There would be no storybook ending, however. The Illini drove more than 60 yards in the final moments of the game and kicked a 25-yard field goal with eight seconds remaining, giving them a 9–7 victory.

It was a bitter loss for Harley, who had also lost just one football game in high school—the final one of his career. He was reportedly so despondent that he sat in the Ohio State locker room for several hours after the game had ended, still in his mud-caked uniform, simply staring at the floor.

Nevertheless, Harley's exploits could not be diminished. He had led the Buckeyes to a 6–1 record, good for a second-place finish in the conference behind Illinois, and had scored 71 of his team's 176 points that year. He wound up his marvelous career with twenty-three touchdowns, eight field goals and thirty-nine PATs. His three-year total of 201 points would stand as a school scoring record for thirty-six years, until Howard "Hopalong" Cassady broke it with 222 in four seasons from 1952–55.

He also had earned a third All-America honor, becoming the first Buckeye to earn that distinction, and was credited with popularizing Ohio State football, to the point that university officials accepted an ambitious plan to construct a huge stadium on the banks of the Olentangy River. The structure was named Ohio Stadium, but its nickname for much of its early years was "The House That Harley Built."

After the 1919 football season, Harley joined the Buckeyes' basketball team and helped OSU to a 17–10 record, establishing a new school record for victories in a single season. In the spring, he rejoined the baseball team and became that program's first-ever four-year letterman.

Harley was good enough in baseball to receive contract offers from the St. Louis Browns and the Chicago White Sox. He chose instead to play pro football in his hometown of Chicago, and he led the Decatur Staleys in passing in 1921.

SITE OF OHIO FIELD (1903–21)
WHERE CHARLES W. "CHIC" HARLEY,
ALL-AMERICAN HALFBACK IN
1916-17-19, PERFORMED THOSE
FEATS WHICH MADE HIM AN OHIO
STATE FOOTBALL LEGEND AND
SPARKED THE PUBLIC ENTHUSIASM
WHICH LED TO THE CONSTRUCTION
OF OHIO STADIUM.

PLAQUE designating the site of Ohio Field, along with a god-like description of Chic Harley's gridiron exploits.

But he began a lifelong battle with depression, and despite returning to Ohio State for a charity football game in 1923 and serving briefly as a volunteer assistant coach under Wilce, Harley simply could not shake his personal demons. After what was termed in those days a "nervous breakdown," Harley entered the Veterans Administration Hospital in Danville, Illinois, in 1938. With very few exceptions, it would be his home for the next thirty-six years.

Harley returned to Columbus only a handful of times. After the gala parade in 1948, he returned in 1953 and was honored at Ohio Stadium for his induction into the College Football Hall of Fame. In 1951, Harley was a member of the inaugural class of inductees to the college hall, honored with such other legends as Sammy Baugh, George Gipp, Knute Rockne, Glenn "Pop" Warner, Grange, Stagg, and Camp.

Harley also returned to Columbus a year later to mark the 35th reunion of the 1919 team.

He continued to follow the Buckeyes through the late 1950s and into the middle '60s, attending games occasionally until declining health kept him hospitalized during most of his final years.

Harley died on April 24, 1974, in Danville, Illinois, at the age of 78.

His body was returned to Columbus for memorial services and was driven past Ohio Stadium one last time on its way to burial in Union Cemetery on Olentangy River Road, the same cemetery that serves as the final resting place for longtime Ohio State head coach Woody Hayes. Two-time Heisman Trophy winner Archie Griffin served as one of Harley's pallbearers.

In 1977, Ohio State honored him in its first-ever class of inductees into the university's athletic hall of fame. And there have been calls for Ohio Stadium to be renamed Harley Stadium many times throughout the years.

GAMEDAY HAUNTS

Buckeye Hall of Fame Café Food, drink, games, tons of Buckeye memorabilia. What more could you ask for from a place that is also within walking distance of the stadium?

But the Buckeyes' first true football star had largely become forgotten until the university honored Harley during the 2004 season and retired his jersey.

As for Harley's place in historical perspective, Homan believes Ohio Stadium stands as the largest monument to what the program's first real star meant to the evolution of college football in Columbus and the stature of Ohio State around the country.

"It would be very difficult to measure Harley against players of other eras because the game of football is so different now than what it was then," Homan said. "I would say this: He would have to be among the very best because he only played in one losing game in the Big Ten during the three years of his career. Not very many players can make that statement.

"You must also remember that when Harley played, players were expected to play 60 minutes and play just as well on defense as on offense. So for all of those reasons—not to mention the fact that the stadium was built because of him—he would have to be among the greatest greats Ohio State has ever had."

HARLEY'S RUNNING MATE—PETE STINCHCOMB

You may not know his name, but you no doubt know his face.

Gaylord Roscoe "Pete" Stinchcomb was born June 24, 1895, near Sycamore, Ohio, a tiny village just northeast of Upper Sandusky, and he became a football, basketball, and track star at nearby Fremont High School.

Because Ohio State was experiencing its first taste of recognition on the national scene thanks to halfback Chic Harley, who had led the team to a perfect 7–0 record in 1916 and the school's first conference championship, Stinchcomb was enticed to continue his playing career for the Buckeyes.

Stinchcomb joined the varsity squad in 1917 and combined with Harley to make one of the most lethal backfield tandems in college football. According to newspaper accounts of the day, "Harley lit the fire and Stinchcomb fanned the flames."

In the '17 season opener against Case, the Buckeyes suffered a potentially devastating blow when Harley suffered an injury and spent most of the afternoon on the sidelines. But Stinchcomb took over at halfback and scored a couple of touchdowns as Ohio State rolled to a 49–0 victory.

Two weeks later, in the conference opener against Northwestern, Harley was back at full strength and provided the blocking for three touchdown runs by Stinchcomb during a 40–0 win.

Ohio State eventually stormed its way to another undefeated season, going 8–0–1 (the lone blemish being a 0–0 tie against Auburn) and outscoring its opposition by a whopping 292–6 margin. More importantly, the Buckeyes had clinched another conference title, their first back-to-back outright championships. That feat has been equaled only twice since—in 1954 and 1955, and again in 2006 and 2007.

Harley and Stinchcomb each missed the 1918 season while serving in World War I, but they made a triumphant return the following year. With Harley at halfback and Stinchcomb moving to quarterback, the Buckeyes won their first six games, including their first-ever victory over Michigan, a 13–3 win at Ann Arbor. Unfortunately, the duo missed out on another Western Conference championship when the team suffered a 9–7 upset loss to Illinois in the 1919 season finale.

After the season, Harley and Stinchcomb earned first-team All-America honors. It was the third award for Harley and the first for Stinchcomb. After Harley graduated, Stinchcomb moved back to a halfback position in 1920 and finished his collegiate career with another undefeated regular season and conference championship. He scored three times in the team's 55–0 season-opening win over Ohio Wesleyan, then returned a kickoff 95 yards for a touchdown the following week to help the Buckeyes to a 37–0 victory over Oberlin.

Against Wisconsin in the conference season opener the next week, Stinchcomb scored on touchdown receptions of 36 and 48 yards—the latter with just fifty seconds remaining—to key a 13–7 win over the Badgers. It was Wisconsin's only loss that season.

The Scarlet and Gray continued their winning ways, topping off the regular season with a 7–0 win at Illinois. With just 0:04 showing on the game clock, Ohio State scored when Stinchcomb was used as a decoy to draw several Illini defenders to the wide side of the field before quarterback Harry Workman connected with end Cyril "Truck" Myers for a 37-yard touchdown. Stinchcomb kicked the extra point to account for the final point of the contest.

The victory propelled the Buckeyes into their first-ever appearance in the Rose Bowl, a game that resulted in a 28–0 loss to California that so thoroughly disappointed university officials the school would not accept another invitation to Pasadena for twenty-nine years.

The loss wasn't exactly Stinchcomb's fault, though. He ran for a team-high 82 yards on 11 carries before exiting the game in the second half with an injury.

Stinchcomb finished his Ohio State football career with a 21–2–1 record and earned his second straight All-America honor in 1920.

Football wasn't the only thing that defined Stinchcomb, however. He capped his collegiate athletic career in the spring of 1921 by winning the NCAA long jump championship and also served as president of the OSU Student Council during his senior year.

After graduation, Stinchcomb rejoined Harley and played for the Chicago Staleys of American Professional Football Association (the precursor of the National Football League) and the former Ohio State teammates won themselves another championship. Stinchcomb ran for 180 yards and a team-high four touchdowns in 1921, while Harley played quarterback and completed 8 of 13 passes for 120 yards and three TDs.

The following year, Harley left the team, but Stinchcomb remained and was among the team leaders in rushing, receiving, punt returns, and scoring, as the Staleys became the Chicago Bears. Following the 1922 season, Stinchcomb departed Chicago and played with pro teams in Columbus, Cleveland, and Louisville, before retiring from the game in 1925.

He returned to Ohio State in 1935 for a brief stint as running backs coach on Francis Schmidt's staff before entering into private business. He lived in Upper Arlington in suburban Columbus for several years before returning to northern Ohio and beginning a successful construction business in Findlay.

Stinchcomb continued to make regular appearances at Ohio State football games, especially for the annual captains' breakfasts, until his death in 1973 at the age of 78. That same year, he was inducted into the College Football Hall of Fame.

In the thirty-five years since his death, Stinchcomb's legacy has been largely lost. But it had been reborn several times in recent history because of an iconic

PETE STINCHCOMB. A versatile player for the Buckeyes in the early '20s, Stinchcomb and Chic Harley combined to make a nearly unstoppable combination. In recent years, this photograph has immortalized the OSU great.

photograph taken after a muddy game in 1920. One of the most recent showings of the photo came during a second-season episode of the long-running sitcom "Everybody Loves Raymond," in which fictional New York Newsday sportswriter Ray Barone remodels his basement as a home office.

Adorning one wall, located just above Raymond's desk, is the photo showing the mud-caked, smiling face of Pete Stinchcomb.

JACK WILCE—THE "REAL" ARCHITECT OF BUCKEYE FOOTBALL

Most Ohio State fans credit Woody Hayes with shining the national spotlight on Buckeye football as we know it today. In reality, the foundation for Ohio State football as a perennial powerhouse was laid in 1913, the year Hayes was born in Clifton, Ohio.

The driving force behind the Scarlet and Gray as they took their place as a college football power was Jack Wilce, who spent sixteen seasons in Columbus from 1913 to 1928 and took the Buckeyes from a fledgling club sport to a program with nationwide prestige.

John Woodworth Wilce was born March 12, 1888, in Rochester, New York, and got his first taste of the Western Conference (later the Big Ten) when he became a three-sport letterman at the University of Wisconsin. Wilce earned all-conference honors as a fullback with the Badgers in 1909 and then went into coaching.

Following his graduation from Wisconsin, he took over the program at La Crosse High School before returning to his alma mater as an assistant professor of physical education and an assistant football coach. The Badgers were one of the country's top programs at the time and had won the 1912 Western Conference title with an undefeated record.

Meanwhile, Ohio State was struggling to get traction with its program. The Buckeyes had been playing football since 1890 and had enjoyed some success playing mostly instate rivals. But that was about to change when the school was invited to join the Western Conference beginning with the 1913 football season.

Not only was OSU taking a step up in competition; the university also needed some stability at the head coaching position. Eleven men had served as head of the program in just twenty-three years, and none had stayed longer than four seasons. In fact, by 1913, the Buckeyes were in search of their fourth new head coach in as many years.

Enter Wilce, who at the tender age of twenty-five was given the task of building Ohio State football into an intercollegiate program capable of competing with stronger, more established teams. Easier said than done. When Wilce took over the program, the Buckeyes held a respectable 126–72–17 record against all-time opponents, but they were only 7–23–4 against out-of-state rivals.

During the new coach's initial season in 1913, the Buckeyes turned in a 4–2–1 overall record including a 58–0 win over Northwestern in the season finale. It was the team's first conference victory, and it wound up with a 1–2 league record and sixth-place finish.

Wilce saw incremental improvement the next two years, as Ohio State finished in a fourth-place tie in 1914 and a third-place tie in 1915, before the program's breakout season came in 1916. The coach had signed one of the country's top prospects from East High School in Columbus, and Charles "Chic" Harley led the Buckeyes to their first-ever Western Conference championship as a sophomore. OSU set a host of school records that season, including a 128–0 win over Ohio Wesleyan—the most points ever scored by the Buckeyes in a single game.

The Wilce-Harley combination also produced Ohio State's first-ever win over archrival Michigan. The 13–3 victory in Ann Arbor in 1919 ended a previous fifteen-game drought against the Wolverines that had produced no victories and only two ties.

Wilce would guide Ohio State to two more conference titles in 1917 and 1920 and three runner-up finishes in 1919, 1921, and 1926. He also coached ten All-Americans, a pretty fair accomplishment especially in an age when the majority of All-Americans hailed from Ivy League schools.

During Wilce's tenure, the Buckeyes were transformed from a team with only a regional following into a national force that played its home games in cavernous Ohio Stadium. And while coaches such as Knute Rockne, Pop Warner, and Amos Alonzo Stagg are more renowned today for the impact they had on football's early days, Wilce doesn't receive nearly enough credit for being one of the game's top tacticians of his time.

His teams played tenacious defense, and Wilce was one of the first coaches ever to adopt the strategy of rushing the passer. He is also believed to be the first ever to utilize the five-man defensive line, unveiling it during a game at Princeton in 1927.

In addition to his innovative pass defense, Wilce also specialized in a wide-open passing attack. While most teams played ball-control with their triple option formations, Wilce allowed his players to throw extensively throughout the game. During the 1920 season, the Buckeyes defeated Illinois and won the conference title by throwing the football. In that game, quarterback Harry "Hoge" Workman passed to Cyril "Truck" Myers for the winning touchdown on the final play of the game, giving the Buckeyes a 7–0 win.

Earlier that season, Ohio State had come from behind to beat Wisconsin when Workman threw two late touchdown passes to All-American Gaylord "Pete" Stinchcomb. Walter Camp was in attendance and later wrote that the game was the "most thrilling I have ever seen."

The Wilce-Harley combination also produced Ohio State's first-ever win over archrival Michigan.

Wilce also tried to marry the physical and mental aspects of the sport. He was constantly trying to reform the way his players talked on and off the field, and he is credited with coining the phrase "intestinal fortitude." He first used the term in 1916 while lecturing his team on anatomy and physiology.

Wilce coached at Ohio State for sixteen seasons, a record that wouldn't be surpassed until Woody Hayes spent twenty-eight seasons in Columbus from 1951–78. After the 1928 season, Wilce resigned, citing a personal struggle of trying to balance the ideals of athletics with the increasing financial requirements needed to field a team that could compete annually for national honors.

"I figured football was becoming more and more of a business proposition than I wanted to go into," Wilce said years later. "I saw the game being taken away from the boys. I was a faculty-type coach. I had always stressed educational aspects of the sport. This, to me, was far more important than winning the game.

"I don't want to give the impression that I'm critical of football the way it is played today. It came about through no one's fault in particular. It followed the normal trend of things and was brought about by the public's demand. I just didn't want to become an active part of that type of football, so I quit."

JOHN W. WILCE compiled a 78-33-9 record over his 16 seasons as head coach of the Buckeyes. He is a member of the College Football Hall of Fame

Wilce could have ridden off into the sunset with his legacy intact. He was inducted into the College Football Hall of Fame in 1954 and wrote several books on football, many of which became primers for coaches who followed him into the profession. He was an honorary life member of the American Football Coaches Association, served as the group's first secretary, and received the Stagg Award in 1959, the association's highest honor for "perpetuating the example and influence of the great coach in football."

But Wilce went on to another career and had as much success—if not more—than he enjoyed on the gridiron.

He had continued his studies of medicine at Ohio State while serving as head coach and received his medical degree in 1919. After his resignation, Wilce took post-graduate classes at Columbia and Harvard, as well as the National Hospital for Diseases of the Heart in London, and then returned to Ohio State in the 1930s as a professor of preventive medicine at the university's College of Medicine. He later became one of the country's leading heart specialists, and he also served as director of Student Health Services at OSU from 1934 to 1958. The John W. Wilce Student Health Center, built on the Ohio State campus in 1969, is named after him.

Wilce retired to his Westerville home in 1958 and continued to remain active in numerous Columbus charitable organizations until he suffered a stroke in 1962. He was hospitalized twice over the next several months, and died at home on May 17, 1963, just five days after his 75th birthday.

Wilce's legacy lived on through his grandchildren. Anne Krause was one of Colorado's best-loved sports and outdoor photographers until her death of pancreatic cancer in 2006, and Dr. James M. Wilce Jr. is one of the world's top linguistic anthropologists and is currently a professor at Northern Arizona University.

KNUTE ROCKNE—HEAD COACH OF THE BUCKEYES?

The legendary Jack Wilce was preparing in the summer of 1928 for what would be his final season as head football coach at Ohio State.

Wilce had coached the Buckeyes since 1913 and brought the program its first glory. During his tenure, OSU had beaten archrival Michigan for the first time, achieved its first-ever unblemished season, and captured its first conference championship. His seventeen years of service as head coach was by far a school record at the time—no one else had served more than five seasons—and Wilce would finish with a record of 78–33–9.

Sam Willaman, Wilce's right-hand man for the previous three seasons, was named his successor as head coach, in a move everyone thought was a foregone conclusion. In fact, at the end of the 1928 season, several Columbus newspapers called it "a mere formality." Nothing could have been further from the truth.

Notre Dame head coach Knute Rockne was already a legend by 1928, having piloted the Fighting Irish since 1918 and compiling an 81–8–5 record in the process. Even with all of that success, Rockne was grossly underpaid and had repeatedly tried in vain to negotiate a better contract in South Bend.

Rockne finally decided to look elsewhere and let Ohio State officials know that he might be persuaded to make a change. He discussed particulars with OSU athletic director Lynn St. John at the American Football Coaches Association meeting in January 1929 and reportedly agreed to terms to take over the Ohio State program that fall. The agreement was contingent, however, on Notre Dame releasing Rockne from his current contract.

The rest, of course, is history. Notre Dame came up with enough money to keep Rockne in South Bend, and Ohio State named Willaman as its new head coach. Neither man would be able to savor his accomplishment for very long.

Rockne coached at Notre Dame through the 1930 season and was killed in a plane crash on March 31, 1931. He was 43.

Willaman, an Ohio native and Ohio State alum, lasted five seasons with the Buckeyes, posting a 26–10–5 record. But the stress of the job got to him. Despite

SCHOOL TRADITIONS

The Illibuck Trophy A tradition since 1925, the Illibuck is a replica of a turtle and is presented to the winner of the Ohio State-Illinois game. The trophy is presented at halftime of the game, to the previous year's winner.

recruiting several All-America players, including Wes Fesler and Sid Gillman, Ohio State never won a conference title under his tutelage. Making matters worse was a 2–3 record against Michigan.

Willman resigned under pressure following the 1933 season, accepting the head coaching job at Western Reserve. Less than two years later, he died following emergency intestinal surgery. He was 44.

So while Willaman certainly was not a failure, it is an interesting footnote in OSU history: What might have been had Rockne taken the helm of the Scarlet and Gray?

Chapter 3

LITTLE-KNOWN FACTS ABOUT OHIO STATE'S FOOTBALL COACHES

Throughout the course of its 100-plus-year history, OSU has employed twenty-two coaches. Success comes from the top, and Ohio State's illustrious history owes much to the excellent coaches who have patrolled the sidelines. Here are a few facts every Ohio State Die-Hard should know about the OSU coaches from years past.

ALEXANDER S. LILLEY (1890–1891)—In 1890, Ohio State senior George Cole took up a collection from fellow students to purchase a regulation football and a book of football rules from the Spaulding Athletic Supply Co. That was the beginning of the football program at The Ohio State University.

Cole later asked his friend Lilley, who had played organized football at Princeton, to serve as coach without pay. Lilley agreed, riding a pony to practice each day. The Buckeyes won their first game, beating Ohio Wesleyan by a 20–14 score on May 4.

That was the team's only win in its inaugural season, however. They lost their final three contests to Wooster, Denison, and Kenyon by a combined score of 96–0.

JACK RYDER (1892–1895, 1898)—Born Frederick Bushnell Ryder in Oberlin, Ohio, Ryder was Ohio State's first paid head coach. In his first season, he was paid the handsome sum of $15 per week. He led the Buckeyes to their first winning season in history, a 5–3 mark in 1892, and is credited with being the first coach to hold closed practice sessions.

Ryder eventually left the coaching profession and became a sportswriter, first at the old *Ohio Journal* in Columbus and later at the *Cincinnati Enquirer*. During his tenure at the *Enquirer*, he was the first to call University of Cincinnati sports teams "the Bearcats." Ryder died of a heart attack in 1936 at the age of 64.

CHARLES A. HICKEY (1896)—Hickey was hired after the 1896 season began and took over for interim coach Sid Farrer, a medical student who had played college football at Princeton. Hickey was only one year removed from his own college playing career, having been captain of the Williams College team in 1895.

The team finished 5–5–1 in Hickey's only season, and he was dismissed by the university. It didn't seem to matter to him, though. He had already left town and had to be informed of the school's decision by telegram.

DAVID F. EDWARDS (1897)—Another Princeton graduate became head coach when Edwards took over the job. But he got it only when Fielding Yost—the same Yost who went on to legendary status at Michigan—had a less-than-sterling interview for the position.

Yost, who had been head coach at Ohio Wesleyan, wanted to coach at Ohio State, but during a visit to campus was a little overzealous. It seems that he showed a couple of his patented plays to a student and a faculty member, knocking both to the ground.

The Buckeyes selected Edwards over Yost, and then Edward proceeded to turn in one of the program's poorest records at 1–7–1. Even the lone victory was tainted—Ohio Medical was leading by a touchdown but left the field after protesting an OSU touchdown. Officials later awarded the win by forfeit to the Buckeyes.

JOHN B. ECKSTORM (1899–1901)—Eckstorm was the first "professional" coach to pilot the Buckeyes, and his approach to the game produced the program's first undefeated season. The team posted a 9–0–1 mark in 1899, outscoring its opponents by a 184–5 margin. All nine wins were shutouts, and the only blemish on the season was a 5–5 tie against Case.

After the season, Eckstorm was rewarded with another program first. The university rehired him for the next two years, making him the first Ohio State coach in history to sign a multiyear contract.

PERRY HALE (1902–1903)—Hale, a former star player at Yale, took over the program when critics were calling for its abolishment. During the 1901 season, OSU center John Sigrist suffered a neck injury during a 6–5 win over Western Reserve and died two days later. A resolution to cancel the rest of the season and abolish the program was defeated by an 18–8 vote of the Athletic Board.

Hale brought several new ideas to the Buckeyes, innovations that were seen as safer than traditional methods, although the coach was credited with perfecting the "flying wedge," a formation that led to a number of major injuries throughout college football.

E. R. SWEETLAND (1904–1905)—Edwin Regur Sweetland was a native New Yorker who coached football, basketball, track and rowing at nine different colleges and universities during his career. He was a graduate of Cornell, where he played football for legendary head coach Glenn "Pop" Warner.

During his first season with the Buckeyes in 1904, the team achieved a program first when it finally scored points against archrival Michigan. (In five previous games, Michigan had outscored Ohio State by a lopsided 177–0.) The 1904 score came on a 50-yard fumble return by Bill Marquardt and was the only bright spot for OSU in a 31–6 defeat to the Wolverines.

Sweetland left coaching after the 1918 season and went into politics. He died in 1950 at the age of 75.

A. E. HERRNSTEIN (1906–1909)—A native of Chillicothe, Ohio, Herrnstein presided over the first Ohio State team to play an entire season without giving up a touchdown.

In finishing 8–1 in 1906, the Buckeyes recorded six shutouts, surrendered only two field goals (worth four points in those days) during a 12–8 win over Ohio Medical, and lost a 6–0 verdict to Michigan when the Wolverines scored on a field goal and a safety. The Buckeyes also attempted their first forward pass during the 1906 season.

Herrnstein is also the only Michigan graduate ever to serve as Ohio State head coach.

HOWARD JONES (1910)—Born in Middletown, Ohio, Jones was a college football star at Yale when the Bulldogs won three straight national championships from 1905–07. He wasn't sure he wanted to be a coach, though. He spent one-year stints at Syracuse, Yale and Ohio State, going 6–1–3 with the Buckeyes before deciding to go into private business.

Jones returned to coaching six years later and enjoyed success at both Iowa and Southern California. He won back-to-back Big Ten titles with the Hawkeyes in 1921–22, the only time in history Iowa has won consecutive league crowns. Later, Jones captured seven conference championships and went a perfect 5 for 5 in Rose Bowl appearances in sixteen seasons with the Trojans.

He retired following the 1940 season and died at the age of 55 the following summer. In 1951, ten years after his death, Jones was included in the inaugural class of inductees in the College Football Hall of Fame.

HARRY VAUGHN (1911)—Vaughn, who had no previous coaching experience, was another former player from Yale, and he got the Ohio State job solely on Jones's recommendation. But he didn't seem too interested in the job.

He guided the Buckeyes to a 5–3–2 record but left after the season to resume his law studies at Yale. OSU was rapidly getting the reputation for being unable to hold onto its coaches, searching for its eleventh different head coach in just twenty-three seasons of organized football.

JOHN R. RICHARDS (1912)—Richards packed a bunch of firsts into his only season as head coach. Hired also as the university's first-ever director of athletics, he did away with closed practice sessions, encouraging fans to attend and even suggest plays. It helped usher in a new era of enthusiasm for the program, enthusiasm that spiked even more when Richards installed lights on the practice field for nighttime drills.

Unfortunately, after a 6–3 record, Richards abruptly resigned following the 1912 season. In retrospect, he might have done Ohio State a favor. His resignation led to the hiring of Lynn St. John as athletic director and John W. Wilce as head football coach.

JOHN W. WILCE (1913–1928)—John Woodworth Wilce was a native of Rochester, New York, who lettered in three sports at Wisconsin. Ohio State, however, was the school that gave Wilce his first chance to be a head football coach, and he stayed in Columbus for sixteen seasons, the second-longest tenure in program history.

Under Wilce's guidance, the Buckeyes earned their first conference championship (1916), received their first-ever invitation to play in the Rose Bowl (1920), and began play in Ohio Stadium (1922).

Wilce retired following the 1928 season and became a professor of preventive medicine at the Ohio State College of Medicine, specializing in research and treatment of heart diseases. He also served as director of Student Health Services from 1934 to 1958. Wilce died in 1963 just five days after his 75th birthday.

SAM WILLAMAN (1929–1933)—While Willaman posted a rather nondescript 26–10–5 record during his four seasons as head coach of the Buckeyes, he achieved much better success as a player. He was a star halfback for the Buckeyes from 1911–13, and in 1921 was selected as second-team halfback on Ohio State's all-time team just behind Chic Harley.

Willaman also played professional football for the Canton Bulldogs, starring the same backfield alongside Jim Thorpe.

Also, Willaman hired one of his former players as an assistant coach in 1931. That former player was Richard Larkins, who would eventually succeed St. John as Ohio State athletic director in 1947 and serve in that position until 1970.

Records

SEASON-BY-SEASON

1890: 1–3	**1910:** 6–1–3	**1930:** 5–2–1
1891: 2–2	**1911:** 5–3–2	**1931:** 6–3
1892: 5–3	**1912:** 6–3	**1932:** 4–1–3
1893: 4–5	**1913:** 4–2–1	**1933:** 7–1
1894: 6–5	**1914:** 5–2	**1934:** 7–1
1895: 4–4–2	**1915:** 5–1–1	**1935:** 7–1
1896: 5–5–1	**1916:** 7–0	**1936:** 5–3
1897: 1–7–1	**1917:** 8–0–1	**1937:** 6–2
1898: 3–5	**1918:** 3–3	**1938:** 4–3–1
1899: 9–0–1	**1919:** 6–1	**1939:** 6–2
1900: 8–1–1	**1920:** 7–1	**1940:** 4–4
1901: 5–3–1	**1921:** 5–2	**1941:** 6–1–1
1902: 6–2–2	**1922:** 3–4	**1942:** 9–1*
1903: 8–3	**1923:** 3–4–1	**1943:** 3–6
1904: 6–5	**1924:** 2–3–3	**1944:** 9–0
1905: 8–2–2	**1925:** 4–3–1	**1945:** 7–2
1906: 8–1	**1926:** 7–1	**1946:** 4–3–2
1907: 7–2–1	**1927:** 4–4	**1947:** 2–6–1
1908: 6–4	**1928:** 5–2–1	**1948:** 6–3
1909: 7–3	**1929:** 4–3–1	**1949:** 7–1–2

* national champions

1950: 6–3

1951: 4–3–2

1952: 6–3

1953: 6–3

1954: 10–0*

1955: 7–2

1956: 6–3

1957: 9–1*

1958: 6–1–2

1959: 3–5–1

1960: 7–2

1961: 8–0–1*

1962: 6–3

1963: 5–3–1

1964: 7–2

1965: 7–2

1966: 4–5

1967: 6–3

1968: 10–0*

1969: 8–1

1970: 9–1*

1971: 6–4

1972: 9–2

1973: 10–0–1

1974: 10–2

1975: 11–1

1976: 9–2–1

1977: 9–3

1978: 7–4–1

1979: 11–1

1980: 9–3

1981: 9–3

1982: 9–3

1983: 9–3

1984: 9–3

1985: 9–3

1986: 10–3

1987: 6–4–1

1988: 4–6–1

1989: 8–4

1990: 7–4–1

1991: 8–4

1992: 8–3–1

1993: 10–1–1

1994: 9–4

1995: 11–2

1996: 11–1

1997: 10–3

1998: 11–1

1999: 6–6

2000: 8–4

2001: 7–5

2002: 14–0*

2003: 11–1

2004: 8–4

2005: 10–2

2006: 12–1

2007: 11–2

2008: 10–3

FRANCIS A. SCHMIDT (1934–1940)—Schmidt may have had one of the most unique nicknames ever in college football history. Because most of his teams were known for high scoring, newspapers began calling him Francis "Close the Gates of Mercy" Schmidt.

He is known for beginning several traditions at Ohio State, including the Gold Pants Club—each member of the program receives a small gold pants charm for beating Michigan.

The club came about by accident when Schmidt asked in his first season at OSU about playing the Wolverines. Despite the fact the Buckeyes had won only six of the previous thirty games with their archrivals, Schmidt replied, "Those fellows put their pants on one leg at a time, same as everyone else."

OSU beat Michigan 34–0 in Columbus that year and shut the Wolverines out in each of the next two years, making Schmidt the first—and still only—coach in school history to beat Michigan in each of his first three tries.

PAUL BROWN (1941–1943)—It's difficult to uncover much about a man who is credited with changing the way football is played today. However, here are a couple of things you may not have known.

Brown played quarterback in high school at Massillon, Ohio, following Harry Stuhldreher, who went on to become one of Notre Dame's legendary "Four Horsemen." Brown later played his college football at Miami (Ohio) but not before first enrolling at Ohio State. As a 145-pound freshman quarterback for the Buckeyes, he soon found out his body couldn't take the pounding of a Western Conference schedule, and Brown transferred to Miami. He graduated there in 1930 with an undergraduate degree in education then got his Masters a decade later from Ohio State.

Finally, let's dispel the myth that the Cleveland Browns are named after Paul Brown. In reality, they are named after former heavyweight boxing champion Joe "The Brown Bomber" Louis. The team was originally named the Brown Bombers, which was later shortened to simply the Browns.

CARROLL C. WIDDOES (1944–1945)—Widdoes was Brown's hand-picked successor at Ohio State with the understanding he would simply hold the job while

CARROLL WIDDOES.
Although he compiled a 16–2 record over two seasons, Widdoes abruptly resigned as OSU coach following the 1945 season.

Brown served in the U.S. Navy during World War II. But two things conspired against Widdoes—first was his easy-going, soft-spoken nature; second was the fact he simply wasn't Brown.

After the Buckeyes went 9–0 in Widdoes's first season, they slipped to 7–2 in 1945, and the natives weren't happy. Widdoes abruptly resigned and didn't coach again until four years later, when he resurfaced at Ohio University. He stayed in Athens for nine seasons, going 42–36–5 with the Bobcats and winning the Mid-American Conference championship in 1953.

PAUL O. BIXLER (1946)—Bixler is the sixth head coach in Ohio State history to serve only one season and—so far—the most recent. His brief tenure was marred by a 4–3–2 record that included a 58–6 thrashing at the hands of Michigan.

Bixler resigned after the '46 season, citing pressure of the job as the major reason.

The Mount Union graduate landed on his feet, though. He later spent five seasons as head coach at Colgate, then followed Brown to the NFL and served several years as director of player personnel for the Cleveland Browns.

WESLEY E. FESLER (1947–1950)—One of the finest all-around athletes the Youngstown area has ever produced—and it has produced more than its share—Fesler was a three-time, first-team All-America end for the Buckeyes from 1928–30 and also starred on the OSU baseball and basketball teams. He was good enough in basketball that he became that program's first consensus first-team All-America selection in 1930.

Despite overtures from the NFL to continue his playing career, Fesler wanted to coach and began as an assistant on Willaman's staff in 1931. He later coached at Harvard, Princeton (where he was also head basketball coach), and Pittsburgh before returning to his alma mater in 1947.

Fesler would last only four seasons with the Buckeyes, though, resigning under pressure after a 9–3 loss to Michigan in the 1950 Snow Bowl. He resurfaced the following year at Minnesota before leaving coaching and pursuing a career in real estate.

WOODY

Photo by (TSN Archives) ZUMA Press

MIKE TOMCZAK and Earle Bruce

Fesler died of complications due to Alzheimer's disease in California in 1989 at the age of 81.

WOODY HAYES (1951–1978)—Think you know everything there is to know about Woody? How about this: He wasn't only a student of military history; he lived it. He enlisted in the U.S. Navy in July 1941, six months before the Japanese attack on Pearl Harbor. During World War II, Hayes commanded two different Navy ships—submarine chaser PC-1251 during the Palau Islands invasion and destroyer-escort USS *Rinehart*, which served in both the Atlantic and Pacific oceans.

If you insist that your nuggets be restricted to football, ask your buddies if they know who succeeded Woody at Miami (Ohio) when he became head coach of the Buckeyes. The answer is Ara Parseghian.

EARLE BRUCE (1979–1987)—When Bruce was recruited by Penn State during his senior season of high school in Cumberland, Maryland, Nittany Lions head coach Joe Bedenk sent an assistant coach to make first contact. That assistant's name—believe it or not—was Earl Bruce.

Bedenk was head coach at Penn State for only the 1949 season, after which he requested to return to his old position as line coach. Bruce (the one without the "e" at the end of his first name) served as interim coach for spring practice until new head coach Rip Engel was hired away from Brown. Engel, of course, brought with him to Happy Valley a young assistant coach named Joe Paterno.

JOHN COOPER (1988–2000)—It seems like Cooper has spent all of his life in the coaching profession, beginning as a college assistant in 1962 and serving at eight different schools over the next thirty-nine years.

Before that, he was a gritty running back and safety at Iowa State. After graduating from high school and spending two years serving in the U.S. Army, Cooper enrolled at Iowa State on a football scholarship and quickly became one of the Cyclones' best players. He played both offense and defense and was a member of the school's famed "Dirty Thirty," the 1959 squad that finished 7–3, including upsets of Nebraska and Colorado.

JIM TRESSEL.
Since 2001, Tressel has carried on OSU's tradition of excellence, to date winning 5 Big Ten Championships to go along with his 2002 National Championship trophy.

Cooper was a sophomore on that team and went on to captain the 1961 team most remembered for beating Oklahoma in Norman, the Cyclones' first win there in thirty years.

JIM TRESSEL (2001–PRESENT)—Like Hayes, it's difficult to come up with anything about Tressel that isn't already well-known. But we'll try.

For example, did you know Tressel graduated cum laude from Baldwin Wallace with a degree in education?

Did you know that during his tenure at Youngstown State, he shifted a game against Akron to Friday night one season when it was originally scheduled for the same day as the OSU–Michigan game?

Did you know that his boyhood idol was Rex Kern?

And did you know that Lee and Jim Tressel make up the only father–son combination ever to win NCAA national championships?

Chapter 4

WOODY COMES TO COLUMBUS

The story of the man who built the Ohio State football program into a major powerhouse began in humble surroundings. Wayne Woodrow Hayes was born February 14, 1913, to Wayne Benton and Effie Jane Hayes in the tiny town of Clifton, Ohio, a small village near Springfield on the Greene and Clarke county line.

His family moved to Selma, Ohio, when Hayes was two, after his father took the position of superintendent of schools. Five years later, the family moved again, this time to Newcomerstown, Ohio, when his father accepted a job as school superintendent there. Hayes and his two siblings—brother Isaac, who was two years older than Woody, and sister Mary, eight years Woody's senior—lived in a white frame house overlooking what was left of the historical Ohio Canal.

As a youngster, Hayes mowed lawns and delivered newspapers to earn extra money but spent most of his spare time reading. It was a pastime that served him well later in life as he became a noted historian, especially on military history.

His father had studied at six different colleges and universities before earning his degree at Wittenberg University, and Hayes understood the value of a college education. In his book *You Win With People*, he described his favorite teacher, Clyde Bartholomew, who taught Hayes in the sixth and seventh grades.

"He taught English so thoroughly," Hayes wrote, "that from that time forward I never had any difficulty with it, and I ended up with a major in English."

There was also time for sports as well. Hayes professed to be a good football player but not a great one. Nevertheless, he captained his high school team in Newcomerstown and played basketball and baseball as well.

Woody graduated high school and enrolled at Denison University in Granville, Ohio, where he went out for the Big Red football team. He was a hard-nosed, 200-pound tackle on a team that wasn't very good. Denison posted a 2–6 season during Hayes's sophomore season and a 2–5–1 record the following year. By his senior season, he had switched to the center position, and the Big Red finished 6–1–1 under head coach George Rich.

Hayes was a three-time letterman at Denison from 1932–34, but he also excelled in academics. He majored in history and English and briefly considered a law career. With the country in the midst of the Great Depression, pursuing a law degree was financially impossible, so Hayes became a high school teacher and football coach.

His first job was as an English teacher and assistant football coach at Mingo Junction, Ohio, a tough little town on the Ohio River across from the West Virginia panhandle and just south of Steubenville. Woody later wrote how that first year of teaching and coaching had a tremendous influence on him.

"I taught seventh grade with supposedly slow learners," he said. "But they weren't. Those youngsters were merely *neglected* learners."

After one year at Mingo Junction, Hayes accepted a job as history teacher and assistant coach at New Philadelphia, Ohio. During the summer between his Mingo Junction and New Philadelphia assignments, Woody decided to enroll in graduate school at Ohio State. He wanted to enter law school but found there were no summer sessions. Instead, he decided he would follow in his father's footsteps and get his master's degree in educational administration.

The following summer, while attending graduate school classes, Hayes met another young coach, Paul Brown, who was then head coach at Massillon High School. The two devoted countless hours to talking football and forged a friendship that would last the rest of their lives.

Hayes spent three seasons as a line coach on Johnny Brickels's staff at New Philadelphia before succeeding Brickels as head coach in 1938. His first two teams with the Quakers won 18 of 19 games before graduation took a heavy toll and his 1940 squad went just 1–9.

Like most other young men of the era, Hayes enlisted in the military as World War II was brewing. He attended the U.S. Navy's officers training school and rose to the rank of lieutenant commander, and eventually commanded a ship in the Palau Islands invasion in the Pacific and the destroyer-escort USS *Rinehart* in both the Atlantic and Pacific operations.

When the war was over in 1945, Hayes pondered his future. He had married the former Anne Gross in 1942, and the couple had a young son, Steven, and he needed a job. Woody thought about returning to New Philadelphia, but a letter from his alma mater settled things.

Tom Rogers was an assistant coach at Denison when Hayes played there, and Rogers had taken over the head coaching position in 1935. The university had briefly suspended the football program during World War II, and was having trouble getting it started back up again. Rogers, who had left the program in 1941, wanted to know if Hayes was interested in returning to Denison to become head coach.

Woody eagerly accepted the offer and began what would be a long and colorful college coaching career.

With the war just over, Hayes had to start from scratch, and Denison struggled through a 2–6 season in 1946. The following year, with basically the same roster, the Big Red marched to a perfect 9–0 record and then followed with an 8–0 mark in 1948. During those two seasons, Hayes began to perfect his coaching philosophy, and his team responded by averaging 32.4 points per game on offense while allowing a scant 6.3 points on defense.

The 1947 and 1948 seasons were the first and only undefeated seasons in Denison football history, a program that began play in 1889.

Those two unbeaten seasons also helped put Hayes on the coaching fast track. He took over the program at Miami University of Ohio in 1949, and after a 5–4 record that first year, the Redskins posted a 9–1 mark in 1950 and won the Mid-American Conference championship. Miami finished that season with a 34–21 victory over Arizona State in the Salad Bowl (the precursor to today's Fiesta Bowl), and Hayes was a hot commodity again in the coaching market.

One month after his team's bowl win, Woody was on the move again. This time, though, he was headed for Ohio State—a place that was rapidly getting the reputation as being "The Graveyard of Coaches."

Former three-time All-American Wes Fesler was hired as head coach of the Buckeyes in 1947 amid tremendous fanfare from Scarlet and Gray alumni. They welcomed Fesler back to Columbus as a favorite son and conquering hero after his playing days in 1928, 1929, and 1930 had produced tough defenses and a pair of victories over archrival Michigan.

But while Fesler enjoyed some success as head coach at his alma mater, including guiding Ohio State to its first-ever Rose Bowl victory, a 0–3–1 record against Michigan after his fourth season quickly soured fans. The breaking point came after the 1950 rivalry game, now known as "The Snow Bowl." Fesler had called for a controversial third-down punt late in the first half, and when Michigan blocked the kick and recovered it in the end zone, it provided the winning points in a 9–3 Wolverine victory.

Fesler was roundly criticized for the decision to punt, and a few weeks later, he bitterly and abruptly resigned, leaving OSU looking for its fifth new head coach in just ten seasons.

Several prominent candidates were mentioned for the opening, most notably longtime Missouri head man Don Faurot. He accepted the job in Columbus on a Friday and went home to clean out his office. Less than 48 hours later, however, Faurot changed his mind and remained at Missouri.

With spring football only a few weeks away, Ohio State officials quickly reorganized and settled on a field of seven candidates—one professional coach, four coaches from the college ranks, and two Ohio high school coaches.

The pro coach was Paul Brown, who had previously coached the Buckeyes from 1941–43 and produced the school's first national championship in 1942. Brown had already flirted with returning to Ohio State following World War II but instead took a job as head coach of the Cleveland Browns. The coach had led the Browns to championships in each of his first five seasons in Cleveland—four in the All-America Football Conference and the 1950 crown in the NFL.

Brown was the hands-down favorite of Ohio State fans and students to replace Fesler. Approximately 1,500 fans cheered his arrival in Columbus for a meeting with the search committee in late January, a meeting during which Brown reportedly told OSU athletic director Richard Larkins that he was "anxious to leave professional football."

Larkins was not swayed, however. The AD later revealed that a number of influential Columbus businessmen did not want Brown to return. They felt he had reneged on a deal to return to Ohio State after the war, and that he signed with Cleveland without notifying the university.

Nevertheless, newspaper reports continued to trumpet Brown as the front-runner for the vacancy. Also receiving formal interviews were OSU freshman coach Harry Strobel, Cincinnati head coach Sid Gillman, Warren Gaer of Drake, and Hayes, as well as high school coaches Chuck Mather of Massillon and Jim McDonald of Springfield.

In early February, the field had reportedly been pared to three: Brown, Mather, and Hayes, with Strobel as a possible dark horse candidate. Brown was the choice of the fans and Mather was backed by the Ohio High School Coaches Association. Meanwhile, Strobel was the original choice of the athletic department, but Hayes had supplanted him after a stellar interview.

An announcement was to be made around February 14—Hayes's thirty-eighth birthday—but all seven members of the Ohio State Board of Trustees had to agree on the new coach, and the university couldn't seem to get the entire panel together at the same time. In the meantime, the six-man search committee and twelve-member athletic board had settled on Hayes.

The official decision was postponed for another week as speculation ran rampant. What if Hayes was rejected by the trustees? Would the athletic board then throw its support behind Strobel, or would some back-room maneuvering pave the way for Brown to return to Columbus after all?

While speculation continued to surround the coaching search, Ohio State football itself was being adversely effected. Dick Syzmanski, a high school All-America lineman from Libbey High School in Toledo, switched his allegiance from the Buckeyes and decided to enroll at Notre Dame. At the same time, the annual Big Ten meetings were rapidly approaching, leading some to suggest that longtime assistant Ernie Godfrey be named "pro-tem coach" so that the Buckeyes could be properly represented.

The OSU Board of Trustees finally got together to end the speculation on Sunday, February 18. Thanks to an impassioned speech from Senator John W. Bricker, the board formally hired Hayes as the university's nineteenth head football coach. Hayes received a one-year, $12,500 contract in accordance with university policy, but received a five-year "gentleman's agreement" from university president Howard L. Bevis.

Before its Sunday meeting, the board reportedly remained split between Hayes and Brown. That was until Bricker made a ten-minute speech to his fellow trustees opposing Brown and boosting Hayes.

Despite the days and weeks of wrangling before being offered the job, Hayes didn't seem the least bit dismayed by the decision.

"I have wanted this job very much," he told reporters. "It's the greatest coaching opportunity in the country."

> ❝I have wanted this job very much. It's the greatest coaching opportunity in the country.❞
>
> —Woody Hayes

WOODY WAS NOT BUCKEYES' FIRST CHOICE

After the 1950 Michigan game, the contest which has come to be known as the "Snow Bowl," Ohio State officials and fans couldn't wait to get rid of head coach Wes Fesler. Unfortunately, their first choice as a replacement decided against taking the job.

WOODY HAYES. Although initially not the Buckeyes first choice, Hayes certainly turned out to be the best choice as head coach. He helmed the OSU squad for 28 seasons, winning 5 National Championships and 13 Big Ten Championships along the way.

When Fesler was hired by OSU as Paul Bixler's replacement following 1946, the Buckeye Nation could not have been happier. He was a three-time All-American end for the Buckeyes from 1928–30, becoming only the second man in program history after Chic Harley to achieve that feat.

During his playing days, Ohio State never finished higher than fourth in the Western Conference standings, but Fesler enjoyed two victories over archrival Michigan in his three seasons. That included a 7–0 win in 1929 at Ann Arbor, only the third time in fourteen trips up North that the Buckeyes had come back victorious.

When Fesler graduated from Ohio State in the summer of 1931, he spurned several offers to play professionally in the fledgling National Football League, deciding instead to begin a coaching career. He began as an assistant on Sam Willaman's staff at OSU and spent two seasons with his alma mater before accepting an offer from Harvard to become backfield coach for the football team as well as head coach of the men's basketball team. (Fesler had also been an All-American guard in basketball while at Ohio State.)

He stayed at Harvard for eight seasons until getting the urge to try his hand at being a head coach in football. Fesler returned to Ohio to become head coach at Ohio Wesleyan in 1941, but the school interrupted its athletic program the following year because of World War II, and Fesler was out of a job.

By 1945, he had landed the positions of assistant football coach and head basketball coach at Princeton, then moved to Pittsburgh a year later to take over the Panthers' football team. One season later, after going just 3–5–1 at Pitt, Fesler returned to his alma mater and became the eighteenth head coach at Ohio State.

During his first two years, university officials and fans wondered if bringing back the old football star as coach was a mistake. Fesler's teams combined to go just 8–9–1 in his first two seasons and never finished higher than fourth in the conference standings. Worse yet, they had lost back-to-back games to Michigan—21–0 at Ann Arbor in 1947 and 13–3 in Ohio Stadium the following year.

It didn't matter that the Wolverines entered both of those games ranked as the No. 1 team in the nation. The Buckeyes wanted results, and they wanted them quickly.

WOODY at
Michigan in 1975

Fesler managed to stem the tide of criticism in 1949 when his team went 7–1–2, tied for the conference title, and notched a 17–14 win over California in the 1950 Rose Bowl, the program's first-ever win in Pasadena. But keeping a lid on the enthusiasm was a 7–7 at Michigan, a game that prevented the Buckeyes from capturing the outright Big Ten title.

When the 1950 team finished with a 6–3 record, topped off by the bizarre 9–3 loss to Michigan in the Snow Bowl, Fesler's fate was sealed. He resigned after the season to take the head coaching job at conference rival Minnesota.

Fesler knew that his resignation came one step ahead of a pink slip from the university, which already had picked out his successor. OSU athletic director Richard Larkins had already focused his attention on luring Don Faurot away

THE WIT AND WISDOM OF

★ ★ ★

WOODY HAYES

"Any time you give a man something he doesn't earn, you cheapen him. Our kids earn what they get, and that includes respect."

"There's nothing that cleanses your soul like getting the hell kicked out of you."

"I've had smarter people around me all my life, but I haven't run into one yet that can outwork me. And if they can't outwork you, then smarts aren't going to do them much good. That's just the way it is. And if you believe that and live by it, you'd be surprised at how much fun you can have."

"Without winners, there wouldn't even be any civilization."

"That was about as bad an opener as we have ever played. When you get into the passing game, you can expect that sort of thing to happen."

from Missouri. Ten years earlier, when Larkins was working under longtime athletic director Lynn St. John, Faurot was a finalist for the job when it went to a young Ohio high school football coach by the name of Paul Brown.

Faurot was a native Missourian who had played his college football in Columbia in the mid-1920s. He had returned to the Tigers as head coach in 1935 and had compiled a fine 78–44–8 record that included a couple of Big Eight championships. During that time, he devised a new kind of offensive formation that allowed for multiple options out of the same alignment. It was the Split T formation, and Faurot is credited for its invention.

Despite all he had accomplished, Faurot was 48 and beginning to wonder what the world was like outside Missouri. He was intrigued by the possibility of coaching at Ohio State, especially since the Buckeyes had the reigning Heisman Trophy winner in Vic Janowicz returning for his senior season.

If he was ever going to make a career move, now was the time.

In Columbus, Larkins coordinated a six-man search committee that selected seven finalists for Fesler's vacated spot, but the interview process was supposed to be a mere formality. Faurot met with the selection committee on a Saturday in early February 1951 and was immediately offered the job. He accepted and went home to Missouri to clean out his office.

Less than 48 hours later, as Larkins was preparing to call a news conference to announce the hiring of Faurot as the new head coach, his office telephone rang. It was Faurot, telling Larkins that he had changed his mind. He was staying at Missouri.

The AD went back to the selection committee and asked for a second choice. The name that was suggested was Woody Hayes, then the head coach at Miami University. After some initial back-room negotiations, Hayes was offered the job, he accepted immediately, and the rest, as they say, is history.

Ironically, all three principals in the story eventually were elected to the College Football Hall of Fame.

Fesler made it first, inducted as a player in 1954 along with an illustrious class that included Michigan running back Tom Harmon, Jay Berwanger of Chicago, the first Heisman Trophy winner, and the trophy's namesake, longtime coach John Heisman.

Faurot was inducted in 1961, and Hayes was enshrined in 1983.

Faurot continued to coach at Missouri until 1956, when he became the school's athletic director. During his career, he worked with such assistant coaches as Bud Wilkinson and hired the likes of Frank Broyles and Dan Devine while he was AD.

In 1972, five years after retiring from the athletic department, Missouri renamed its football field Faurot Field. He remained a fixture in Columbia until his death in October 1995 (during homecoming week) at the age of 93.

WHERE WOODY GOT HIS "THREE YARDS AND A CLOUD OF DUST" PHILOSOPHY

Do you know who Gomer Jones was? If you're an Ohio State football fan, you should. He wasn't only an outstanding lineman for the Buckeyes in the 1930s; he also helped make the program what it was under legendary head coach Woody Hayes.

Gomer Thomas Jones was born February 26, 1914, in Cleveland, and was a star football player at South High School. At 5' 8" and 210 pounds, Jones was built like a fire hydrant—and was just about as difficult to move out of the way.

He got to Ohio State in the fall of 1932 as a freshman and played varsity ball for the Buckeyes beginning the following season. Playing mostly center and linebacker, Jones helped the team to a 7–1 record in 1933 and second-place finish in the Western Conference.

Unfortunately, the lone loss on the schedule was a 13–0 defeat at Michigan. Then as now, losses to the Wolverines were fatal to OSU head coaches, and fifth-year coach Sam Willaman resigned under pressure at season's end.

In his place, the university hired a brash innovator named Francis A. Schmidt, whose razzle-dazzle approach to the game excited fans. With Jones now a junior and anchoring both the offensive line and linebacker corps on defense, the Buckeyes again finished 7–1 but scored a convincing 34–0 knockout of Michigan.

In his senior season of 1935, Jones was selected captain by his teammates, and the Buckeyes won the conference championship for the first time in 15 years. The only blight was an 18–13 loss to Notre Dame in the so-called "Game of the Century," but there were also plenty of highlights, including another shutout of Michigan, this one a 38–0 verdict in Ann Arbor. It marked the first time the two archrivals had played one another in the final game of the regular season and began a tradition that holds to this day.

After the season, Jones earned first-team all-conference and first-team All-America honors at center. He also became one of the first Buckeyes selected to play in the East–West Shrine Game, an all-star contest for college seniors.

Following his graduation, Jones was drafted No. 15 overall by the Chicago Cardinals of the NFL, but he decided there was more money in coaching football than playing it. He landed a job as an assistant on Schmidt's staff, and when Schmidt was let go by OSU after the 1940 season, Jones became an assistant at John Carroll University before moving to Oklahoma in 1947.

There, he became line coach under the legendary Bud Wilkinson and stayed in Norman throughout Wilkinson's entire 17-year tenure. During that time, the Sooners posted a record of 145–29–4 and won 14 Big Eight titles and three national championships.

In the spring of 1952, Wilkinson had taken ill, and Jones was in charge of putting the team through its spring practice drills. A young coach from the Midwest had asked to come to Norman and watch the Sooners take part in those drills, and he paid special attention to the way Jones coached his offensive linemen. Since the coach was from his alma mater, Jones decided to hold nothing back. He proceeded to show Woody Hayes the kind of philosophy and technique he used to produce All-American linemen.

"Gomer Jones, who had been an All-American at Ohio State, was extremely helpful to me along with the rest of the Oklahoma staff," Hayes later wrote in *You Win With People*, the coach's bestseller from 1973. "I came back to our spring practice and put in the Split T (formation) exactly the way it had been explained to me.

"Going out to Oklahoma in the spring of 1952 (was) where I really learned the basis of our running game which to this day is the hub of our offense."

Hayes used the Split T formation to win national championships in 1954 and '57, and a form of that running style—which later became known as "three yards

A YOUNG WOODY HAYES. To this day, Hayes is one of the most revered men in college football history.

and a cloud of dust"—can be traced back to what Jones taught the Ohio State coach in the spring of 1952.

When Wilkinson retired following the 1963 season, Jones was his hand-picked successor at Oklahoma. Jones lasted only two years as head coach, however, resigning after the 1965 season to concentrate on being athletic director at OU. It was a post in which he remained until his death in 1971 at the age of 57.

That same year, the university established the Gomer Jones Coronary Care Unit within Owen Stadium, an on-site facility for emergency coronary care. There is also a Gomer Jones Residence Hall, an on-campus dormitory that houses OU student-athletes. However, a $12.5 million construction project currently under way at Oklahoma will create new housing on the campus and replace Jones House as well as a dorm named for Wilkinson, who died in 1994.

Although most of his acclaim in later life came while he was at Oklahoma, when Jones was inducted into the College Football Hall of Fame in 1978, it was because of his playing career as a Buckeye. And while many fans of the Scarlet and Gray have long forgotten Jones, they have no trouble remembering his legacy, since he taught Woody Hayes how to run the football.

WOODY'S BIGGEST BOOSTER

When Wayne Woodrow Hayes was born on Valentine's Day in 1913, he became the youngest of three children born to Effie Jane and Wayne Benton Hayes.

Mary was the oldest child by eight years, and Isaac was two years older than Woody.

Mary was an accomplished pianist and studied classical piano at the Ithaca (N.Y.) Conservatory. When she completed her studies, she went to New York and found work in vaudeville. She later became a leading lady on Broadway, acting in such hits as *The War Song* starring alongside George Jessel.

In later life, Mary became the first female radio announcer at WMCA in New York and wrote radio shows for several years until her retirement.

Meanwhile, Isaac turned a boyhood love for horses into a lucrative career in veterinary medicine. Woody once said, "The most colorful person I have ever known was my brother Ike. He had three loves in this world—horses, football, and family."

Ike volunteered for military duty in 1941, five months before Pearl Harbor, and as a captain in the cavalry division was in charge of some 1,500 horses at a base in New Guinea.

Before the war, Ike was an excellent football player.

"Ike was the most intense and the most competitive football player I ever knew," Woody wrote in *You Win With People*. "In high school after the season was over, he cried because he couldn't play more football."

After he graduated from high school, Ike didn't want to continue his education. Woody always reasoned that his older brother refused to go to college because of trouble Ike had had growing up the son of a school superintendent. Tired of having education shoved down his throat, Ike decided to go with his heart and worked with horses for three years.

Finally, after being persuaded by a local farmer on the advantages of a college degree, Ike relented and enrolled at Iowa State. Not only did he become a distinguished student in veterinary medicine, earning distinction as the "Most Representative Man" in his class, Ike resumed his football career and became a star guard for the Cyclones.

Despite his diminutive 5' 6", 158-pound frame, Ike earned first-team all-conference honors in 1934 and '35, and received second-team All-America mention in 1935. He also served as team captain of the Iowa State squad.

To say Woody Hayes idolized his older brother would be something of an understatement.

"Each person who met him regarded Ike as his closest friend," Woody wrote. "He had a personal aura about him that was unbelievable, and it was not the least bit phony. Friends of mine who met him would immediately spend more time with him than they would with me. I have to believe that if it weren't for his attitude and relationship to me, I wouldn't have amounted to much. . . . He was the greatest booster that I ever had."

Not that Ike coddled his younger brother. After watching a game between Miami (Ohio) and Cincinnati, a game in which the Woody-coached Redskins absorbed a lopsided loss, Ike was waiting outside the stadium. He told his brother, "Wood, you got outcoached today and your team got outfought. I'm going to be on this exact spot a year from today, and if you don't beat them, I'm going to beat the hell out of you!"

Woody later said, "Would he have done it? No, but he would have tried. The next year, he had no reason to try for we won, 28–0."

After his graduation from Iowa State, Ike settled in Waterloo, Iowa, and set up a successful veterinary practice. Periodically, he returned to Ohio to watch his brother coach football teams at New Philadelphia (Ohio) High School as well as Denison, Miami, and Ohio State.

Ike proudly traveled with his family to Pasadena for the 1955 Rose Bowl and watched the Buckeyes roll to a 20–7 victory over the University of Southern California to win the 1954 national championship. Then he returned home to resume his veterinary practice.

Less than a month later, he was dead.

"No one enjoyed that [Rose Bowl] victory more than Ike did," Woody said. "Then a couple of weeks later, I got a call one morning from his wife, Lucy, and she said very simply, 'I'm sorry to tell you but your brother just passed away.'"

Ike had gotten up early on the morning of January 25, 1955, and complained that he wasn't feeling well. A few moments later, he collapsed after suffering a massive heart attack. He was only 43.

The funeral was attended by a huge number of people, all of them touched in some way by Ike. Upon returning to Columbus, Woody related the eulogy of a man who helped his brother with horses.

"I can't understand why Ike's been taken from us," the man told Woody, shaking his head. "I guess the Lord has a mighty sick horse."

WOODY'S FINAL GAME

More than thirty years after the incident many believe to be one of the most seminal moments in Ohio State football history, emotions continue to run deep.

On the evening of December 29, 1978, the long and storied coaching career of Woody Hayes ended in the blink of an eye. Near the end of his team's two-point Gator Bowl loss to Clemson that night, the legendary coach threw a punch at Tigers middle guard Charlie Bauman in full view of a national television audience.

Less than eight hours later, Hayes had been fired.

"If you look back at all of milestone moments in Ohio State football history, I would probably have to rank that Gator Bowl incident with Coach Hayes at No. 1," said longtime OSU football historian Jack Park. "After all of the victories and championships, and all of the things Coach Hayes did for the university, it was a shame his career had to come to such an abrupt and tragic end."

Many of the principal players on stage for the last act in that tragedy would rather not be reminded of that soggy night in Jacksonville.

"Why can't people let this rest?" Bauman told the *Florida Times-Union* in December 2008. "It's been 20-something years. Thirty now, I guess. If nothing else happened after the interception, nobody would have ever remembered it. It's really no big deal. It wasn't a big deal for me then, and it's not a big deal now."

Former Ohio State athletic director Jim Jones was senior associate athletic director in 1978, and was seated next to athletic director Hugh Hindman when the incident occurred.

"I'm not even sure why this has to be rehashed," Jones said. "You're asking me how I felt when it happened? You're talking about a guy who was where he was because of Coach Hayes. How in the world do you think I felt? Not very good."

It is probably understandable why three decades' time has not healed some of the deepest wounds from that rainy night in northern Florida.

"We've had situations where coaches were forced to resign under pressure. And, of course, I have always thought Earle Bruce's situation was mishandled," Park said.

"But the way the incident with Coach Hayes played out ...I can remember watching it on television on a Saturday night and being in a state of total disbe-

> **Any time you give a man something he doesn't earn, you cheapen him. Our kids earn what they get, and that includes respect.**
>
> —Woody Hayes

lief. It was probably the next Monday before it really hit me, and I wasn't close to Coach Hayes the way some others were. I can see why many of them would probably be reluctant to dredge up old feelings."

Nearly everything that surrounded the 1978 Gator Bowl seemed to portend ill will for Hayes and the Buckeyes. The invitation to play in the game came after a tumultuous season during which the team had finished 7–3–1 and ended a school-record streak of six consecutive Big Ten championships or co-titles.

At the beginning of the season, Hayes had installed freshman Art Schlichter as the starting quarterback, moving incumbent Rod Gerald to a receiver position. The move did not sit well with many senior members of the team, especially since Gerald was extremely popular and had earned first-team All-Big Ten honors the year before.

The Buckeyes struggled during the early part of the season, going just 2–2–1 through their first five games. But they strung together five consecutive wins and had a chance to tie for another Big Ten championship before finishing the regular season with a 14–3 home loss to Michigan.

Following that game, the players were emotionally spent, and a chance to play one more game was the furthest thing from their minds.

"We didn't want to go," said former OSU player Ernie Andria, who alternated at the left offensive guard position for the Buckeyes in 1978. "We'd been used to the Rose Bowl, the Orange Bowl, the Sugar Bowl. And now they wanted us to play in the Gator Bowl? What the hell is the Gator Bowl? We didn't even know where it was played.

"So the team got together, had a vote and we decided we just wanted to stay home. But Woody came to us and said the university told us we had to go. It was too much money to pass up."

Perhaps to placate his players, Hayes decided to hold most of his bowl preparations in Columbus. For the first time in eleven bowl trips during the coach's tenure, the team waited until after Christmas to head for its postseason destination.

The Buckeyes arrived in Jacksonville just three days before the Gator Bowl was to be played, and their moods weren't enhanced very much by the cool, wet weather that quickly turned their practice field at a Jacksonville Beach high school into a quagmire.

One day after the team's arrival, would-be burglars ransacked the hotel room occupied by Gerald and senior co-captain Ron Springs. Nothing was taken, but that didn't prevent the intruders from rifling through everything from dresser drawers to mattresses.

"They were probably looking for money or jewelry and didn't find it," Gerald told reporters. "I usually keep my valuables on me, not in the room. Everything's straightened up now."

A gag gift at the annual luncheon the day before the game proved to be one final irony. While introducing Hayes, ABC sportscaster Keith Jackson presented the coach with a pair of boxing gloves, retired Clemson head coach Frank Howard's attempt at a joke regarding Hayes's combative nature. Hayes did not appear amused.

Ohio State was supposedly overmatched in the game against Atlantic Coast Conference champion Clemson. The Tigers had posted a 10–1 record, were the No. 7 ranked team in the nation, and entered the game with a nine-game winning streak.

Once the game began, however, the two-point underdog Buckeyes more than held their own. Following a scoreless first quarter, OSU got on the board first with a 27-yard field goal from freshman kicker Bob Atha. Clemson answered with a 4-yard touchdown run by quarterback Steve Fuller, but the Buckeyes came back less than four minutes later with a 4-yard run by Schlichter.

Unfortunately, the extra point attempt after Schlichter's touchdown failed, and when the Tigers got a 47-yard field goal from sophomore kicker Obed Ariri on the final play of the first half, Clemson took a 10–9 lead into the locker room.

Freshman running back Cliff Austin's 1-yard touchdown run with 2:16 remaining in the third quarter pushed the Tigers' advantage to 17–9, but Schlichter ran 1 yard for a touchdown at the 8:11 mark of the final period to make it 17–15. The OSU quarterback's attempt at running for the tying two-point conversion was stopped by Clemson defensive tackle Jim Stuckey, setting up the ill-fated finish.

THE ST. JOHNS RIVER ABOUT 1900

OHIO STATE vs **CLEMSON**

34th Annual Gator Bowl

THE THIRTY-FOURTH ANNUAL PLAYING OF THE GATOR BOWL CLASSIC DECEMBER 29, 1978

SALUTING THE CITY OF JACKSONVILLE FLORIDA

PRICE $ 2.00

GATOR BOWL PROGRAM. Woody's Last Game. It was an unfitting ending to an otherwise illustrious and storied career.

The Tigers seemed intent upon killing the clock and marched from their 35-yard line to the Ohio State 36. But on a third-and-4 play, one of Fuller's running backs crossed up the quarterback, resulting in a pitchout that went to no one. By the time the loose football was corralled by OSU nose guard Tim Sawicki, it was a 20-yard loss and the Buckeyes were back in business at the Clemson 44 with 4:22 remaining.

"We were just going to take it down and win the game," Schlichter said. "We made a couple of first downs and were in pretty good shape."

As the clock wound down to the two-minute mark, the Buckeyes had pushed their way to the 24-yard line and had a third-and-5 coming up. Memories vary greatly on exactly what happened next.

Team manager Mark George was in the press box charting plays and has repeated the same story over the years.

"I still have the notebook, and the play was a Y-77 Cross," George said. "Art was supposed to drop back, and tailback Ron Springs was to come out of the backfield and cut across the middle for a little 5-yard dump pass."

Schlichter remembered the play as "24-Tuba, which was a tailback delay. Ron was going to go over the middle and I was going to dump it to him."

Andria, who rotated with teammate Jim Savoca bringing in plays from the sideline, said, "The play I got was 37-Streak. What I'm thinking is that there was another call for the receivers. And maybe the call Woody gave was different than the one I got. But I've been telling this story for 30 years and it was 37-Streak."

One facet of the play that everyone seems to agree upon—the cautionary last words spoken by assistant coach Alex Gibbs, who was relaying the plays to Andria and Savoca.

"I told Art exactly what Coach Gibbs told me," Andria said. "I said, 'No interceptions. If it's not there, throw it away and we'll kick the field goal.' I think it's pretty obvious that I jinxed him right there."

Schlichter also has a vivid memory of that final admonition.

"Oh, yeah, I remember that pretty well," the former OSU quarterback said. "Those words were ringing in my ears: 'Whatever you do, don't throw an interception.' And of course, I did. I was drifting a little bit to the right and just made a bad play."

As Schlichter moved to his right, he tried to get the ball downfield to Springs, who had circled out of the backfield and cut to the middle of the field before changing course to his right. But Bauman flashed between Schlichter and Springs. The Clemson middle guard had started the play rushing the passer, but then dropped back into zone coverage tracking Schlichter and made the easy interception as Schlichter threw up both hands in disbelief.

As Bauman headed upfield with the football, the OSU quarterback came over to make the tackle on the Ohio State sideline.

Then, almost in the blink of an eye, it happened.

"I ran over and tried to tackle the guy, and when I rolled over I stayed down because I had a cramp in my leg," Schlichter said. "The next thing I knew, all hell was breaking loose around me."

As Bauman popped to his feet, he stood facing the Ohio State sideline with the football in his left hand. Hayes suddenly appeared and struck the Clemson player, throwing a right foreman just below Bauman's facemask. The coach tried to keep his hold on Bauman, but senior co-captain Byron Cato grabbed Hayes, and with help from offensive lineman Ken Fritz and defensive coordinator George Hill, spun the coach around and yanked him away.

"I was just trying to be protective of him—not to let him get hurt," Fritz said. "At that time, it was chaos."

Photographs and videos of the incident appear to show Hayes continuing to flail away as Fritz restrained him, leading many to mistakenly believe the coach was attacking his own player.

"He had no idea what he was doing," Fritz said. "He was just kind of like in a daze."

The rest of the evening was a blur. Benches emptied as mini-skirmishes broke out, but order was quickly restored. The incident with Bauman drew a 15-yard unsportsmanlike conduct penalty against the Buckeyes, and several minutes later Hayes still hadn't regained his composure. He called timeout after Clemson had run a play, but complained bitterly that the clock had run too long before officials

Photo courtesy of Buckeye Sports Bulletin

BOB HOPE AND WOODY. These legends are two of the few
people chosen as honorary "i-dotters" of the OSU band's Script Ohio.

stopped it. That protest earned Hayes another flag for unsportsmanlike conduct. The Tigers were then able to run out the rest of the clock to preserve the 17–15 victory.

Hill was sent to address the media following the game, but the Ohio State defensive coordinator was unable to satisfy reporters eager for Hayes's version of what occurred on the sideline.

"I have no idea what happened," Hill told reporters. "I was with the defense, getting them ready to go back in."

Pressed further by reporters who saw Hill as one of several coaches and players who tried to restrain Hayes, the OSU assistant insisted, "I didn't see it. Whatever I say would be wrong."

Over in the winning locker room, Clemson head coach Danny Ford withheld comment about the incident. When asked if he wanted to say anything about what he saw, Ford replied, "No, nothing until we look at the films. And even then I'd want to be careful."

The 65-year-old Hayes remained in a secluded portion of the OSU locker room for more than an hour following the game. He had only two visitors—first Hindman and then *Columbus Dispatch* sportswriter and longtime friend Paul Hornung.

Hindman entered the locker room grim-faced and related later, "I told him, 'Coach, we've got a problem. I'm in a position where I've got to go to the president. You need to expect the worst possible decision.'"

Hindman exited and then Hayes summoned Hornung, who later wrote that his meeting with the coach was "a soliloquy of anger and frustration." He added, "Woody punctuated his monologue by hurling a metal folding chair at a covey of lockers with a resounding clatter."

Finally, Hayes emerged from the locker room and was escorted to the team bus by three special-duty policemen, although the protection didn't seem necessary. All but a few fans had already left the Gator Bowl, and those who remained looked on with sympathetic gazes seemingly knowing the coach's long and storied career was over.

"We knew he was done," Andria said. "A lot of guys will tell you that they were surprised when they heard the official announcement, but we knew in the locker room right after the game. Nobody had to tell us. Nobody had to say a word."

By the time Hayes exited the locker room and headed back to team hotel, Hindman was on his way to meet with Ohio State president Harold Enarson and several of his administrative associates. Their decision was a swift one—Hayes's 28-year tenure as head coach of the Buckeyes was over.

But there were still some important distinctions to be made, so Hindman drafted two news releases for the following morning—one that indicated Hayes had decided to retire, the other announcing that the longtime coach had been fired.

"I was sitting right next to Hugh in the press box when it happened," Jones said. "I asked, 'Did you see what I just saw?' I don't think he ever answered the question. He just stared straight ahead for a couple of seconds before heading down to the locker room."

The incident and what transpired after was particularly painful for Hindman. He played for Hayes at Miami University and was an assistant coach on his staff at Ohio State from 1963–69. In 1970, Hindman moved from the sideline to the athletic department, and was named director of athletics in 1977, many times mentioning Hayes as a personal mentor and close friend.

Nevertheless, Hindman delivered the news to the coach at 7:30 the next morning. After a contentious few minutes, Hayes reportedly asked if he would be allowed to retire.

"I told him he had that right," Hindman recalled years later. "But then he said, 'No, goddammit. You bastards are going to have to fire me.'"

Several years later, Hindman admitted, "The only thing I've had to do that was tougher was bury my dad. I still had great admiration and respect for him."

Less than a half-hour after his meeting with Hindman, Hayes had evidently cooled off enough that he called Hornung, who by that time had returned home to Columbus. According to Hornung, the coach told him, "I always promised that when I decided to retire, you would be the first to know. I'm retiring as of now."

As a result, the first edition of the December 30, 1978, *Dispatch* front page carried the huge banner headline reading, "WOODY HAYES RESIGNS." In later editions, after an early-morning press conference called by Hindman, the word "RESIGNS" was replaced by "FIRED."

Speaking of his tenure for an oral history by the university in 2002, Enarson said he and Hindman agreed that Hayes had to be dismissed. But since Hayes refused to apologize for his behavior, he was given no formal opportunity to resign.

As the official Ohio State charter made its initial descent into the Columbus airport the following morning, Hayes grabbed a microphone and spoke to his team over the plane's intercom system.

"That in and of itself really wasn't that unusual," Jones said. "After a road trip or bowl game, Coach Hayes always spoke to the team about getting to class or when the next practice would be. He did that this time, too, and then added one other thing."

Schlichter remembered it was difficult to hear the coach's voice and several players telling their teammates to quiet down.

"All of a sudden, he said he wasn't going to be our coach anymore," the former QB said. "You could have heard a pin drop."

As soon as the plane landed, Hayes calmly exited where an Ohio Highway Patrol cruiser was waiting. He was taken to his Cardiff Road home in Upper Arlington, where he remained out of sight for several weeks.

In the meantime, Ohio State conducted a two-week search for his successor. Former OSU assistant Lou Holtz was the early favorite, but Holtz quickly took his name out of the running, deciding to remain head coach at Arkansas. The university eventually interviewed several candidates before settling on Iowa State head coach Earle Bruce, another former Hayes assistant.

On the evening before Bruce was formally introduced as Hayes's successor, the new coach was treated to dinner at Enarson's residence. During the evening, Hindman interrupted the proceedings to say that Bruce had a phone call.

"It was Woody," Bruce said. "I was struck by how upbeat he sounded. He said he was happy that I'd been chosen and he would be there for me whenever I needed support. To this day, I have no idea who called Woody to tell him I was at the president's house. I just know it was a gracious gesture and gave me a great feeling about coming to Ohio State."

Despite the abruptness with which his coaching career ended, Hayes continued to be an iconic figure at Ohio State for the remainder of his life. He was made a professor emeritus by the university and retained an office in the old Military Science building, just a stone's throw from Ohio Stadium.

In 1983, he was inducted into the College Football Hall of Fame. That same year, he became one of only a handful of "civilians" to dot the "i" in Script Ohio when he performed the honor at halftime of the homecoming game against Wisconsin.

"When you get recognition like that, or any reward," Hayes said the next day, "you start looking back at all the people who have had a part in it—your players, your coaches, the administration, the university, the fans.

"I found out that I did become emotional out there yesterday because I thought of all the great victories we've had and all the great people we've had. It makes you realize how doggone lucky you are."

Hayes suffered a heart attack in 1985, and his health began to deteriorate. One of his final public appearances occurred March 14, 1986, when Ohio State awarded him with an honorary Doctorate of Humanities degree. During commencement ceremonies, a frail Hayes gave a heartfelt speech that stressed the value of education, the worth of a diploma, and the need for good acts in the community. It resonated with even his harshest critics.

"Today," he began, "is the greatest day of my life. I appreciate so much being able to come here and talk to a graduating class at The Ohio State University—a great, great university."

Hayes died March 12, 1987, at the age of 74. Some 15,000 people attended a memorial service at Ohio Stadium in his honor, and among the mourners at Hayes's funeral was former U.S. President Richard Nixon, who gave the eulogy.

"The incident at the Gator Bowl in 1978 would have destroyed an ordinary man," Nixon said. "But Woody was not an ordinary man. Winston Churchill once said, 'Success is never final. Failure is never fatal.' Woody lived by that maxim. He was never satisfied with success; he was never discouraged by failure.

"Two thousands years ago, the poet Sophocles wrote, 'One must wait until the evening to see how splendid the day has been.' We can all be thankful today that in the evening of his life, Woody Hayes could look back and see that the day had indeed been splendid."

WOODY'S COMMENCEMENT SPEECH given in March of 1986, one year before his death.

Chapter 5

THE HOUSE
THAT HARLEY BUILT

HORSESHOE HISTORY

The year was 1919, and Ohio State football was bursting at the seams—figuratively and literally. All-America halfback Chic Harley had led the Buckeyes to undefeated records and Western Conference championships in 1916 and 1917, and after a year away while serving in the military during World War I, looked to be on his way to accomplishing those feats a third time in 1919.

Harley had already engineered the program's first-ever win over Michigan, a 13–3 decision in Ann Arbor, and had become a matinee idol of epic proportions in Columbus. Residents who had never paid any attention to football until then suddenly began to call themselves Buckeye fans. As the team's season finale—a showdown with powerful Illinois—drew near, the evidence was clear that the Buckeyes had outgrown their home.

The contest at Ohio Field against Illinois, Harley's final game as a Buckeye, produced an unprecedented ticket demand. The game had been sold out for weeks, and Ohio State athletic director Lynn St. John estimated the university could have sold 60,000 tickets for the contest.

On November 22, 1919, nearly 20,000 jammed into a facility that had been built to hold only about one-fourth of that crowd. Fans filled the wooden bleachers long before game time, and stood fifteen to twenty deep in both end zones. Others stood in windows of buildings across the street, while several more climbed trees to catch a glimpse of the game. The *Ohio State Monthly* reported that when the Buckeyes took the field, residents as far as a mile away could hear the roar.

Although Harley and his team came up short that day, losing 9–7 when Illinois scored a field goal with just eight seconds remaining in the game, university officials couldn't help taking note of how the football team had grown in popularity. The day after the OSU–Illinois game, St. John and other Ohio State officials gathered to discuss plans for a new, modern stadium.

Those at the meeting were somewhat surprised to learn plans for the new facility were already well under way. Engineering department head and OSU athletic board president Thomas E. French was credited with fathering the idea of a new stadium as early as 1915.

French, whose brother Edward was co-captain of the 1896 football team, was a proponent of all athletic endeavors. He had previously chaired the committee that guided the expansion of Ohio Field from 6,000 to 10,000 in 1909, and predicted six years later that a new concrete stadium was needed. Later that year, during an address to the Columbus Chamber of Commerce, French said he believed Ohio State football crowds would one day number as many as 50,000. His speech was received with a huge amount of skepticism.

Nevertheless, when the Buckeyes captured the Western Conference championship in 1916, French pressed ahead with his idea for a new stadium. He asked university engineer Clyde Morris to prepare sketches for a new stadium, and Morris designed an oval-shaped facility that would seat approximately 40,000. The new stadium would be located in what was then a wooded area north of the Oval and west of Ohio Field.

> " My idea of a good hit is when the guy wakes up on the sidelines with train whistles blowing in his head. "
>
> —Jack Tatum

OHIO STADIUM, a landmark of both OSU and NCAA football, it sits along the Olentangy River at 411 Woody Hayes Drive.

French submitted the plans to the OSU Board of Trustees, which approved them. However, University President William Oxley Thompson had reservations about the plans. The new stadium would have been ten feet taller than any other campus structure, giving the impression that athletics took precedent over academics. Thompson asked that new plans be drawn, and university architect Joseph Bradford took over the project.

Bradford came up with the horseshoe-shaped innovation, in part so that the facility could also hold field events of track and field meets in the open end of the stadium. He also decided the new facility should be moved to a much larger tract of land, farther south along the Olentangy River.

These new plans, which called for capacity of around 50,000, were much more to Thompson's liking, and they were quickly approved by the board of trustees. However, plans for the new stadium were put on hold as the country was thrust into World War I.

In the summer of 1918, as the war was winding down, French brought renowned architect Howard D. Smith on board with the project. Smith was a 1907 Ohio State graduate and faculty member in the School of Architecture, and he was asked to refine Bradford's drawings.

Smith, who had spent time in Europe studying ancient Roman and Greek architecture, employed many of the characteristics of those works in his plans. For example, instead of employing numerous columns like those at Harvard Stadium, Smith designed double columns that allowed for more space between columns. He added arches in the style of the Roman Colosseum, and the rotunda at the north end of the stadium, which is now adorned with stained glass murals, was designed to look like the dome at the Pantheon.

Smith also employed a number of revolutionary techniques during the building of the stadium. Since the stadium sits on a flood plain, Smith designed a slurry wall at the base to keep out the waters from the Olentangy River. Additionally, rather than building a large, bowl-like structure like the previously constructed Yale Bowl, Ohio Stadium was designed to have an upper deck that would hang over part of the lower deck, giving the facility its familiar "A," "B," and "C" decks. The American Institute of Architects would award Smith a gold medal for such a unique and innovational design.

Smith completed his plans in the summer of 1920, and in October, a public campaign to fund the stadium began and quickly raised over $1 million in pledges by the following January.

Still, there was opposition to the stadium project. Many university officials disagreed with building such a large and expensive facility for the football team. The stadium's original capacity was designed to be 66,210, and several faculty members feared the facility would never come close to being filled to capacity. Others maintained the total $1.5 million cost of construction was astronomical for a facility that would be used for only five or six games each year.

Nevertheless, the project began August 3, 1921, with an official ground-breaking ceremony. Ohio Governor Harry L. Davis turned the first shovel of dirt, and an ambitious thirteen-month construction schedule began. Approximately 300 workers were on-site each day, with structural steel installation lasting well into the winter until the following spring when they began pouring some 85,000 tons of concrete.

By the first week of October 1922, most of the stadium construction was complete. The first game in the stadium was played October 7, 1922, and the Buckeyes took a 5–0 win over Ohio Wesleyan. Workers and university officials, including Thompson, worked all day Friday and well into the night to clear the stands of any leftover debris so the stadium would be ready.

Unfortunately, only about 25,000 fans were on hand to witness history, and the half-empty facility brought a new round of criticism to university officials, especially Thompson, French, and St. John. But those critics were silenced two weeks later when Ohio State hosted archrival Michigan in the stadium's official dedication game.

The official crowd was announced at 72,000, but no one is really sure how many people made it into the stadium. The number could have been closer to 80,000, as many fans who were unable to buy tickets forced their way in through a fence at the south end of the stadium.

Another attendance mark was set in 1926 when 90,411 showed up to watch the Buckeyes play Michigan. As was the case four years earlier, the attendance figure was probably low, since an estimated 10,000 fans that were outside the stadium before the game stormed the gates and surged inside. It marked the last

STADIUM

Dedication
Game Program
(1922)

time standing room only tickets were ever sold for an Ohio State game at Ohio Stadium.

Even with the large crowds that turned out for Michigan games, the stadium did not regularly sell out until after World War II. One notable exception was the 1935 contest with Notre Dame, with more than 81,000 in attendance.

The stadium has been renovated several times over the years. The most recent renovation occurred over a two-year period beginning in 1999, when the press box was replaced and expanded, additional seating was installed above the existing upper deck, and eighty-one luxury suites and 2,500 club seats were added. In addition, the cinder track ringing the football field was removed, and the field of play was lowered some fourteen and a half feet to add additional seating closer to the field. Also, the temporary bleachers in the south end zone were replaced with permanent seating; however, the south end of the stadium remains partially open, thus allowing the stadium to maintain its unique horseshoe configuration.

The result of the $194 million renovation project was a capacity that rose to 101,568.

Since its inaugural contest in 1922, Ohio Stadium has played host to more than 500 Ohio State games, and nearly 400 of those have resulted in wins for the Buckeyes. Because of its fans making their regular pilgrimages to the Horseshoe, Ohio State has been among the top four NCAA schools in attendance in each of the last sixty years.

More than 39.5 million fans have witnessed a game inside Ohio Stadium, whose capacity is now listed at 102,329. That figure has been eclipsed fifty times, including the all-time attendance mark of 105,711, set in October 2008 when Penn State came to Columbus for a rare night game.

GAME-DAY TRADITIONS

Attending a game in Ohio Stadium is every Buckeye football fan's dream. But there is so much more to the experience than the game itself. So many long-standing traditions are associated with fall Saturday afternoons at the Horseshoe that the game itself sometimes becomes an anticlimax.

Traditions begin several hours before kickoff, when the sweet smells of a variety of tailgate foods begin wafting through the air. Exactly two hours before kickoff, formal festivities begin.

SKULL SESSION

Fans begin tuning up in earnest as the Ohio State Marching Band hosts its "Skull Session" inside St. John Arena, the old basketball arena just across Woody Hayes Drive from Ohio Stadium.

Each week, the band's different "cheer groups" perform a song to go along with the football team's opponent of the week. The cheer groups are selected from their respective sections: Trumpet Cheers (the oldest Cheer Group), Trombone Cheers, Horn Cheers, Baritone Cheers, Stadium Brass (an instrument from every part of the band except percussion), Percussion Cheers (playing "Wipeout"), and the Tuba-Fours.

As the Skull Session begins, members of the football team begin their walk as a single group from the Blackwell Hotel to St. John Arena. Once they enter the arena, the band plays "Fanfare for a New Era."

After the team's entrance, a senior player addresses the fans, followed by a quick pep talk from OSU head coach Jim Tressel. After the football team exits St. John Arena, the band plays several more songs, including the university fight song "Across the Field"—first softly and slowly, and on the repeat of the chorus, at well beyond normal tempo.

Outside the arena, fans line up to provide a tunnel for the team members to make their way to their Ohio Stadium locker room.

BRUTUS BUCKEYE

It may sound strange to this generation of Buckeye fans, but the university did not have an official mascot until the mid-1960s. Not that Ohio State and its students didn't try.

Several possibilities were suggested as early as the 1890s, including a ram, an elk, a moose, and a male deer (a Buck to be exact). However, due to the skittish nature of real deer, the idea of a mascot was tabled until January 1941, when "Chris," a German police dog owned by an assistant cheerleader, made an appearance at a basketball game. The dog seemed to be the university's de facto mascot for a few years, but OSU remained without any official mascot until 1965.

During the homecoming game against Minnesota that season, a smiling buckeye nut with furry eyebrows and human legs made his debut, much to the delight of fans in attendance.

It wasn't until nearly three weeks later that the new mascot was named. A campus-wide contest to determine the name settled on Brutus Buckeye, an entry submitted by OSU student Kerry Reed.

Brutus remained unchanged for the next decade until September 1975, when he received a makeover that slimmed him down and put a crown on his head. The makeover was not well-received, however, as students, alumni, and fans criticized the new version's squinting eyes and seemingly vicious sneer. The university quickly scrapped the new Brutus, and the friendly nut was resurrected.

Two years later, Brutus received another facelift. This version retained the happy face, which went to waist level of the performing person, but added a ball cap to rest on top of his head.

That model remained until the early 1980s, when Brutus received another makeover. The cumbersome head, which weighed nearly eighty pounds, was replaced by smaller, plush headgear that fit on the wearer's shoulders. For the first time, the mascot donned a Scarlet and Gray striped shirt with "Brutus" on the front and "00" on the back. His pants were scarlet, with the name of his school embroidered on the sides.

That's the way Brutus stayed until just before the 1998 season, when he returned in the fall with an updated look that included a more buff appearance, a tan, and new facial features.

RAMP ENTRANCE

With most football programs, the loudest cheers are reserved for when team members take the field. On game day in Ohio State, that honor is reserved for

BRUTUS BUCKEYE

Photo courtesy of Jeff Brehm/Buckeye Sports Bulletin

members of "The Best Damn Band In The Land," (TBDBITL) and their ramp entrance from the north end of the stadium is one of the most highly anticipated.

Appearing first is the percussion section—not to music or cadences, but to cheers at the precise tempo of 180 beats per minute. A series of elaborately timed flanking maneuvers leads members of the section to their respective rows in the block.

That is followed by "ramp cadences," which are played exactly seventeen times, as the rest of the band members file down the ramp, onto the field, and into their respective positions. Once a row is placed, the members mark time until all rows are into position.

As the final two rows file in, their squad leaders nod to the two bass row squad leaders, who sound a loud blast on their whistles. The entire band responds to this call with a deafening yell of "Whistle!" Then, after the last ramp cadence and a roll-off is played, the band starts into the intro of "Buckeye Battle Cry" while marking time.

During the intro and first verse, the drum major moves through the band and comes to the front of the ranks where he executes a back bend, forming his or her body into the shape of an O. As the drum major's hat plume touches the grass, the band starts to play two choruses of "Buckeye Battle Cry" while moving toward the south stands. The drum major reaches the end zone and tosses the baton through the goal post as the band finishes the downfield march.

The opposing team's fight song is played as a salute to their university, returning the band to midfield before completing the pregame performance.

TUNNEL OF PRIDE

One of the newer game day traditions features former players gathering on the field to form a "Tunnel of Pride" for current team members to run through prior to home Michigan games.

The Tunnel of Pride was the brainchild of former OSU athletic director Andy Geiger and 1968 national championship quarterback Rex Kern, who worked together to come up with a way to connect current Buckeyes with those who played before them.

The first tunnel appeared before the 1994 Michigan game when all former players in attendance took to the field to salute the current-day players. Ohio State rallied for a 22–6 victory over the Wolverines that day, ending a six-year winless streak in the series. In each home game against Michigan since, the tradition has been repeated.

The Tunnel of Pride was also formed for the 1995 Notre Dame game, and that resulted in a 45–26 win over the Fighting Irish.

SCRIPT OHIO

Script Ohio is the signature formation of TBDBITL, and it is performed before or after home games or during halftime.

The formation was first performed October 10, 1936, when Ohio State hosted Pittsburgh. It was devised by then band director Eugene J. Weigel, who based the looped "Ohio" script design on the marquee sign of the Loew's Ohio Theatre in downtown Columbus.

The script is an integrated series of evolutions and formations. The band first forms a triple "Block O" formation, then slowly unwinds to form the letters while playing "Le Régiment de Sambre et Meuse," a military march written in 1871 and played at U.S. Military Academy graduations.

The drum major leads the outside O in a peel-off movement around the curves of the script, every musician in continual motion. Slowly, the three blocks unfold into a long, singular line which loops around and forms the word "Ohio" in script letters.

Each time the formation is performed, a different fourth- or fifth-year Sousaphone player receives the honor of dotting the "i." The dotting of the "i" has been ranked the greatest college football tradition by several outlets, including Athlon Sports and ESPN.

Over the years, there have been a handful of honorary "i"-dotters, including former head coach Woody Hayes, comedian Bob Hope, and golf legend Jack Nicklaus. This is considered the greatest honor the band can bestow to any non-band member and is an extremely special and rare event, since the Sousaphone

SCRIPT OHIO at 2006 Fiesta Bowl

player selected to dot the "i" for that specific game must give up their spot in order for an honorary member to exercise the privilege.

BLOCK O

Block O was founded in 1938 by Ohio State cheerleader Clancy Isaac and serves as the official student cheering section in Ohio Stadium.

Prior to the stadium renovation project in 1999–2000, the Block O section traditionally resided in the north end of the stadium, but it has since been relocated to section 39A in the south stands.

Block O is made up primarily of upperclassmen that perform elaborate card stunts. The section annually sells out its 1,200 tickets within hours of ticket sales opening and leads the stadium in many cheers and songs, including the "O-H!" "I-O!" cheer.

In 2008, Block O opened a new section in the north end of the stadium. Block O North, primarily featuring underclassmen, was located in section 1A.

HANG ON SLOOPY

A relatively obscure pop song from 1965 has become a staple of game days in Ohio Stadium, thanks to TBDBITL member John Tatgenhorst.

"My Girl Sloopy" was a song written in the early 1960s by Wes Farrell and Bert Russell as a tribute to singer Dorothy Sloop, who went by the stage name "Sloopy." The song was a modest hit in 1964 for The Vibrations, but it didn't reach the top of the charts until a year later, when The McCoys recorded it and changed the title of the song to "Hang On Sloopy."

That fall, Tatgenhorst convinced Ohio State Marching Band director Dr. Charles L. Spohn that the song would be a crowd-pleaser at football games. Tatgenhorst put together a hasty arrangement for the all-brass band, and TBDBITL first played it October 9, 1965. It was not an immediate sensation, however. Crowd response was mediocre at best, as the band was not allowed to take the field because of heavy rain.

The next game was a different story. The band played the song the following week and the crowd went crazy, yelling "Sloopy!! Sloopy!! Sloopy!!" and singing along with the song's offbeat lyrics. "Hang On Sloopy" has been a part of Ohio State football Saturdays ever since.

In 1985, the Ohio General Assembly voted to make "Hang On Sloopy" the official rock song of the State of Ohio.

The song is now played at least once each game, typically before the start of the fourth quarter.

"CARMEN OHIO"

"Carmen Ohio" has the distinction of being one of the oldest and newest traditions in Ohio State football.

It is the university's alma mater and is the oldest school song still used by the university. On the train ride home from an 86–0 loss to Michigan in 1902, freshman football player Fred Cornell wrote lyrics to the melody of an old Spanish hymn. One year later, the Men's Glee Club performed the song, but it didn't gain popularity until after being publicized in the October 10, 1906, issue of the university newspaper the *Lantern*.

The following week, the words to "Carmen Ohio" were published in the official game program and the song has been a staple of home football games ever since.

Until 2001, however, the song was performed before the game by the marching band. Since Tressel took over as head coach, the entire football team and the remaining crowd sing the first verse of "Carmen Ohio" after every home game, accompanied by the band.

VICTORY BELL

Ohio Stadium's distinctive Victory Bell is rung after every Ohio State victory by members of Alpha Phi Omega, a tradition that began after the Buckeyes defeated California on October 2, 1954.

The bell is situated 150 feet high in the southeast tower of Ohio Stadium and was the gift of the classes of 1943, '44 and '45. It weighs 2,420 pounds.

The Victory Bell traditionally rings for approximately fifteen minutes after each home victory—or up to thirty minutes after a win over Michigan.

BUCKEYE GROVE

No trip to Ohio Stadium would be complete without a visit—either before or after the game—to the Buckeye Grove, a stand of trees commemorating each OSU player who has won first-team All-America honors.

FRED A. CORNELL
WEIRSDALE, FLORIDA

Fifty Years Ago a Freshman Wrote —

CARMEN OHIO

Oh come lets sing Ohio's praise
And songs to Alma Mater raise
While our hearts resounding Thrill
With joy which death alone can still.
Summer's heat or winter's cold
The seasons pass the years will roll
Time and change will surely show
How firm Thy Friendship — Ohio.

these jolly days of priceless worth
By far the gladdest days of earth
Soon will pass and we not know
How dearly we love Ohio.
We should strive to keep Thy name
Of fair repute and spotless fame
So in college halls we'll grow
To love Thee better — Ohio.

Though age may dim our memory's store
We'll think of happy days of yore
True to friend and frank to foe
As sturdy sons of Ohio.
If on seas of care we roll
'Neath blackened sky, o'er barren shoal
Thoughts of Thee bid darkness go
Dear Alma Mater — Ohio.

Fred Albert Cornell w'06.
(Now LXX)

HANDWRITTEN
lyrics to Carmen Ohio

The practice of planting a Buckeye tree for each All-American began in 1934. The grove was first located just southeast of the stadium, but during the 1999–2000 renovation project, the trees were relocated near the southwestern corner between the stadium and Morrill Tower.

Each player who wins first-team All-America honors is recognized by the planting of a buckeye tree and installation of a plaque in the Buckeye Grove. New trees are planted during special ceremonies held prior to each year's spring game.

THE HORSESHOE'S GREATEST GAMES

Some refer to it as their Saturday afternoon home away from home, while others believe it's a cathedral where Scarlet and Gray worshipers congregate each fall. It's been called "The House That Harley Built," "The Old Gray Lady of the Olentangy," and "The Horseshoe."

No matter what image it conjures in your mind, or what you call it, Ohio Stadium is the home of the Ohio State football team and evokes almost as much emotion for Buckeye fans as the young men who graced its gridiron over the past eight-plus decades. There are those who were lucky enough to attend their first game in the stadium before they could walk and haven't missed a game since. Others who have never walked through the stadium turnstiles can still quote chapter and verse about what has happened inside those fortress-like walls.

It was the site of Ohio State's first-ever Big Ten win in 1924, where Paul Brown and Woody Hayes were carried off the field in victory, the personal playgrounds of Les Horvath and Vic Janowicz, Hop Cassady and Archie Griffin, Eddie George and Troy Smith. It is where championships have been won, Rose Bowl berths have been cemented, and national title dreams have been born.

As the Buckeyes readied themselves for the 2009 season, more than 39.5 million people—39,574,083 to be exact—had attended the 511 games played at Ohio Stadium. That computes to an average attendance of 77,444 per game, 385 of which have been OSU victories.

Built with an original capacity of 66,210, the stadium had its initial critics who said it was much too large. Since an ambitious renovation project between

BUCKEYE GROVE, where a Buckeye tree is
planted for every OSU first-team All-American

Photo courtesy of Mark Rea

1999 and 2001 increased capacity to 102,329, there have been more than fifty crowds in excess of that number, including thirty of 105,000 or more.

Over the years, those record crowds have feasted on some of the most notable games in college football history. Here are some of the most memorable.

OFF TO A WINNING START (1922)

Ohio State christened its new stadium on October 7, 1922, with a 5–0 win over old rival Ohio Wesleyan. Construction crews hurried to complete work on the structure and enlisted the Friday night help of university officials, including president William Oxley Thompson, to help clear away any remaining debris.

A crowd of approximately 25,000 was in attendance, somewhat disappointing since the new stadium was built to hold more than 60,000 fans. Still, the gathering was the largest crowd ever to witness a football game in the state of Ohio.

The Buckeyes won the opening coin toss and elected to defend the south goal with a slight wind at their backs. All of the scoring occurred in the first quarter as OSU scored a safety and a field goal.

RUN, RUN, RUN (1930)

Ohio State head coach Sam Willaman spent most of the offseason implementing significant changes in his offensive attack, and it paid off handsomely in the 1930 season opener against Mount Union.

Willaman was intent on scrapping his triple option attack for the wingback formation, a speed-based attack first employed by legendary coach Glenn "Pop" Warner, who won four national championships. Willaman switched two-time All-America end Wes Fesler to a fullback position, while senior Dick Larkins moved from tackle to end, and junior Stuart Holcomb went from fullback to halfback.

The result paid immediate dividends as the Buckeyes rolled to a 59–0 victory over the Purple Raiders. Eight different players scored touchdowns during the contest, and Ohio State rolled up 718 yards on the ground, a single-game team record that still stands.

THE GAME OF THE CENTURY (1935)

Fans from Ohio State and Notre Dame had been waiting a long time for their respective schools to meet on the gridiron, and it finally happened November 2, 1935.

The Irish entered the game with victories over Kansas, Carnegie Tech, Wisconsin and Navy, while the Buckeyes had beaten Kentucky, Drake, Northwestern, and Indiana. Ticket demand to see the two unbeaten teams was unprecedented, and OSU athletic director Lynn St. John estimated 200,000 tickets could have been sold.

Ohio State struck first when fullback Frank Antenucci intercepted a pass and then lateraled to halfback Frank Boucher, who raced 65 yards for a touchdown. A second-quarter score gave the Buckeyes a 13–0 lead at halftime, but the Irish came back with a trio of fourth-quarter TDs. The game-winner came on a 19-yard pass from backup quarterback Bill Shakespeare to Wayne Millner with less than thirty seconds remaining.

Many spectators remained in their seats thirty minutes after the game had ended, too stunned to move. Meanwhile, Irish fans jubilantly tore down the goal post at the stadium's south end and marched it all the way downtown to the lobby of the Deshler Wallick hotel, where they celebrated well into the night.

Those in attendance called the game easily the most exciting they had ever witnessed, and many sportswriters coined it "The Game of the Century." In South Bend, the celebration continued for several days. Classes at Notre Dame were dismissed early the first three days the following week, allowing students more time to celebrate the victory.

A NEW 'SCRIPT' (1936)

A crowd of 71,711 was on hand to witness history October 10, 1936, but it had little to do with the intersectional matchup between Pittsburgh and Ohio State.

During its halftime show, the Ohio State Marching Band unveiled a new formation that spelled out the word "Ohio" in cursive letters. The new "Script Ohio" was devised by band director Eugene J. Weigel, and E-flat cornet player John Brungart became the first person to dot the "i."

As far as the football game was concerned, the Buckeyes and Panthers participated in a defensive struggle that Pittsburgh finally won by a 6–0 score. The Panthers, who did not throw a single pass during the game, tallied the lone touchdown on a 35-yard run by sophomore halfback Harold Stebbins late in the fourth quarter.

VIC'S BIG DAY (1950)

The Dad's Day crowd of 82,174 showed up on a balmy late October afternoon to witness one of the finest single-game performances in Ohio State football history.

Junior halfback Vic Janowicz had a game for the ages, leading the Buckeyes to an 83–21 blowout of Big Ten rival Iowa. Before the contest was six minutes old, Janowicz had already accounted for three touchdowns—one rushing, one passing and one on a 61-yard punt return—kicked three extra points, and recovered two fumbles on defense.

OSU had run out to a 35–0 lead after the first quarter and a 55–14 advantage by halftime. Janowicz, who would go on to win the 1950 Heisman Trophy, played very little in the second half but still managed to score two touchdowns, complete 5 of 6 pass attempts for 133 yards and four TDs, kick 10 extra points, punt twice for an average of 42.0 yards per kick, and recover two fumbles at his defensive safety position.

The 83 points by the Buckeyes remains the highest total ever scored against a Big Ten opponent.

QUITE A DEBUT (1952)

College football rules were changed in 1952 permitting freshmen to play on varsity teams, and Howard "Hopalong" Cassady made one of the most exciting debuts in Ohio State history.

DID YOU KNOW?

Incredibly, eight players have made All-American three times for the Buckeyes: **Chic Harley, Wesley Fesler, Lew Hinchman, Merle Wendt, Archie Griffin, Tom Skladany, Mike Doss**, and **James Laurinaitis**.

The Buckeyes had been pointing toward their season opener with Indiana for eleven months after the Hoosiers had cruised to a 32–10 victory the year before. This time, OSU turned the tables and ground out a systematic 33–13 win over their Big Ten foes.

Cassady got his college career off to a good start by making a leaping touchdown catch midway through the second quarter. The 27-yard scoring play erased a one-point Indiana lead and pushed the Buckeyes in front at 13–7.

The Hoosiers tied the score at 13 by halftime, and after a scoreless third period, Ohio State erupted for 20 points in the final quarter. Cassady got his second touchdown of the game on a 5-yard sweep to make it 20–13, and then after a 27-yard romp from fullback John Hlay, Cassady scored again from the Indiana 3 to put the game on ice.

Cassady's debut game was the touchstone for a brilliant career that included a national championship, two outright Big Ten titles, three victories over Michigan, and the 1955 Heisman Trophy.

PICK SIX KEYS COMEBACK (1954)

Ohio State had designs on the Big Ten championship in 1954, but Wisconsin stood in its way. The second-ranked Badgers were one of the nation's top defensive teams, and they invaded Columbus on October 23 for the annual homecoming game.

Wisconsin jumped out to a 7–3 lead, and after protecting that advantage well into the third quarter, threatened to put the game away. With a second-and-4 at the OSU 20, Wisconsin quarterback Jim Miller faked a handoff and then tried to whip a quick pass into the flat.

Cassady flashed into the area and intercepted Miller's pass at the 12-yard line. What transpired then was described by many as the finest broken-field run in stadium history. Cassady picked up a couple of blocks and then streaked down the field with a spectacular 88-yard touchdown return. It marked Miller's first interception of the season and the first time that year the Badgers had been scored upon in the second half.

The interception return broke open the game as the Buckeyes tallied three more touchdowns in the fourth quarter to run away with a 31–14 decision.

With the victory, Ohio State jumped to No. 1 in the national polls the following week, and the Buckeyes remained in the top spot the rest of the season, giving Woody Hayes his first national championship.

WELCOME TO THE WHITE HOUSE (1957)

Fifth-ranked Iowa was installed as a six-point favorite to defeat sixth-ranked Ohio State in a game that would decide the Big Ten championship, and a then-record stadium crowd of 82,935 (which included U.S. Vice President Richard Nixon) showed up to see the Buckeyes prove the oddsmakers wrong.

The game was a seesaw affair that saw the lead change hands three times before the Hawkeyes seized a 13–10 advantage in the third quarter.

With just 7:51 remaining in the game, Ohio State took possession at its own 32-yard line and proceeded to ride fullback Bob White's back to victory. On an eight-play, 68-yard scoring drive, White carried seven times for 66 of the yards.

He got things started with a 4-yard plunge over right tackle before going over left tackle for 9 yards and a first down. White next broke through over right guard and wasn't pulled down until he had tacked on another 29 yards and moved the ball to the Iowa 26. With the crowd on its feet and the noise level deafening, half-back Dick LeBeau ran for 2 yards before White returned for gains of 6, 10, and 3 yards. The final carry in the sequence for White was a 5-yard touchdown burst over left tackle, giving the Buckeyes an eventual 17–13 win.

After the game, Iowa head coach Forest Evashevski gave credit to White, saying, "We knew what was happening, but we were just powerless to stop it. It was fantastic."

AERIAL CIRCUS (1980)

Ohio Stadium has seen its share of big rushing games, but it had seldom seen anything like what transpired November 8, 1980. Ohio State and Illinois combined for 905 yards through the air as the Buckeyes outlasted the Fighting Illini by a 49–42 score in one of the wildest games ever in the Horseshoe.

The Buckeyes jumped out to a 28–0 advantage midway through the second quarter and nearly let it slip away as Illinois quarterback Dave Wilson had a record-setting day. Wilson finished the game with 43 completions in 69 attempts for an NCAA-record 621 yards and six touchdowns.

Five of Wilson's scoring passes and 344 of his passing yards came in the second half, overshadowing what was one of OSU quarterback Art Schlichter's finest games. The junior QB connected on his first 11 attempts and finished 17 for 21 for 284 yards and a career-high four touchdowns.

Ohio State took what seemed to be a comfortable 49–35 lead with 10:55 remaining in the game, but Wilson kept his team in the game. He might have even rallied the Illini for the victory if not for two costly turnovers—a fumble inside the OSU 10-yard line and an interception in the end zone at the 3:06 mark.

Thanks to Wilson's efforts, Illinois piled up 36 first downs—26 of them through the air—and amassed 659 total yards. Each of those figures remains an all-time single-game high for an Ohio State opponent.

UNDER THE LIGHTS (1985)

Ohio Stadium was ushered into a new era September 14, 1985, when the first night game was held. Pittsburgh provided the opposition, and the Buckeyes scratched their way to a come-from-behind 10–7 victory.

OSU was hampered by the lack of a running attack due to the loss of senior tailback Keith Byars. The Heisman Trophy candidate broke a bone in his foot during a non-contact practice drill just twelve days before the opener, and the Buckeyes were held to just 48 yards rushing against a veteran Pitt defense.

Quarterback Jim Karsatos came to the rescue, though, throwing for 246 yards including the winning touchdown, a 1-yard strike to sophomore receiver Cris Carter, with just 4:19 left to go in the game.

Sophomore cornerback William White was the defensive hero of the game for Ohio State. He made a key interception at the OSU 44-yard line to stop the Panthers' final drive at the 1:43 mark of the fourth quarter.

KNOCKING OFF NO. 1 (1985)

A steady downpour couldn't dampen the spirits of another record stadium crowd as 90,467 cheered the Buckeyes to a 22–13 victory over top-ranked Iowa.

The Hawkeyes entered the game with a perfect 7–0 record and were installed as 1 1/2-point favorites, making Ohio State underdogs at home for the first time in eight years. That fact was not lost on senior co-captain Keith Byars, who delivered an emotional pregame speech that was punctuated by upsetting food trays, shattering a water glass against a wall and kicking over chairs.

The Buckeyes grabbed an early 5–0 lead after Rich Spangler kicked a 28-yard field goal, and roverback Sonny Gordon blocked an Iowa punt that went out of the end zone. Tailback John Wooldridge added a 57-yard touchdown romp in the second quarter to stretch OSU's lead to 12–0, and Spangler added another field goal to make it 15–0.

The Hawkeyes managed to cut the deficit to 15–7 by halftime and then threatened to seize momentum early in the fourth quarter. But Ohio State linebacker Chris Spielman dropped Iowa tailback Ronnie Harmon for no gain on a crucial fourth-and-1, and the Hawkeyes never seriously threatened again.

Spielman came up huge in the contest as the sophomore middle linebacker registered nineteen tackles and two interceptions.

IRISH EYES AREN'T SMILING (1995)

The Buckeyes and their fans had been waiting sixty years for payback against Notre Dame, and they weren't disappointed. Finally erasing memories

GAMEDAY HAUNTS

Plank's Café Tucked away on Parsons Avenue in German Village, Plank's is a great gathering place for Ohio State fans before, during, and after games. And it has the best pizza in Columbus.

FIRST NIGHT GAME at Ohio Stadium. The Buckeyes, led by running back Keith Byars, defeated Pittsburgh 10–7.

of the 18–13 loss in "The Game of the Century" in 1930, Ohio State overcame an early 10–0 deficit and rolled to a 45–26 victory.

Stars were plentiful on both sides of the ball for the Buckeyes. Senior tailback Eddie George, on his way to the 1995 Heisman Trophy, carried 32 times for 207 yards and a pair of touchdowns, while quarterback Bobby Hoying completed 14 of 22 passes for 272 yards and four scores. Wide receiver Terry Glenn caught four balls for 128 yards and two TDs, including an 82-yarder that was the second longest scoring pass in OSU history.

On defense, middle linebacker Greg Bellisari had a team-high 12 tackles, while fellow linebacker Ryan Miller and defensive tackle Luke Fickell had 10 each. Defensive end Mike Vrabel also had an excellent game, including a fumble-inducing tackle early in the third quarter that helped turn momentum of the game over to the Buckeyes.

The 45 points were the most ever scored against a Notre Dame team coached by Lou Holtz, and the most scored against any Fighting Irish team since a 58–7 loss in the 1985 season finale to Miami (Florida).

TRIPLE OVERTIME THRILLER (2003)

Ohio State extended its unbeaten streak to seventeen games in a row, but not before a pulse-pounding, triple overtime 44–38 thriller against North Carolina State. It was the first overtime game in Ohio Stadium history and also the longest game ever for OSU, lasting four hours and seventeen minutes.

The Buckeyes held what seemed to be a comfortable 24–7 lead in the fourth quarter before Wolfpack QB Philip Rivers ignited a comeback. Rivers threw for a pair of touchdowns, and N.C. State added a field goal in the final 8:26 of regulation to knot the game at 24.

Then things got really interesting. Ohio State quarterback Craig Krenzel ran for a 6-yard touchdown in the first overtime period before Rivers tossed his fourth TD pass of the game to send the action into a second extra session. The teams traded touchdowns again in overtime No. 2, setting up the climactic third OT.

Krenzel threw a 7-yard touchdown pass to receiver Michael Jenkins but then misfired on the two-point conversion, leaving the Wolfpack with a chance at the victory. But on fourth-and-goal at the 1, OSU defenders A. J. Hawk and Will Allen stopped N.C. State tailback T. J. McLendon just short of the goal line to preserve the win for the Buckeyes.

The two quarterbacks combined to throw for eight touchdowns and nearly 600 yards. Krenzel was 26 for 36 for 273 yards and four scores, while Rivers completed 36 of 52 attempts for 315 yards and four TDs.

MILESTONE VICTORY (2008)

It may not have been the prettiest victory ever witnessed in the stadium, but the September 6, 2008, game against Ohio University had its share of historical significance.

The 26–14 victory was No. 800 in program history for Ohio State, making it only the fifth school in college football to achieve that milestone. The others: Michigan, Yale, Notre Dame, and Nebraska (Penn State joined the elite group on November 22, 2008, with a 49–18 win over Michigan State).

Ohio held a surprising 14–12 lead over OSU after three quarters, but the Buckeyes recovered a fumbled punt—one of five turnovers they created during the afternoon—to score a touchdown early in the fourth quarter and then got a 69-yard punt return for a touchdown from Ray Small to finally put the Bobcats away.

The contest marked the sixth all-time meeting between Ohio State and Ohio University, and the Buckeyes have won all six. The win pushed the Buckeyes' all-time record to 176–48–15 against in-state opponents, with the most recent defeat a 7–6 loss to Oberlin in 1921. The closest any in-state rival has come since was a 7–7 tie achieved by Wooster in 1924.

CLASH OF THE TITANS

Ohio Stadium fans were treated to huge momentum swings, outstanding offensive plays, and dynamite defensive performances September 10, 2005, as a battle between second-ranked Texas and No. 4 Ohio State lived up to its advanced billing.

In the end, the Buckeyes—who had scratched back from an early 10-point deficit and were holding a lead heading into the final three minutes by their fingernails—simply couldn't hold off the Longhorns, and Texas pulled out a 25–22 victory.

It marked the first meeting ever between the two college football titans, each of which was among the top five winningest Division I-A programs of all time. It also was Ohio State's first nonconference loss in the Horseshoe since 1990 and the program's first loss at home in seven night contests.

Texas was the highest rated team to visit Ohio Stadium since No. 1-ranked Iowa lost to the Buckeyes in 1985 by a 22–13 score.

Ohio State head coach Jim Tressel praised his team but lamented the abundance of missed opportunities that ultimately cost the Buckeyes dearly.

"I think you have to start with the fact that our kids played their hearts out. It was a well-fought football game," Tressel said. "I'm disappointed that we had several opportunities and didn't cash in on enough of them to win. We're going to have a good football team, but obviously we have to be more consistent."

Four times, the Buckeyes started a possession inside Texas territory, and four other times they started inside their own 40-yard line. Yet all OSU could get from those eight possessions was five field goals. The other three possessions wound up in punts.

There were other opportunities as well. Ohio State special teams veteran Antonio Smith missed a second-quarter tackle on Longhorns kickoff returner Ramonce Taylor in the end zone that would have been a safety. The score was 10–10 at the time.

In the third quarter, a sure touchdown pass bounced off normally sure-handed tight end Ryan Hamby, and the Buckeyes had to settle for a field goal. The Buckeyes then allowed the Longhorns to get a cheap field goal before halftime, pooching a kickoff in the waning seconds and then getting slapped with a personal foul penalty on the end of the run.

"We had our opportunities—we just couldn't cash in," OSU offensive lineman Rob Sims said. "It's very disappointing to get into the red zone and come away with only three points. Offensive production in the red zone—that's it right there. We didn't get it done."

Although OSU got some tough yards against a staunch Texas defense, it still only managed 111 rushing for the game and didn't appear to have the ability to pick up yardage when it was absolutely necessary.

"This was a tough loss, especially considering how we had them against the ropes throughout most of the game," OSU center Nick Mangold said. "It just seemed like we couldn't get that one big play we needed when we needed it."

The game was also supposed to solve the quarterback conundrum facing the Buckeyes but probably only added to the controversy of whether Justin Zwick or Troy Smith should start.

Zwick started and completed 9 of 15 passes for 66 yards. But when he couldn't move the team early and the Buckeyes fell behind 10–0, Smith entered the game and immediately sparked a surge. But he, too, fell victim in the second half to an offensive attack that could not cross the goal line, and Zwick returned to the lineup midway through the third quarter. In the end, Zwick led six series, and the Buckeyes netted 114 yards and three points. Smith piloted seven possessions, worth 121 yards and 19 points.

The game featured a host of excellent plays on both offense and defense from both teams. In the beginning, however, it was Texas making the most of the big plays. In fact, the Longhorns seemed to blow right through Ohio State in the early going.

After the Buckeyes went three-and-out on the game's first possession—thanks to dropped passes by Ted Ginn Jr. and Anthony Gonzalez—Texas embarked upon an 11-play, 64-yard drive that was nearly all Heisman Trophy winning quarterback Vince Young.

The 6' 5", 233-pound junior scrambled for 52 of those yards and helped set up the first score of the game, a 42-yard field goal by David Pino at the 10:03 mark of the first quarter.

And there was to be more of the same. OSU punter A. J. Trapasso pinned the Longhorns back at their own 16-yard line, but Young came out firing again, this time directing a 10-play drive that resulted in a touchdown. The UT quarterback showcased his arm instead of his legs, throwing for 58 yards during the march, the last five to receiver Billy Pittman, to give his team a 10–0 advantage with 1:37 remaining in the opening period.

By that time, not only were the Longhorns holding a 10-point lead; they looked to be on the verge of a blowout. They had already piled up 148 yards and eight first downs while the Buckeyes had 26 yards and just one first down.

But OSU got some life on the ensuing kickoff when Santonio Holmes returned it 47 yards to near midfield, and then Texas was hit with an unsportsmanlike conduct penalty. That gave the Buckeyes possession at the Texas 36-yard line, and Smith entered the game. But a holding penalty stunted the drive, and the team had to settle for a 45-yard field goal from Josh Huston.

That score seemed to spark the defense, which finally got a stop, and the Buckeyes went back to work. This time, Smith engineered an 80-yard drive that covered eight plays, including a 14-yard run by Antonio Pittman on a second-and-10 play and a 12-yard toss from Smith to Gonzalez on a third-and-5.

The most important play came, however, on a third-and-8 when Smith threw a perfect pass in the corner of the end for Holmes, who took the ball away from Texas cornerback Cedric Griffin. That touchdown play covered 36 yards and tied the score at 10 with 8:11 remaining in the first half.

More importantly, it triggered a huge momentum swing for the Buckeyes. Three plays into Texas's next drive, OSU linebacker A. J. Hawk stepped in front of a Young pass and returned the interception 24 yards to the UT 18. On the possession after that, Hawk recovered a fumble by Texas tailback Selvin Young to give the Buckeyes the ball at the Longhorns 30.

Unfortunately, Ohio State couldn't muster any offense on either opportunity. With Smith still at the controls, the Buckeyes actually went backward on the first possession and netted just 22 yards on the second, squandering a first-and-goal situation at the Texas 6. Huston bailed them out on both occasions, hitting a 36-yard field goal and then a 25-yarder to give the Buckeyes 16 unanswered points and a six-point advantage with just 35 seconds left until halftime.

The OSU kicker was instructed to pooch the ensuing kickoff, and Brown fielded it at the 19. He returned it 12 yards, but the Buckeyes were assessed a costly personal foul penalty that gave Texas the ball at their own 46. On first down, Young connected for 36 yards to freshman tailback Jamaal Charles, and the Longhorns got into position for Pino to boot a 37-yard field goal right before the half.

The OSU defense came to the field inspired in the second half. Safety Nate Salley picked off Young on the second play of the third quarter, giving the Buckeyes excellent field position again at the Texas 37.

Again, the offense fizzled with only 11 yards in six plays, and again Huston was called upon. His 44-yard field goal pushed the Buckeyes' advantage back to six points.

The teams exchanged field goals and the game settled into a battle for field position. The Buckeyes seemed to be winning that battle as Trapasso continually pinned the Longhorns back inside their own 20-yard line. The OSU redshirt freshman punted four times in the game, each time dropping his kick inside the opponent's 20.

The Buckeyes nearly put the game out of reach at the five-minute mark of the fourth quarter, moving from their own 30-yard line to the Texas 29. But the drive stalled—in fact, it lost four yards from there—and Huston was forced to try a 50-yard attempt, which sailed just outside the right upright.

That gave the Longhorns one final chance, and Young was up to the task. Starting at his own 33, the Texas QB got his team going with a 9-yard pass to Charles on a third-and-6 play, then sneaked through the line on a third-and-1 to sustain the march. The dagger came at the 2:37 mark. Texas receiver Limas Sweed was let go at the line of scrimmage by OSU cornerback Ashton Youboty, then Salley was just a hair late on help coverage. Young's pass was perfectly thrown, Sweed made a twisting catch, and the Longhorns scored a 24-yard touchdown. Pino's PAT provided the eventual winning point although the game wasn't quite over.

The Buckeyes got the ball back, but on a first-down scramble Zwick fumbled and the Longhorns recovered. OSU's defense held near the goal line on fourth down, but on the next play, Smith was sacked in the end zone for a safety to account for the final score.

Young finished the game with 270 yards and two touchdowns through the air and added another 76 yards on the ground. Zwick and Smith combined to throw for 144 yards and one score, but added only 38 more yards rushing. On defense, Hawk played an exceptional game for the Buckeyes. He had a game-high twelve tackles, including three for loss and two sacks to go along his fumble recovery and interception. Bobby Carpenter added 11 stops, while Donte Whitner and Anthony Schlegel had eight apiece.

Chapter 6

THE BEST OF THE BEST

HEISMANS AND NATIONAL CHAMPIONSHIPS

O ver its long and glorious history, the Ohio State football program has enjoyed more than its share of outstanding players and great teams. Nearly 350 Buckeyes have earned status on the All-Big Ten first team, and more than seventy-five have earned consensus All-America honors. Moreover, the College Football Hall of Fame has twenty-seven representatives who either played or coached for the Buckeyes.

In terms of team accomplishments, the university boasts thirty-three Big Ten championship trophies, as well as the awards brought home for winning eighteen postseason games, including six Rose Bowls.

There is no doubt that those players and teams gave Ohio State football the rich tradition it enjoys today. Mixed among their numbers, however, are players and teams who transcended greatness to become the best of the best.

Six young men have brought seven Heisman Trophies—college football's most prestigious individual prize—back to Columbus, while seven teams have ascended to the pinnacle of the sport by capturing national championships.

Each Heisman winner and each national title team hold special places in the hearts of all Buckeye fans, and we take pride in introducing them to you once more.

JEWELS IN THE CROWN: OHIO STATE'S HEISMAN WINNERS

LESLIE HORVATH (1944)

The great 1942 team, loaded with good players and commanded by the peerless Paul Brown, was helped immeasurably by a fellow who was born in—of all places—South Bend, Indiana.

Raised in Cleveland, Leslie Horvath was like other Buckeye award winners: athletic and brainy. In fact, his entrance into dental school in 1943—after the stellar team achievements of the season before—almost derailed him from becoming Ohio State's first Heisman winner.

After playing quarterback and halfback on offense, and safety on defense, Horvath began to think of life beyond the gridiron. Dental school proved to be "quite taxing," so Les concentrated on that full time. When head man Carroll Widdoes approached him in the pivotal year of 1944, though, Les thought about it. Would he return for his senior year and play ball again?

Yes, he would, and the rest, as they say, is history.

Horvath played brilliantly during the 1944 season for the Buckeyes, leading his team to a perfect 9–0 record and the number two ranking in the nation behind a powerful Army team that had many of the best players from across the country. Horvath logged time at quarterback, halfback, and defensive back that season, and played 402 of a possible 540 minutes. He rushed for 924 yards, threw for 344 more, and scored 72 points, earning the team's most valuable player award, an honor bestowed upon him by a vote of his teammates.

In addition, he earned first-team all-conference honors and went on to become the league's most valuable player. After the season, Horvath joined three other Buckeyes—Hackett, Dugger, and Bill Willis—as consensus All-Americans.

LESLIE HORVATH. OSU's first Heisman winner. Horvath played three positions for the Buckeyes: Quarterback, halfback, and defensive back.

Photo by Newscom/TSN/Icon SMI

To top things off, he was announced December 1 as the 10th recipient of the Heisman Trophy, the first Ohio State player ever to win the prestigious award. He beat out Army's two outstanding sophomore backs Felix "Doc" Blanchard and Glenn Davis, who would go on to win the 1945 and 1946 awards, respectively.

Horvath won the award despite finishing first in only one of the five U.S. voting sections. Davis, who was from California and played at West Point, won in the West and the East, while Blanchard, who was from Texas, won in the Southwest. Horvath took the Midwest and had a huge amount of second- and third-place votes that pushed him above Davis and Blanchard.

"It was a very big thrill back then," Horvath said years later. "But to tell you the truth, it means even more when you look back on it. I owe it all to my teammates.

"We had a very unusual squad that year. We had four or five starting freshmen in our starting lineup every game. We didn't really expect that much to begin with, but week after week, those freshmen got better. They just didn't realize how good they really were. Then, to go undefeated was a remarkable feat."

For his college career, Horvath carried the ball 290 times for 1,546 yards, an average of 5.3 yards per carry, and scored 12 touchdowns. He also completed 25 of 50 passes for 509 yards.

After winning the Heisman Trophy, Horvath took his diploma and enlisted in the U.S. Navy. That enlistment took him to the Great Lakes Naval Base where he reunited with Brown and became an assistant coach on his staff in 1945. The following two years, Horvath was stationed in Hawaii and attached to the U.S. Marine Corps.

Upon being discharged in 1947, he settled on the West Coast and began a brief professional football career. He played with the Rams, who had moved from Cleveland to Los Angeles, for two seasons before reuniting with Brown one last time in 1949 to play for the Cleveland Browns.

By that time, he had married his wife, Shirley, who admittedly didn't know much about her husband's athletic exploits. In fact, she asked him one day about the large bronze trophy that was prominently displayed in their living room. When Horvath tried to explain that it was the Heisman Trophy, Shirley nodded and smiled, then asked why it had to be so ugly.

Les finally convinced her of the trophy's importance, but after they visited their friends' homes—friends like the Tom Harmons and the Doc Blanchards—Shirley discovered that they also had the same bronze trophy in their living rooms.

Horvath always loved to relate the story of what happened next.

"Les," Shirley said, "you told me that football trophy of yours was really something special, but it turns out that everyone we know has one."

Horvath retired from football following the 1949 season, and spent more than 40 years in the Los Angeles area as a dentist. In 1969, he was inducted into the College Football Hall of Fame in a star-studded class that included Penn lineman Chuck Bednarik and legendary Oklahoma head coach Bud Wilkinson. Eight years later, Horvath would be included in the inaugural class of inductees into the Ohio State Athletic Hall of Fame, joining such luminaries as Chic Harley, Jerry Lucas, Jack Nicklaus, and Jesse Owens.

Horvath died on November 14, 1995, at his home in Glendale, California. He was 74.

VIC JANOWICZ (1950)

Born in 1930 in Elyria, Ohio, Victor Felix Janowicz was a pure, natural athlete from day one.

His legend began first at Holy Cross Elementary School, then at Elyria High School. In fact, a life-sized painting of Vic still hangs in the lobby of the school.

At 20, Vic became Ohio State's second Heisman winner as a single wing tailback. But he did much more as a runner, passer, placekicker, punter, and safety on defense. Woody Hayes also noted on several occasions that his superstar was an excellent blocker.

His best year statistically was that memorable 1950 season, during which he scored 16 TDs and gained 875 yards of total offense. Another remarkable thing about Janowicz's ability was that he also completed 32 of 77 passes for 561 yards and 12 TDs that season.

Janowicz's overall greatness is best remembered for two games in 1950. On October 28 in Ohio Stadium, he had a game for the ages when he accounted for five first-half touchdowns during an 80–23 win over Iowa. Before the break, Vic

VIC JANOWICZ truly did it all. He ran, passed, and caught, but he didn't stop there. Janowicz also punted, place-kicked, returned punts, and manned a defensive safety positon.

Photo courtesy of OSU Photo Archives

the Quick had rushed twice for 19 yards, including an 11-yard score; passed four times, completing three (all for TDs) for 77 yards; and returned a punt 61 yards for another score. He also punted for a 33-yard average, kicked off nine times, and converted seven PAT kicks.

Four weeks later, Janowicz put on an incredible punting and kicking display against Michigan in the famous Snow Bowl. In that game, Janowicz booted a 27-yard field goal through a driving snowstorm to provide the Buckeyes' only points in a bitter 9–3 defeat. That field goal, as well as his school-record 21 punt attempts in the game, remains an iconic moment in Buckeye football history.

Despite the fact the season ended on a sour note, Janowicz earned the Silver Football Trophy, symbolic of the Big Ten's most valuable player, and went on to become the school's second Heisman Trophy winner. He won the award in a landslide, more than doubling the vote total of his nearest competitor, SMU senior halfback Kyle Rote.

Janowicz went on to play two seasons of major league baseball with the Pittsburgh Pirates before switching back to football. He played in 1954 and 1955 with the NFL's Washington Redskins, but during training camp in 1956, he was nearly killed in an automobile accident. He suffered serious head injuries that left him partially paralyzed, ending his athletic career.

But Janowicz did not give up. After years of rehabilitation, he overcame the paralysis and spent many years as administrative assistant to the state auditor. He was elected to the College Football Hall of Fame in 1976, and one year later was in the inaugural class of inductees into the Ohio State Athletic Hall of Fame.

In 1992, he received perhaps his highest honor when the Columbus Downtown Quarterback Club named him Ohio State's greatest athlete of the previous fifty years.

Janowicz continued to be much in demand as a public speaker, especially at schools where he would cheerfully display his Heisman. He took great delight in telling children to rub the back leg of the player on the trophy for good luck.

He continued to tour the state as a goodwill ambassador for the university until his death from cancer on February 27, 1996.

HOWARD "HOPALONG" CASSADY (1955)

When a 150-pound freshman halfback from Columbus Central entered the first game of the 1952 season—against the Indiana Hoosiers—Ohio State fans knew they were in for an exciting four years.

Young Howard Albert Cassady scored three touchdowns during that 33–13 win, and Columbus sportswriters who watched him that day said the freshman "hopped all over the field like the performing cowboy." That was a reference to cowboy film star Hopalong Cassidy, and the nickname stuck.

Cassady went on to prove his durability in thirty-six career games. He led the Buckeyes to a 10–0 record and a national championship in 1954 and became a consensus All-American. The season ended with a smashing 20–7 win over Southern California in the Rose Bowl.

During that 1954 season, Cassady finished third in the Heisman balloting with Wisconsin halfback Alan Ameche winning the award although the Buckeyes defeated the Badgers by a 31–14 tally while holding Ameche to only 42 yards. Cassady scored on an 88-yard interception return that keyed a second-half rally for the Buckeyes.

The next year, Woody Hayes had his first Heisman winner as Hopalong ran for 958 yards and 15 TDs. In late November when the votes were tabulated for the 1955 Heisman Trophy, it wasn't even close. Cassady became the first player ever to amass 2,000 points in the Heisman scoring system and bested runner-up Jim Swink of Texas Christian by a whopping 1,477 points, the largest margin of victory to that time.

The following month, the *Associated Press* named Cassady its "Athlete of the Year for 1955," beating out such other notables as heavyweight boxing champion Rocky Marciano and Cleveland Browns quarterback Otto Graham.

Hop went on to establish new career marks for Ohio State with 2,466 yards rushing and 37 touchdowns while playing sterling defense. It was said that in his four years in the Buckeye secondary, Cassady never had a pass completed behind him. And his stardom wasn't only limited to the football field. He was also a three-year letterman for the Ohio State baseball team and earned a Big Ten baseball championship in 1954 to go along with his national title in football.

HOWARD "HOPALONG" CASSADY.
Another two-way player, Cassady solidified his spot among OSU greats by winning the Heisman in 1955.

The Detroit Lions made Cassady their first-round selection in the 1956 NFL draft, and he was a starter for the Lions for six seasons. He was later traded to Cleveland for the 1962 season and also played for Philadelphia that year, then returned to Detroit for the 1963 season. He retired after 8 NFL seasons and finished with 1,229 yards and 6 touchdowns rushing and 111 receptions for 1,601 yards and 18 TDs. He also returned 43 punts for a 7.9-yard career average and ran back 77 kickoffs, averaging 20.7 yards per return.

Following his retirement from football, Cassady translated his gridiron success into business success. He formed his own company, which manufactured concrete pipe, and sold it in 1968 when he moved into selling steel with Hopalong Cassady Associates. Howard later worked for American Shipbuilding in Tampa, Fla., where he struck up a friendship with the company's owner George Steinbrenner. Cassady later became a scout and coach for the New York Yankees and spent several seasons as first base coach for the Columbus Clippers, the Yankees' Triple-A farm club.

Cassady was selected as part of the inaugural class of the Ohio State Athletic Hall of Fame in 1977 and was inducted into the College Football Hall of Fame two years later. In the fall of 2000, he returned to Ohio State when the university retired his jersey No. 40.

ARCHIE GRIFFIN (1974 AND 1975)

Archie Mason Griffin is quite simply the king of the Heisman Trophy. Methodical and spectacular, he set a slew of school and NCAA records and became the face of Buckeye football in 1970s. In many respects, he retains that stature to this day.

In just the second game of his career, Griffin smashed the school's single-game rushing record with 239 yards against North Carolina. That broke Ollie Cline's old mark of 229 yards that had stood for twenty-seven years.

Griffin would go on to 867 yards that freshman season, helping the Buckeyes to a conference co-championship and a berth in the Rose Bowl. It was the beginning of quite a career. He would break his own single-game rushing record the following year with 246 yards against Iowa, and would rush for 100 yards or more

ARCHIE GRIFFIN. Now the head of the OSU Alumni Association, Griffin is still the only player to win two Heisman trophies.

Photo courtesy of OSU Sports Information

in a game thirty-five times in his career, including an NCAA-record thirty-one contests in a row.

Griffin would go on to set several other records. He became the first and only player ever to start in four consecutive Rose Bowls. He won back-to-back Big Ten most valuable player honors, becoming only the second player ever to accomplish that feat. And he rushed for 5,589 yards during his career at Ohio State—no other Buckeye running back has ever come close. Eddie George ranks second all-time, 1,821 yards behind Griffin.

In 1974, Griffin reached the pinnacle of his sport when he was named winner of the 40th annual Heisman Memorial Trophy. He became only the fifth junior to win the award and easily outpointed the second-place finisher, senior running back Anthony Davis of Southern California. Griffin received 1,920 points in the balloting to 819 for Davis.

The following year, Griffin became the first and only player to repeat as Heisman Trophy winner, this time besting California running back Chuck Muncie by a margin of 1,800 points to 730.

After graduation, Griffin was a first-round draft choice of the Cincinnati Bengals, who took him as the twenty-fourth overall selection in 1976 NFL draft. He played seven seasons for the Bengals, and played in the team's Super Bowl XVI loss to San Francisco. Griffin retired after the 1982 season with career statistics that included 2,808 yards and seven touchdowns rushing, as well as 192 pass receptions for 1,607 yards and six TDs.

Griffin returned to Columbus in 1984 and joined the Ohio State athletic department, eventually working his way to assistant athletic director and later associate director of athletics. In 1981, he was enshrined in the OSU Athletic Hall of Fame, and five years later received induction into the College Football Hall of Fame. That was followed with the ultimate honor in October 1999 when Griffin's familiar No. 45 became the first jersey number ever officially retired by Ohio State.

In 2004, Griffin left the university's athletic department but didn't stray very far. He was named president and chief executive officer of the Ohio State Alumni Association and continues to be one of the best goodwill ambassadors the Scarlet and Gray has ever had.

EDDIE GEORGE (1995)

Philadelphia-born Edward Nathan George Jr. remains one of the greatest "elegant" power backs of all-time.

At 6'3" and 230 pounds, Eddie George was smooth, powerful, and a workhorse—one of those backs that gets stronger as the game goes on.

The same could be said about his career at Ohio State.

After slowly working himself into the tailback mix as a freshman during the first four games in 1992, George fumbled twice near the goal line against Illinois in game five. One of his fumbles was returned 96 yards for an Illini touchdown that ultimately accounted for the losing margin in an 18–16 final.

The fumbles proved disastrous for George, who found himself on the bench for much of the rest of the 1992 season, and for a good part of his sophomore campaign as well. He had only 37 carries for 176 yards in 1992 and just 42 more the following season for 223 yards.

He thought about how a fresh start elsewhere might be what he needed but was talked out of transferring by several teammates. During the offseason between his sophomore and junior years, George dedicated himself to a weight training regimen that reshaped his body and his spirit. As a result, he became the go-to guy for the Buckeyes in 1994 as he carried 276 times for 1,442 yards and 12 touchdowns. He also added 16 receptions for 117 yards after never having caught a pass in his OSU career.

That set the stage for a superlative senior season. After rushing for 99 yards in the opener against Boston College, George totaled 100 or more yards in each of the Buckeyes' final 12 games, including 207 yards and a pair of touchdowns in a 42–26 win over Notre Dame and a school-record 314 yards during a 42–3 victory over Illinois.

By the time he had finished his final season at Ohio State, George had broken the OSU single-season mark with 1,927 yards. He followed that by winning Big Ten player of the year honors, earning consensus All-America merit, and capturing the 61st annual Heisman Trophy, easily outdistancing Nebraska quarterback Tommie Frazier for the honor.

George went on to an illustrious professional career, starring for several seasons for the Tennessee Titans. He was NFL rookie of the year in 1995, was named

EDDIE GEORGE set OSU's single-season rushing record en route to winning the 1995 Heisman Trophy.

to four consecutive Pro Bowls from 1997–2000, and retired following the 2004 season with 10,441 yards and 68 touchdowns on the ground and another 268 receptions, 2,227 yards, and 10 TDs on 268 receptions.

In addition to his triumphs on the gridiron, George has enjoyed success off the field with several lucrative businesses, including a popular Columbus restaurant located just across High Street from the Ohio State campus.

But he is clearly defined by the legendary status he achieved while wearing Scarlet and Gray. In 2006, George was inducted into the university's athletic hall of fame. Five years earlier, he was honored when his No. 27 jersey was retired.

TROY SMITH (2006)

Jim Tressel is a great evaluator of talent, a skill that separates many good coaches from a few great ones. He knew when he watched a great athlete at Cleveland Glenville High School that this was a guy Ohio State had to have.

Troy Smith had been coached in high school by another guy who knew something about great athletes—Ted Ginn Sr. Before his senior year, Smith was invited to the Elite 11 quarterback camp. There he distinguished himself, and on February 6, 2002, he became Ohio State's final signee that winter.

It was perhaps fate that Smith would wind up playing for Tressel and his Buckeyes, since he had been mentored by Ginn and, in a twist that seems providential, by Irvin White, coach of the Glenville A's midget football team. Smith, having been raised by his mother, began his playing career as a tight end and running back, until White moved him to quarterback. Eventually, he would also move in with the Whites.

With all this male mentorship, Smith blossomed into a tremendous quarterback prospect—although his Ohio State career took a little time to take off.

As a redshirt freshman for the Buckeyes in 2003, Smith saw most of his playing time as a kickoff returner. By the next season, he was the backup quarterback until a midseason injury to starter Justin Zwick. After that, Smith led his team to a 4–1 record down the stretch, and really emerged against Michigan with 386 yards total offense during a 37–21 win.

The next year, he led OSU to another great win over Michigan and a smashing win over Notre Dame in the Fiesta Bowl.

His brightest moments were still ahead of him, though.

During his senior year, Smith led his team to a 12–0 regular-season record with a school-record 30 touchdown passes. However, his greatest achievement was engineering a third straight victory over Michigan. In a classic 42–39 win over the second-ranked Wolverines, Smith had another 300-yard total offense game. His career stats of 1,151 yards of total offense and nine TDs against Michigan prove that he was at his best on the biggest stage.

Following his senior season, Smith earned a host of individual honors, including the Walter Camp and Davey O'Brien awards, as well as being named college football player of the year by the *Associated Press* and *Sporting News*.

In December, he added to his long list of awards when he won the 2006 Heisman Trophy in a landslide over Arkansas running back Darren McFadden and Notre Dame quarterback Brady Quinn. Smith received 801 first-place votes and won the Heisman by 1,662 points. Each figure represents the second-highest total in the 75-year history of the award. USC running back O. J. Simpson totaled 855 first-place votes in 1968 and won the trophy by a margin of 1,750 votes over runner-up Leroy Keyes of Purdue.

Smith finished his career with his name all over the Ohio State record books. He has the best all-time pass efficiency rating (157.1) and is second all-time in career completion percentage (62.7), third in touchdown passes (54), third in total offense (6,888), and fifth in passing yardage (5,720).

Smith was a fifth-round selection by the Baltimore Ravens in the 2007 NFL draft.

WE ARE THE CHAMPIONS: RECAPPING OHIO STATE'S NATIONAL TITLE SEASONS

HISTORY IS MADE (1942)

After Paul Brown lost twenty-two players to military service following the 1941 season, there wasn't much expected of the 1942 Ohio State football team. Of course, many other schools around the country were experiencing the same kind of attrition as World War II waged in Europe and the Pacific.

TROY SMITH. This 2006 Heisman winner has his name peppered throughout the Ohio State record books.

Photo courtesy of Mark Rea

The season began with a 59–0 win over Fort Knox, but the Buckeyes had a much taller task in week two against experienced Big Ten rival Indiana. The Hoosiers were set to invade Columbus with one of their all-time greatest teams, including triple-threat halfback Billy Hillenbrand and quarterback Lou Saban, who was voted his team's most valuable player that year.

IU was coached by the legendary Alvin Nugent "Bo" McMillin, who was in his ninth year in Bloomington and 20th overall as a college head coach. McMillin had told friends that he had his "best-manned squad in years," and that Hillenbrand was the greatest back in college football since Illinois star Red Grange. The Hoosiers were the bigger, stronger, and more experienced team, and McMillin reasoned they not only would beat the Buckeyes, they would win rather convincingly.

Brown had a few tricks up his sleeve, however. The Hoosiers went into the fourth quarter trying to protect a 21–19 lead, but fell victim to a pair of late touchdowns by the Buckeyes. Sophomore fullback Gene Fekete tallied one of the OSU scores and quarterback George Lynn tacked on the insurance TD which was set up by a 44-yard interception return by future Heisman Trophy winner Les Horvath.

The Buckeyes used the 32–21 come-from-behind victory over a supposedly superior opponent to touch off a magical season. After dispatching Indiana, Ohio State rolled off three more victories in a row before a 17–7 loss at Wisconsin, a game in which several of the Buckeyes played with dysentery contracted by drinking contaminated water on the train ride to Madison.

They came back, though, the next week with a 59–19 thrashing of Pittsburgh, and then finished the regular season with big home victories over thirteenth-ranked Illinois (44–20) and number four Michigan (21–7).

Ohio State capped off the 1942 season with a 41–12 win over the Iowa Seahawks, a military team that featured several former star college players, and the Buckeyes were named national champions by the *Associated Press*, the first time in school history the team was so honored.

Halfback Paul Sarringhaus, end Bob Shaw, and lineman Lindell Houston earned first-team All-Big Ten accolades that season, and that trio was joined by lineman Chuck Csuri and Fekete as first-time All-Americans. Fekete also finished eighth in the Heisman Trophy balloting that season, and led the Big Ten in scoring with a school-record 92 points. That single-season mark would stand for 26 years until another fullback, Jim Otis, broke it with 102 points in 1968.

At the center of national championship season, however, was Brown. He went on to become a seminal figure in football history with many experts ranking him as one of the greatest coaches the game has ever seen.

THE TEAM THAT SAVED WOODY (1954)

In 28 seasons as head coach at the Ohio State University, Woody Hayes won 205 games, coached 58 All-Americans, and captured four national championships and 13 Big Ten crowns. But Hayes didn't always have the swagger that comes with being the program's winningest coach.

When he was named head man in 1951 just four days after his 38th birthday, Ohio State had the reputation as being "The Graveyard of Coaches," and Hayes quickly experienced why. During his first three seasons in Columbus, the Buckeyes never finished higher than third in the Big Ten, and won only sixteen of twenty-seven games. Worse yet, Hayes had lost two of three games against archrival Michigan, including a 20–0 shutout to end the 1953 season.

As the coach made his annual rounds of the offseason banquet circuit, Hayes began to hear whispers about his job status. Nothing was ever discussed publicly, but the writing was on the wall. The coach knew his team had better contend for the Big Ten championship and beat Michigan in 1954 or there would be a tombstone with his name on it in "The Graveyard."

GAMEDAY HAUNTS

The Little Bar Tons of HD big screens and a jumbo 16-foot indoor TV for your viewing pleasure. Also more beverage stands around the property than you could ask for.

Ohio State was picked by most sportswriters to finish third in the 1954 conference race behind Wisconsin and Minnesota, but the Buckeyes caught fire early. They shut out Indiana in the season opener, and then notched a pair of important wins. They defeated eighteenth-ranked California by a 21–13 score and then avenged a 21-point loss to Illinois from the year before by rolling to a 40–7 victory over the Illini.

Those games were followed by wins over thirteenth-ranked Iowa and second-ranked Wisconsin, and suddenly the Buckeyes were undefeated and the nation's number one team. They added three more victories to their ledger—at Northwestern, in Columbus over number twenty Pittsburgh, and at Purdue—before hosting archrival Michigan in the traditional season finale.

In front of a capacity crowd of 82,438 in Ohio Stadium, OSU overcame an early 7-point deficit and rolled to a 21–7 victory. The Buckeyes followed with a 20–7 win over Southern California in the Rose Bowl to finish off the program's first 10-victory season in history and only its second unblemished record since 1917.

The undefeated season also resulted in the *Associated Press* awarding Ohio State its national championship. It was the second national title in school history and the first of five for Hayes.

Years later, Hayes would say that the 1954 season was one of his greatest accomplishments because the way that team performed allowed him to keep his job at Ohio State.

"Woody gave credit to that team many times over the years for saving his job," said Ohio State football historian Jack Park. "Woody had a lot of people who thought he wasn't up to the job. But that season and the way that team played was what allowed him to keep his job and establish Ohio State as one of the top college football programs in the nation. If it hadn't been for the 1954 season, the history of Ohio State football as we know it would probably have changed dramatically."

FROM RAGS TO RICHES (1957)

When Ohio State opened its 1957 football season, there was little indication the Buckeyes were on the threshold of greatness.

A year before, the university's athletic department had been slapped with a one-year probation by the NCAA because several football players had reportedly accepted improper benefits from a campus official. That official happened to be head coach Woody Hayes, who had casually mentioned in 1955 that he often loaned small amounts of money to players who were in need of financial assistance.

The story eventually made its way into several national magazines, which prompted an NCAA investigation and subsequent one-year penalty for all Ohio State athletic teams.

Hayes was incensed by the ruling, saying the aid was merely token assistance to youngsters in need. Nevertheless, he agreed to abide by the NCAA probation without public appeal. The Buckeyes went on to post a 6–3 record in 1956, getting shut out in its final two games—6–0 at Iowa and 19–0 at home against Michigan—and finished in fourth place of the Big Ten standings.

By the time the 1957 season rolled around, the probation had been lifted, but it didn't seem to matter. The football team wasn't expected to do much, being picked fifth in a Big Ten preseason poll behind Michigan State, Minnesota, defending champion Iowa and Michigan.

More than half of the starting lineup from the previous year had graduated, including two-time All-America lineman Jim Parker, and Hayes welcomed back only 18 returning lettermen.

The preseason forecast for a middle-of-the-pack showing seemed to be correct when the team stumbled coming out of the gate, losing an 18–14 decision to Texas Christian in the 1957 season opener. Ohio State entered the game as a two-touchdown favorite against the Horned Frogs, a team that would go 5–4–1 that year and finish fifth in the old Southwest Conference. The loss also marked Hayes's first opening-game defeat in seven years as head coach of the Buckeyes, and coupled with the two season-ending losses the year before, gave him his first three-game losing streak in Columbus.

No one could have foreseen at that time that OSU would go on to rattle off nine consecutive victories, including a 10–7 win over Oregon in the Rose Bowl, and capture the 1957 national championship.

Although the season began with only a handful of returning veterans, several members of the team became some of the most recognizable names in Ohio State football history.

Manning the tackle positions on the team were Dick Schafrath and Jim Marshall, who went on to become stars in the NFL. Schafrath was a six-time Pro Bowler for the Cleveland Browns from 1959–61, and opened holes for such Hall of Fame running backs as Jim Brown, Bobby Mitchell, and Leroy Kelly. Marshall spent most of his 20-year Hall of Fame career with the Minnesota Vikings, and started an NFL-record 282 consecutive games at defensive end from 1960–79 .

Alongside the young tackles were seniors Aurealius Thomas and Bill Jobko. Thomas was named a first-team All-American following the 1957 season and later earned enshrinement into the College Football Hall of Fame. Jobko, whom many believe was the most underrated player on the team, played such a vital role in the national championship run that his teammates voted him most valuable player.

Also on the line was a sophomore end named Jim Houston, who would go on to become an All-American at Ohio State, a member of the College Football Hall of Fame, and a four-time Pro Bowl linebacker for the Browns.

The backfield featured powerhouses such as Galen Cisco and Bob White at fullback, junior Frank Kremblas at quarterback, and talented stars like Don Clark and Dick LeBeau at halfback. LeBeau, of course, went on to a 14-year NFL playing career with the Detroit Lions and has served as head coach or assistant coach with six teams, including the Pittsburgh Steelers with whom he won Super Bowl championship rings following the 2005 and 2008 seasons.

Cisco served as team captain in 1957 along with fellow senior Leo Brown, who was an end. Cisco went on to become a major-league pitcher with Boston, Kansas City, and the New York Mets, then spent 31 years as a pitching coach in the majors for several different teams.

The Buckeyes' kicker that season was Don Sutherin, whose 34-yard field goal provided for the winning margin over Oregon in the Rose Bowl. Sutherin went on to a hall of fame career in the Canadian Football League where he played in eight Grey Cup championships, winning four.

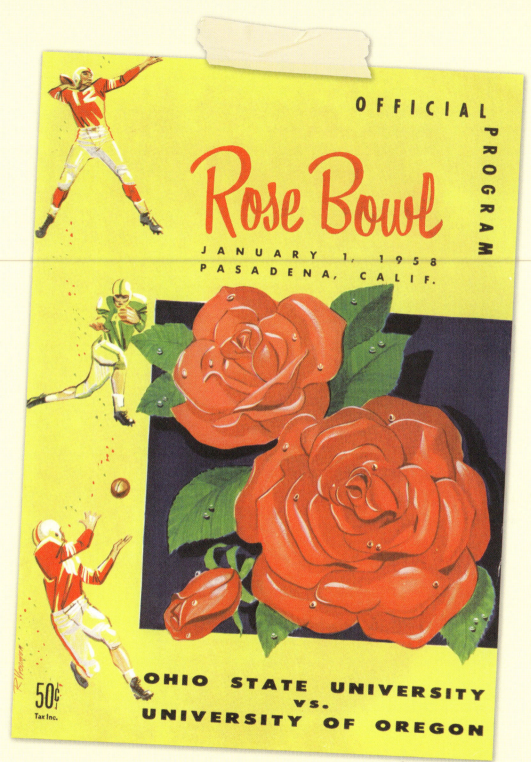

Photo courtesy of Mark Rea

1958 Rose Bowl Program

United Press International awarded its national championship trophy to the Buckeyes—declaring OSU the champion even before the bowl game—and gave Hayes his second title in four seasons. Michigan State, which finished at 7–1 that season but did not play Ohio State, was third in both national polls. Unfortunately, the Buckeyes did not do enough to convince *Associated Press* voters, who awarded their version of the 1957 national championship to undefeated Auburn.

Nevertheless, Hayes was named national coach of the year by several organizations, including the American Football Coaches Association and the Football Writers Association of America, while Thomas earned first-team All-America honors. He joined teammates Brown and Clark on the consensus All-Big Ten team.

'BECAUSE I COULDN'T GO FOR THREE' (1961)

After the national championship in 1957, Ohio State took a step back. The Buckeyes slipped to a 6–1–2 record the following season and 3–5–1 in 1959, one of only two losing seasons in Woody Hayes's tenure.

OSU improved to seven wins against only two defeats in 1960 and then came all the way back in 1961. After being surprised by Texas Christian in the season opener with a 7–7 tie, the Buckeyes steamrolled over eight opponents in a row and averaged better than 30 points per game during that streak.

Despite all the victories, however, Ohio State went into its traditional season finale at Michigan not knowing if a win would be enough to clinch the Big Ten championship. Minnesota, which had shared the 1960 title with Iowa, was hosting a three-loss Wisconsin team and held an edge over the Buckeyes by virtue of playing more conference games that season.

The Wolverines were led in 1961 by College Football Hall of Fame coach Chalmers "Bump" Elliott, who was in his third season in Ann Arbor. Elliott's team entered the game on a three-game winning streak and hoped for revenge against its archrivals for a 7–0 victory the Buckeyes had enjoyed in 1960.

That wasn't to be, however. OSU held the Wolverines on a fourth-and-1 situation early in the game and never looked back. Fullback Bob Ferguson rushed for 152 yards and four touchdowns as the Buckeyes rolled to a 50–20 win. The 30-point margin of victory was Ohio State's widest in the overall series since a

38–0 victory over Michigan in 1935, and the 50 points represented an all-time high for OSU against their archrivals.

The Buckeyes' final touchdown of the game also created more than its share of controversy—not to mention folklore.

With less than thirty seconds to play, Hayes instructed his quarterback to go to the air, and Joe Sparma connected with Paul Warfield on what the OSU speedster would turn into a 70-yard play. Then, with just five seconds left, Sparma threw a 10-yard touchdown pass to backup end Sam Tidmore, who fought the final four yards into the end zone.

Hayes then elected to go for a two-point conversion. The Sparma-to-Tidmore connection worked again, accounting for the Buckeyes' final margin of victory.

When quizzed about the final touchdown and two-point conversion, Hayes offered several different explanations.

He denied that pouring it on at the end was his way of paying back the Wolverines for kicking a field goal in the fourth quarter of a 58–6 win over the Buckeyes in 1946.

"The Bucks don't get steamed up on junk like that," Hayes told the *Columbus Dispatch*. "One writer accused me of running up the score on Bump. I might do that to Fritz Crisler (who was the Michigan coach for the '46 game), but not Bump. Bump Elliott is truly one of the great sportsmen in football."

Elliott later told reporters, "I'm not sure what Ohio State was shooting for—shooting for us, I guess."

Many years later, Hayes finally admitted that he did have the Wolverines' win in 1946 in the back of his mind. Asked why he went for two, the coach simply replied, "Because I couldn't go for three."

The Buckeyes finished the 1961 campaign with an 8–0–1 overall record, and when Wisconsin upset Minnesota on the final day of the regular season, Ohio State won the outright Big Ten championship and earned the right to represent the conference at the Rose Bowl.

At the time, however, the contract between the Big Ten and Pacific Coast Conference had expired, and a new one was still in negotiation. It was a forgone conclusion that the Rose Bowl would offer an invitation to the Buckeyes to play against Pacific Coast champion UCLA. But the 44-member Ohio State Faculty Council, fearing that athletics was overtaking academics on the campus, voted to deny the Buckeyes their trip to Pasadena.

It was a bitter pill for players on the 1961 team to take, one the survivors of the squad continue to struggle with today.

Instead of getting a chance to play in Pasadena, the Buckeyes had to be content with the Football Writers Association of America's version of the national championship for 1961.

A SEASON FOR THE AGES (1968)

Woody Hayes was preparing for his 18th season as head coach of the Buckeyes in the fall of 1968. He was already by far the winningest coach in school history and had notched a consensus national championship in 1954 and parts of two others in 1957 and 1961. But in the previous seventeen years, Hayes's teams had won only four Big Ten championships.

OSU fans were thirsty for more conference titles, and making matters worse was the fact that the Buckeyes were coming off back-to-back down seasons. During a thirteen-game stretch that spanned the 1966 and 1967 seasons, the team had lost eight times. Furthermore, their record in the Big Ten during that stretch was an unsatisfactory 4–6.

To say the natives were getting restless was an understatement. Hayes managed to stem the criticism a bit when his Buckeyes won their last four games in 1967, including a 24–14 victory at Michigan. Still, there was plenty of trepidation as the team headed into the 1968 season.

Hayes was committed to infusing several sophomores from his 1967 recruiting class into the starting lineup, players who had performed superbly the year before as freshmen when pitted in scrimmages against their varsity counterparts. There was only one thing wrong—Hayes hated using first-year players in any capacity, much less as starters.

DID YOU KNOW?

Academy Award nominated actress Natalie Portman has an interesting connection to Ohio State. Portman's father, **Avner Hershlag**, an Israeli doctor specializing in fertility and reproduction, was visiting OSU in the late 1970s when he attended an event at the Jewish student center on campus. Selling tickets to the event was Shelley Stevens. The two met and began a relationship that continued even after Hershlag returned to Israel. The two eventually married and daughter Natalie was born June 9, 1981, in Jerusalem. The family moved to the United States three years later and Natalie began acting in films at the age of 13, taking her grandmother's maiden name Portman as her professional name.

He obviously changed that philosophy in 1968 when the class dubbed the "Super Sophomores" became eligible. Hayes turned the keys to his offense over to Rex Kern at quarterback and even told Kern that he would have the luxury of calling his own plays.

"That's totally unheard of today," Kern said. "A lot of people can't believe Woody would have entrusted the play-calling to any quarterback, much less a first-year starter, but he saw that as his best chance to win and Woody placed winning above everything else."

Kern wasn't the only sophomore who played a vital role for the Buckeyes in 1968. He was joined by classmates such as Jan White at tight end, Bruce Jankowski at receiver, Jim Stillwagon at middle guard, Mark Debevc at defensive end, Doug Adams at linebacker, and Mike Sensibaugh, Tim Anderson, and Jack Tatum in the secondary. In addition, Leo Hayden, Larry Zelina, and John Brockington shared the running back duties with juniors Ray Gillian and Dave Brungard.

Over the years, the sophomores have gotten more than their share of the credit for the national championship run. The truth is they could never have accomplished so much without the help of their more experienced teammates.

"The leadership those older guys gave our team was tremendous," Kern said. "That season was never about one guy or even a group of guys. It was all about the team. That's what I remember most—we had a great group of guys who were great teammates, and that's what allowed us to achieve what we did."

The young OSU quarterback was able to operate freely behind a veteran offensive line that featured seniors Dave Foley and Rufus Mayes at tackle, juniors Alan Jack and Tom Backhus at guard, and dependable senior John Muhlbach at center. It also helped to have the benefit of the running and blocking prowess of junior fullback Jim Otis.

On defense, the Buckeyes relied heavily on senior linebacker Mark Stier as well as junior linemen Paul Schmidlin, Brad Nielsen, Bill Urbanik, Dave Whitfield, and Mike Radtke. Another junior, Ted Provost, helped anchor the young secondary.

The Buckeyes piled up victory after victory that season, including a vital 13–0 shutout of top-ranked Purdue in week three. After the victory, Ohio State rose from number four to two in the national polls. Despite the fact that they kept on winning, however, the Buckeyes couldn't ascend to the top spot. That was reserved for defending national champion USC, which was punishing opponents in its own way behind ultimate Heisman Trophy winner O. J. Simpson.

The two powerhouses finally got to settle things in the Rose Bowl, a match-up featuring two unbeaten teams for the first time in the twenty-two-year history of the contract between the Big Ten and Pac-8.

USC scored first, racing out to a 10–0 lead thanks in part to an 80-yard touchdown burst by Simpson. But the Buckeyes rallied to tie the score by halftime and then pulled away in the second half on a Jim Roman field goal and a pair of Kern touchdown passes.

The Trojans scored a meaningless touchdown in the final minute as Ohio State celebrated a complete 27–16 victory, earning the national championship and completing only the fourth undefeated and untied season in program history.

UPSET LOSS AVENGED (1970)

Strange as it may seem, the senior members of the Ohio State football team looked for redemption just two years after winning the national championship as sophomores.

The Buckeyes had rolled through the 1969 season with eight straight victories and seemed poised for another shot at the national title when they suffered an almost-inexplicable 24–12 upset loss at Michigan. Over the next nine months, that defeat consumed the players and coaches so much that avenging that loss took precedence over everything else—including the national championship.

Head coach Woody Hayes had a veteran team that included the one-two punch of Rex Kern and Ron Maciejowski at quarterback, Larry Zelina, Leo Hayden, and John Brockington in the backfield, the likes of Dave Cheney, John Hicks, and Tom DeLeone on the offensive line, and a defense spearheaded by Jim Stillwagon, Mark Debevc, Stan White, Doug Adams, Tim Anderson, Mike Sensibaugh, and Jack Tatum.

OSU made a statement in the season opener with a 56–13 stampede over Texas A&M, the most points an opponent had scored against the Aggies in their 75-year history. What followed were wins over Duke, Michigan State, Minnesota, Illinois, Northwestern, and Wisconsin with an average 20.5-point margin of victory.

JIM OTIS blocks for QB Rex Kern in a 1968 football game against rival Purdue.

One week before facing Michigan, the Buckeyes nearly got caught looking ahead, but a fourth-quarter, 30-yard field goal into a strong wind from kicker Fred Schram gave Ohio State a 10–7 win at Purdue. That set up a grudge match in Ohio Stadium between the fifth-ranked Buckeyes and the number four Wolverines, marking the first time since 1905 that two undefeated and untied teams had met to settle the Big Ten championship.

A record stadium crowd of 87,331 watched as the teams played almost evenly for the first three quarters until Anderson blocked an extra-point kick to preserve a 10–9 Ohio State lead. In the fourth period, the Buckeyes got a 27-yard field goal from Schram and a 9-yard touchdown run from Hayden set up by a White interception.

During his postgame press conference, Hayes referred to the victory as the greatest game in Ohio State history, and President Richard Nixon telephoned the coach within minutes of the final gun to offer the coach congratulations.

Unfortunately, the euphoria from the redemption win was short-lived. The Buckeyes squandered a late 17–13 advantage in the Rose Bowl and wound up 27–17 losers as Heisman Trophy quarterback Jim Plunkett rallied his Stanford team to the upset victory.

Nevertheless, the National Football Foundation selected Ohio State as its national champion. *United Press International* placed the Buckeyes second behind Texas, while the *Associated Press* had Nebraska at number one and OSU at number five.

Tatum, Debevc, Stillwagon, Cheney, Sensibaugh, DeLeone, Brockington, and linebacker Phil Strickland helped Ohio State dominate the All-Big Ten team, and Stillwagon, Tatum, White, Brockington, Sensibaugh, and Anderson each earned All-America honors.

The following spring, four Buckeyes—Brockington, Tatum, Anderson, and Hayden—were first-round selections in the 1971 NFL draft. Nine of their teammates were also taken in that draft—testament to the talent at Hayes's disposal for the glorious three-year period beginning in 1968.

FITTING END TO THRILLING SEASON (2002)

The Buckeyes ended their long national championship drought in dramatic fashion, setting a school record with 14 victories, many of them in heart-stopping fashion. Seven of the wins came by a margin of seven points or less, including a pulsating 14–9 nail-biter over Michigan and a double overtime title thriller against defending champion Miami (Florida).

The Hurricanes, owners of a 34-game winning streak, were coached by former OSU assistant Larry Coker, who had taken over the program in 2001 and had a spotless 24–0 record. Coker had a star-packed roster headlined by the likes of such future NFL stars as running back Willis McGahee, tight end Kellen Winslow II, middle linebacker Jonathan Vilma, and safety Sean Taylor.

Leading the offense was senior quarterback Ken Dorsey, who had thrown for more than 3,000 yards and 26 touchdowns. Dorsey had been under center for each of the Hurricanes' 34 consecutive victories, and he needed only one more to tie the NCAA record for most wins in a row by a starting quarterback.

Miami had such a high-powered offense and stingy defense that practically no one gave Ohio State a chance to win the national title game. Oddsmakers installed the Hurricanes as prohibitive thirteen-and-a-half-point favorites. Several national college football analysts didn't think it would be that close.

But the Fiesta Bowl crowd of 77,502 that jammed its way into Sun Devil Stadium was witness to a classic, back-and-forth battle that wasn't decided until the final play.

Miami grabbed an early 7–0 lead before the Buckeyes forged a 17–7 advantage midway through the third quarter. The Hurricanes fought back to tie the game, getting a third-quarter TD run from McGahee and a 40-yard field goal from kicker Todd Sievers at the end of regulation.

In the first overtime period, Miami scored a touchdown that was matched by Ohio State. In the second extra session, however, the Buckeyes sealed the championship with a goal-line stand after freshman tailback Maurice Clarett's 5-yard scoring run.

Clarett was named Big Ten Freshman of the Year and earned first-team all-conference honors along with safety Mike Doss, cornerback/receiver Chris Gamble, defensive tackle Darrion Scott, linebacker Matt Wilhelm, punter Andy Groom, and kicker Mike Nugent.

> " I love my kids, and I want what is best for them. I don't care what they do, be it athletics, science or playing the piano as long as they do it to the best of their ability...and they attend The Ohio State University. "
>
> —Keith Byars

CRAIG KRENZEL reacts after sneaking into the end zone to send the Fiesta Bowl against Miami into a second overtime. The Buckeyes would go on to win after Maurice Clarett scored a touchdown and the OSU defense put up a thrilling goal-line stand.

Photo courtesy of Jeff Brehm/Buckeye Sports Bulletin

Doss, Wilhelm, Groom, and Nugent added first-team All-America honors while Jim Tressel was honored as the American Football Coaches Association's coach of the year. Coupled with his 1991 and 1994 awards while at Division I-AA Youngstown State, Tressel became the first coach in NCAA history to be named AFCA coach of the year while at different schools, and also the first to win the award in two different divisions.

Chapter 7

TOP TEN OSU PLAYERS BY DECADE

In the history of Ohio State football, there have been many outstanding players. Home to hundreds of All-Americans and seven Heisman Trophy winners, OSU's tradition of excellence is long and storied. So without further ado, here are the top ten Ohio State players from each decade.

1890–99

1. DEL SAYERS

Sayers was team captain in 1899, the first undefeated season for the Buckeyes. The team scored 184 points that year and surrendered only five. Unfortunately, those five points came in a 5–5 tie against Case. Ohio State's nine other games ended in shutout victories, including a 6–0 win over Oberlin during which Sayers—who played left tackle—scored the game's only touchdown after returning a fumble 25 yards.

2. EDWARD FRENCH

French was a multiyear letterman who played the end position for the Buckeyes in the mid-1890s. He served as captain of the 1896 team that played an ambitious 11-game schedule and finished 5–5–1. French's younger brother, Thomas, would later become a major force behind the construction of Ohio Stadium, and French Field House is named for him.

3. RICHARD T. ELLIS

Ellis played on Ohio State's first three teams and earned varsity letters each season. He was also the program's first two-time captain and presided over the first winning season in program history, a 5–3 showing in 1892 that included a 62–0 win at Akron and an 80–0 wipeout of Marietta. After Ellis, there wouldn't be another two-time captain until Archie Griffin in 1974 and 1975.

4. JESSE JONES

Jones holds the distinction of being the first team captain in Ohio State football history. He was known as the "center rusher" for the 1890 team and helped the Buckeyes beat Ohio Wesleyan in their debut game, played May 3, 1890. Unfortunately, success was fleeting that first season. The team lost its final three games—all played in November—by a combined score of 96–10.

5. RENICK DUNLAP

Dunlap was one of the Buckeyes' first four-year lettermen, earning his initial varsity award in 1891 and repeating from 1893–95. Dunlap captained the 1895 squad, which achieved a couple of program firsts. It was the first OSU team to play to a tie when it settled for a 4–4 deadlock at Oberlin. And the Buckeyes played their first-ever out-of-state contest that season and came home with an 8–6 victory over Kentucky.

6. PAUL HARDY

Hardy was quarterback of the undefeated 1899 team, and although the position was played much differently than it is today, it was still a position that

TWO PIONEERS of OSU football, Edward French (top row, first from left) and Renick Dunlap (middle row, fourth from left).

Photo courtesy of The Ohio State University Archives

demanded expertise and leadership. Hardy excelled in both areas and led the Buckeyes to a 9–0–1 record that included a 6–0 victory over Oberlin. It was the first victory in seven tries against Oberlin, which had outscored OSU by a 200–10 margin in six previous games.

7. B. F. YOST

Nearly two decades before Chic Harley electrified Ohio State fans, Yost was a Columbus product who joined his hometown university team and became an immediate sensation. In his first game as a Buckeye in 1899, Yost rushed for 80 yards from his halfback position during a 30–0 win over Otterbein. He followed that performance with a pair of touchdown runs against Ohio University in late October and finished the 1899 season as one of the team's leading ball-carriers.

8. JAMES KITTLE

A three-time letterman at the turn of the century, Kittle was the starting fullback on the 1899 championship team and also its leading touchdown scorer with seven. Three of his scores came in the season opener, a 30–0 whitewash of Otterbein, and he tallied twice more three weeks later in a 41–0 pounding of Ohio University.

9. HOMER WHARTON

Wharton was one of the top linemen for the Buckeyes in the late 1890s, and he helped the team to its Ohio championship in 1899. Playing mostly left guard, Wharton spent most of his time opening holes for players such as Yost, Kittle, and halfback James Westwater. But he occasionally got into the act of scoring as well, tallying a 1-yard touchdown run during a 34–0 win at Muskingum.

10. JOSEPH LARGE

Large was the quarterback of Ohio State's first football team in 1890, and he was at the controls when the Buckeyes won the first game they ever played, a 20–14 victory over Ohio Wesleyan. In that contest, Large scored the program's first touchdown, which counted for only four points in those days.

1900–09

1. FRED CORNELL

Cornell is long forgotten for what he did on the gridiron as a member of the Ohio State team in 1902. It is what he did on the train ride back from Ann Arbor after the Buckeyes absorbed an 86–0 loss to the Wolverines, still the most lopsided game in series history. As Cornell listened to the clackety-clack of the rail car on the tracks, he began scribbling words to a song that began "Oh come let's sing Ohio's praise." By the time he had arrived back in Columbus, Cornell had penned the lyrics to "Carmen Ohio," which became Ohio State's official alma mater. Cornell went on to a successful career in the automobile and shipbuilding industries, and in 1961 he received the university's Distinguished Service Award for his composition.

2. BILL MARQUARDT

Marquardt, a three-year letterman from 1902–04, etched his name forever into Ohio State football history on October 15, 1904. With his team trailing 5–0 early in the second half, Marquardt scooped up a Michigan fumble near midfield and raced all the way to the end zone for a touchdown. It became the first TD ever scored by an OSU player against the Wolverines. Unfortunately, Marquardt's touchdown was all the Buckeyes had to cheer about that afternoon, as Michigan ran away with a 31–6 victory.

3. WALTER BARRINGTON

During the Buckeyes' 12–0 victory over Wooster in 1906, Barrington earned the distinction of becoming the first Ohio State player to throw a forward pass. The team's second touchdown of the afternoon was a 10-yard scoring pass from Barrington to teammate Harry Carr, the first touchdown reception in school history. Barrington won varsity letters for the Buckeyes from 1905–08 and was captain of the 1908 team, which posted a 6–4 record.

4. MILLARD GIBSON

Gibson was a talented fullback who won letters during the 1906, 1907, and 1908 seasons, and he nearly pulled off an upset of Michigan during the 1908

WALTER BARRINGTON. A varsity letterman, Barrington was the first Buckeye to throw a forward pass—a touchdown to Harry Carr.

Photo courtesy of The Ohio State University Archives

campaign. Lined up in punt formation, Gibson pulled off a fake and rumbled 75 yards for a touchdown to give the Buckeyes a 6–4 halftime lead over the Wolverines. Unfortunately, Ohio State couldn't hold on and lost a 10–6 decision. At the end of the season, Gibson became the first player ever recognized by sportswriter Walter Camp, who each season selected the college All-America team. Gibson was given honorable mention.

5. LESLIE WELLS

Wells was a shifty halfback for the Buckeyes who won letters in 1908, 1909, and 1910. His finest performance came during a late October contest in 1908 against an Ohio Wesleyan team coached by Branch Rickey. Wesleyan had taken a 5–4 halftime lead, but the Buckeyes came roaring back on the strength of three second-half touchdowns from Wells as Ohio State took a 20–9 victory. Wells was also an outstanding kicker for the Buckeyes and captained the 1910 squad that boasted a 6–1–3 record, including a 3–3 tie against Michigan. OSU's only points that afternoon came on a 25-yard field goal from Wells.

6. BILL WRIGHT

Ohio State scored one of its first major intersectional victories late in the 1909 season, taking a 5–0 victory over Vanderbilt. Wright was one of the stars for the Buckeyes, preserving the shutout with a game-saving tackle late in the fourth quarter. Vandy's Bill Neely received a punt deep in his own territory, but eluded a couple of would-be tacklers until Wright—who was a backup sophomore end—made a shoestring stop at his own 20-yard line. Wright went on to win three varsity letters in his career for the Buckeyes.

7. FRED SECRIST

Secrist was a shifty halfback who lettered four times for the Buckeyes from 1905–08. He had an excellent game in the 1906 season finale during an 11–8 victory over Ohio Medical, which was led by former OSU head coach John Eckstorm. Secrist, a speedy sophomore from Chillicothe, Ohio, scored both of Ohio State's touchdowns (which were worth only five points in those days) during the Thanksgiving Day contest and allowed the Buckeyes to secure the undisputed Ohio championship.

8. JAMES LINCOLN

Lincoln was one of the many players who helped establish Ohio State's tradition of excellence on the gridiron. He earned four varsity letters and served as team captain of the 1906 team that went 8–1 with seven shutouts. That team also was champion of the "Big Six," which included Ohio rivals Case, Kenyon, Oberlin, Ohio Wesleyan, and Western Reserve. Lincoln was enshrined in the OSU Athletic Hall of Fame in 1978.

9. JOSEPHUS H. TILTON

Tilton was a four-year varsity player from 1898–1901, and was voted team captain of the 1900 team that posted an 8–1–1 record. Six of the Buckeyes' eight victories were shutouts that season, and the tie was a 0–0 deadlock against Michigan that was played in a driving snowstorm at Regents Field in Ann Arbor. That game marked the first time in the OSU–Michigan series that the Buckeyes did not lose to their archrivals from the north.

10. JOHN SIGREST

Sigrest was a 27-year-old senior who began playing football for the Buckeyes in the late 1890s. He was a well-conditioned athlete and one of the team's top performers in 1901, when tragedy struck. During a 6–5 home victory over Western Reserve, Sigrest suffered a serious neck injury and died two days later in a Columbus hospital. He is the only player ever to die from injuries sustained during an Ohio State football game. In the wake of Sigrest's death, a portion of the faculty and student body favored abolishing football at the university. But when Sigrest's brother, Charles, who was the team's right tackle, strongly defended the game and urged the sport be continued, the university voted to continue fielding a football team.

1910–19

1. CHIC HARLEY

In the long and glorious history of Ohio State football, there have been only eight individuals who have been named All-American three times. The first—and arguably the greatest—was Chic Harley. He came along when Ohio State was struggling to find its place in college football. By the time he had finished his career in Scarlet and Gray, Buckeye football had been changed forever, transformed to the status of perennial powerhouse it continues to enjoy today. Harley led the Buckeyes to their first-ever Western Conference (Big Ten) championship and their first-ever win over Michigan. His popularity also led to construction of Ohio Stadium.

2. IOLAS HUFFMAN

One of the program's first players to win four varsity letters, Huffman was also versatile. He earned All-America honors as a guard in 1920 and as a tackle in 1921. Huffman was the captain of the undefeated OSU team that made the school's first Rose Bowl appearance, and in his senior year, he won the Big Ten Medal of Honor as Ohio State's top scholar-athlete.

3. BOYD CHERRY

Cherry played for the Buckeyes from 1912–14 and became the first player in program history recognized as an All-American. As a senior in 1914, after helping his team to a 5–2–2 record, Cherry earned honorable mention All-America status from sportswriter Walter Camp and received second-team honors from the International News Service (the precursor of United Press International).

4. CHARLES "SHIFTY" BOLEN

Bolen earned consensus All-America honors as a senior end in 1917 and was one of the mainstays of the teams that won Western Conference championships in 1916 and 1917. During Bolen's three varsity seasons, the Buckeyes posted a glittering record of 20–1–2 and outscored its opponents by a margin of 655–74.

5. HAROLD "HAP" COURTNEY

Courtney earned All-America and all-conference honors in 1917 as an end, and also served as co-captain of the squad that season with his brother Howard. Hap was especially efficient on the defensive side of the ball and helped spearhead the Buckeyes' attack that pitched seven shutouts and surrendered only six points all season (two field goals), never allowing an opponent past the goal line in nine games.

BOYD CHERRY
was the first Buckeye honored as an All-American. He was also a stand-out player for his OSU basketball squad.

Photo courtesy of OSU Photo Archives

6. CLARENCE MACDONALD

MacDonald was an excellent end for the Buckeyes in 1916 before missing the 1917 season due to military service in World War I. He returned to Ohio State in 1918 and played two more seasons of college football, serving as co-captain of the team and earning All-America honors in 1918.

7. ROBERT KARCH

Karch was a tackle for the Buckeyes who helped blow open holes for Chic Harley during the 1916 and 1917 seasons, allowing Ohio State to claim their first-ever Western Conference championships. During his senior season in 1917, Karch was named to the All-America team.

8. CAMPBELL "HONUS" GRAF

Graf was a four-year letterman from 1912–15 and the starting fullback on the football team for three seasons. Nicknamed after his boyhood idol, baseball hall of famer Honus Wagner, Graf played in Ohio State's first official Western Conference (Big Ten) game against Indiana in 1913 and served as team captain of the 1914 team. He also played basketball and baseball for the Buckeyes and earned nine varsity letters during his career.

9. SAM WILLAMAN

Willaman gets more recognition as head coach of the Buckeyes from 1929–33, but he was also a hard-nosed halfback, fullback, and end for Ohio State who won three varsity letters between 1911 and 1913. One of Willaman's best games came during an 11–6 victory over Cincinnati in the 1911 season finale. The sophomore scored two touchdowns in the contest (TDs were worth only five points in those days), the first on a 60-yard interception return.

10. CHARLIE SEDDON

The Buckeyes won conference championships during both seasons Seddon played. Playing at only 5'7" and 150 pounds, he was an undersized defensive lineman but a favorite of head coach John Wilce, who called Seddon his "watch charm." Seddon was one of the defensive stalwarts in 1917 that helped Ohio State outscore its nine opponents by a 292–6 margin.

1920–29

1. WES FESLER

Fesler was one of the top defensive stars of his day for OSU squads that were extremely stingy. During his sophomore season of 1928, the Buckeyes gave up only 35 points to eight opponents over the course of the entire season. Four of the team's five victories that year were shutouts. During an 18–6 loss to Northwestern in Ohio Stadium during his junior year, Fesler pounced on a fumble and returned it 95 yards for the Buckeyes' only touchdown in the game. And as a senior in 1930, Fesler served as the team captain and was named the Big Ten's most valuable player. It capped a tremendous career for the player who earned first-team All-America honors three straight times.

2. GAYLORD "PETE" STINCHCOMB

Stinchcomb was a halfback for the Buckeyes who played in the same backfield with Harley and then took over when Harley graduated. He led OSU to a perfect regular season in 1920, helping the team make its first-ever appearance in the Rose Bowl. A two-time All-American, Stinchcomb was also a standout basketball player and the 1921 national intercollegiate long jump champion. He was elected to the College Football Hall of Fame in 1973.

3. WILLIAM BELL

Bell was the Jackie Robinson of Ohio State football. When he joined the Buckeyes in 1929, he became the first African-American to play football for the team. Bell was a three-time letterman and earned honorable mention All-America honors while playing guard and usually opening holes for Fesler. Bell went on to serve as a professor and had a distinguished career in the U.S. Air Force, retiring at the rank of lieutenant colonel.

Photo courtesy of The Ohio State University Archives

WES FESLER. The anchor of the great Buckeye defense of 1928. He was a first-team All-American three straight years. Pictured here wearing a fedora, Fesler went on to coach OSU for four seasons.

4. HARRY "HOGE" WORKMAN

The Buckeyes had used the forward pass as mostly a gimmick play until the strong-armed Workman came onto the scene. He threw several key touchdown passes during the 1920 championship season and then earned All-America honors as a senior in 1923, becoming the first Ohio State quarterback to be so honored. In addition to his offensive prowess, Workman was also an excellent defensive halfback and handled the team's kicking duties.

5. MARTY KAROW

Long before Karow earned fame as the longtime baseball coach at Ohio State, he was a feisty fullback for the Buckeyes in the mid-1920s. Karow was team captain and earned All-America honors in 1926, when the Buckeyes posted a 7–1 record with their only loss a 17–16 setback against Michigan. In that game, Karow scored his team's only touchdown, the first scored by a conference opponent against the Wolverines in two years. A quarter-century after hanging up his football cleats, Karow returned to Ohio State as head baseball coach and led the Buckeyes to 478 victories and five Big Ten titles over the next twenty-five seasons. OSU won its only College World Series title in 1966 under Karow.

6. EDWIN HESS

One of the Buckeyes' early stars, Hess earned All-Western Conference and All-America honors at guard during his junior and senior years in 1925 and 1926. A standout both offensively and defensively, he won the Walter Camp Memorial Trophy in 1925, then the nation's top individual award. Hess was inducted into the Ohio State Athletic Hall of Fame in 1985.

7. LEO RASKOWSKI

Raskowski was a native of Cleveland who anchored the offensive and defensive lines in the late 1920s, earning back-to-back all-conference and All-America honors in 1926 and 1927. He played tackle and helped provide interference for such speedy teammates as Freddy Grim and Byron Eby. Raskowski was also captain of the 1928 team, John Wilce's final season as head coach.

8. CYRIL "TRUCK" MYERS

Myers was a three-year letterman for the Buckeyes from 1919–21 and helped OSU to the Western Conference championship as a junior, playing a major role in a decisive win over defending champion Illinois. He was on the receiving end of a touchdown pass on the final play of the game, giving Ohio State a 7–0 win and propelling the team to its first-ever Rose Bowl appearance. Myers earned all-conference and All-America honors as a senior in 1921, the Buckeyes' final season at Ohio Field.

9. HAROLD "COOKIE" CUNNINGHAM

Cunningham was a two-sport star at Ohio State and earned All-Big Ten honors in both basketball and football. On the gridiron, he was an All-American end in 1924, and his 6'4" frame keyed a defensive effort that allowed only 45 points in eight games that season. Cunningham later played professional football with the Cleveland Bulldogs, Chicago Bears, and Staten Island Stapletons of the NFL, as well as pro basketball, before becoming a college baseball coach at Washington & Lee and North Dakota.

10. LLOYD PIXLEY

Pixley was a four-time letter winner as an offensive and defensive lineman, earning two letters in 1918 and 1919 before returning for two more in 1921 and 1922. He also boasts the distinction of being team captain in 1922 when the Buckeyes began play in Ohio Stadium. Pixley, who usually played the left guard position, was instrumental in a 5–0 victory over Ohio Wesleyan in the first game ever played in the Horseshoe.

1930–39

1. WILLIAM H. H. "TIPPY" DYE

An excellent passer and runner, Dye quarterbacked the Buckeyes to three straight victories over Michigan in the mid-1930s, a feat that wasn't matched until seventy years later by Troy Smith. In the 1935 game against the Wolverines, Dye also returned a punt 78 yards during OSU's 38–0 victory. Dye was also an outstanding basketball talent and was elected to the university's athletic hall of fame in 1984.

2. SID GILLMAN

Gillman is probably better remembered for his hall of fame coaching careers in the college and pro ranks. Before that, however, he was an outstanding end for the Buckeyes. In 1933, Gillman was captain of the football team and earned All-Big Ten and honorable mention All-America honors for a team that posted a 7–1 record and allowed only 26 points in eight games. Gillman later became head coach at Miami (Ohio) and Cincinnati before spending more than twenty seasons at the helm of four different teams in the AFL and NFL. He is a member of both the College and Pro Football halls of fame.

3. LEWIS HINCHMAN

Usually lost in the discussion about great Ohio State halfbacks, Hinchman was good enough to earn a trio of All-America honors in the early 1930s. He was the team captain and MVP during his senior season in 1932. Hinchman's athletic exploits were not limited to the gridiron. He starred in three other sports for the Buckeyes, earning three letters in basketball, two in baseball, and one in golf.

4. GOMER JONES

A fireplug of a man at 5'8" and 210 pounds, Jones anchored the OSU line in the mid-1930s as an All-American center. He also played linebacker, and in 1935, was voted the team's most valuable player. Jones went on to coach at OSU, John Carroll, and Oklahoma, and served as OU's athletic director from 1964 until his death in 1971. The Cleveland native was elected to the College Football Hall of Fame in 1978.

5. ESCO SARKKINEN

You probably remember Sarkkinen as a longtime assistant coach under Woody Hayes, but in 1939, Sarkkinen was helping the Buckeyes to a Big Ten championship as a consensus All-American end. He was also a two-time, first-team All-Big Ten performer, and earned the Big Ten Medal of Honor in 1939. After serving in the U.S. Coast Guard during World War II, Sarkkinen returned to Ohio State as an assistant football coach in 1946 and served in that capacity until 1978. Sark is believed to hold the school record for winning the most pairs of Gold Pants—seventeen as a player and assistant.

6. DON SCOTT

Scott was a two-time All-American, the first Ohio State quarterback to earn that distinction. He led the Buckeyes to the 1939 Big Ten championship and also played on the OSU basketball team that won the conference title that same year. Scott was killed in World War II, and the university airport bears his name.

7. MERLE WENDT

One of only eight Buckeyes to earn three All-America honors, Wendt began his college career as a fullback. But he became so valuable in Francis Schmidt's razzle-dazzle offensive attack that he was switched to an end position to take advantage of his pass-catching skills. He also was a sure-handed tackler from his defensive end position.

8. GUST ZARNAS

A three-sport star at Ohio State, Zarnas earned All-America honors as a guard in 1937 and was voted to play in the 1938 East-West All-Star Game. He also lettered two years in baseball for the Buckeyes and one year in track. Zarnas was elected to the College Football Hall of Fame in 1975.

9. JIM MCDONALD

McDonald played halfback, quarterback, and linebacker for the Buckeyes in the mid-1930s. He was team captain and earned All-America honors in 1937, a season that saw Ohio State surrender only 23 points in eight games. McDonald later earned the distinction of becoming the first OSU player ever taken in the NFL draft, when the Philadelphia Eagles selected him with the second overall pick

LEWIS HINCHMAN. With all the great running backs in
Buckeye history, Hinchman often gets lost in the shuffle, but he was a
three-time All-American and the captain and MVP of the 1932 team.

Photo courtesy of The Ohio State University Archives

in 1938. McDonald was also a team captain for the Buckeyes in basketball and later served as head football coach at Tennessee.

10. NICK WASYLIK

Wasylik was an excellent all-around athlete who played in the backfield for the Buckeyes during the mid-1930s. He earned three letters from 1935–37, helping the team to victories over Michigan in each of those seasons. Wasylik also earned three varsity letters in baseball, serving as team captain in 1938, and spent one season on the OSU basketball team. He was inducted into the OSU Athletic Hall of Fame in 2003.

1940–49

1. BILL WILLIS

Five years before Jackie Robinson broke the color barrier in Major League Baseball and more than thirteen before Rosa Parks refused to give up her seat on an Alabama bus, Willis was breaking down barriers as one of the first African-American football stars at Ohio State. He was an integral part of the 1942 national championship team and earned a pair of All-America honors. Willis also went on to a stellar professional career with the Cleveland Browns, and the Buckeyes continue to annually hand out the Bill Willis Award to the most outstanding OSU defensive player of the year.

2. LES HORVATH

Horvath could be remembered for a lot of things, such as being one of the first four-year lettermen in football, playing halfback on Ohio State's first-ever national championship team, or earning Big Ten most valuable player and All-America honors as a senior. But all of those achievements pale in comparison to the fact that Horvath lays claim to something no other Buckeye can—he was the school's first-ever winner of the Heisman Trophy.

3. WARREN AMLING

A two-time All-American lineman who finished seventh in the 1944 Heisman Trophy balloting, Amling was inducted into the OSU Athletic Hall of Fame in 1981 and the College Football Hall of Fame in 1984. He also played basketball for the Buckeyes and is the only member of the College Football Hall of Fame to start in a Final Four contest.

4. OLLIE CLINE

Nicknamed the "Blond Bomber," Cline was a fullback and linebacker for the Buckeyes. He was a blocking back in 1944 when Horvath won the Heisman Trophy, and then led OSU in rushing in 1945 with a then-record 936 yards. Cline also set the single-game rushing record with 229 yards against Pitt in 1945, a mark that stood until Archie Griffin broke it in 1972.

5. CHUCK CSURI

An All-American at tackle, Csuri was voted the team MVP during the 1942 national championship season. That year, he led a rushing attack that averaged 5.2 yards per carry and 281.2 yards per game in addition to 33.7 points per contest. Csuri left OSU after that season to join the military, but he returned to finish his collegiate career in 1946 and earned his third varsity letter. After graduation, he became a national leader in the field of computer graphics.

6. JACK DUGGER

Dugger excelled at two sports during his college career. He was a starter on the 1942 national championship team as a sophomore, served as captain of the 1943 squad, and earned All-America honors as an end in 1944. As good as he was in football, Dugger was equally as adept at basketball. He was voted MVP of the 1942 basketball team and was a starter in 1944 when the Buckeyes won the Big Ten championship and advanced to the NCAA Final Four.

7. BOB SHAW

Inducted into the OSU Athletic Hall of Fame in 1996, Shaw was one of the top receivers in college football in the early 1940s. He earned All-America honors after helping the 1942 football team to the national championship. During that season, he caught a touchdown pass in the 21–7 win over Michigan. Shaw later played six seasons in the NFL and became the first receiver ever to catch five TD passes in a single game.

8. CECIL SOUDERS

An excellent receiver, Souders was named the Buckeyes' most valuable player in 1946 when he led the team with nine catches for 157 yards. He became only the second end to be named team MVP. He was a member of the 1942 national championship team and the 1944 squad that went undefeated and earned the national "civilian" championship. He was elected to the OSU Athletics Hall of Fame in 2002.

9. WILLIAM HACKETT

As a starting guard in 1943 and 1944, Hackett gained a reputation as a superior blocker and strong defender. In 1944, he earned All-America honors while helping lead the undefeated Buckeyes to a Big Ten championship. He later helped Paul Brown organize the Cincinnati Bengals and became a board member for the team. Hackett was inducted into the OSU Athletic Hall of Fame in 1986.

10. JACK GRAF

Graf led the Buckeyes in rushing and scoring in 1941 and was voted team MVP in a season that produced a 6–1–1 record under first-year head coach Paul Brown. Additionally, Graf was named the Big Ten's most valuable player that season. He was also a star guard for the OSU basketball team and served as captain of the squad in 1942. The following season, Graf joined the basketball coaching staff and began a 26-year career as an OSU assistant, and during that time the Buckeyes won a national championships and nine Big Ten titles. Graf was elected to the university's athletic hall of fame in 1988.

1950–59

1. HOWARD "HOPALONG" CASSADY

There have been many Ohio State football players who exploded onto the scene in their first game as a Buckeye and then leveled off as their careers continued. Cassady had a breakout game in his first game and only continued to get better. In his first game as a fresh-faced freshman in 1952, Cassady scored three times as the Buckeyes rolled to a 33–13 victory over Indiana. By the time his career was finished, he had led the Buckeyes to the 1954 national championship and established new career marks for Ohio State with 2,466 yards rushing and 37 touchdowns. Cassady was also an outstanding defensive halfback, and he won the 1955 Heisman Trophy by a wide margin. He was also a three-year letterman for the Ohio State baseball team and earned a Big Ten baseball championship in 1954 to go along with his national title in football.

2. VIC JANOWICZ

There have been stars, superstars, and megastars that have had outstanding careers in an Ohio State football uniform. But perhaps the one who possesses the most raw athletic talent ever was Janowicz. A professional athlete in two sports nearly fifty years before that feat became fashionable, Janowicz is also one of only six Buckeyes to win the Heisman Trophy. The speedster from Elyria, Ohio, was equally adept at running, passing, kicking, punting, returning kicks, and playing defense, and two of his performances in 1950 remain legendary. During a 41–7 win over Pittsburgh, Janowicz completed all six passes he threw for 151 yards and four touchdowns, and then three weeks later had a record-setting game against Iowa. The OSU junior completed five of six passes for 133 yards and four TDs, rushed for a touchdown, returned a punt 61 yards for another score, kicked 10 extra points, punted for an average of 42.0 yards and recovered two fumbles on defense as the Buckeyes rolled to an 83–21 victory. It was arguably the finest single-game performance of any player who has worn the Scarlet and Gray.

3. JIM PARKER

Ohio State has churned out a variety of outstanding linemen over the years, but the prototype was Parker. Playing at 6'2" and 250 pounds during an era when most linemen were in the 5'11", 185-pound range, Parker was a tremendous athlete, one of the first interior players who combined power and quickness. He excelled as an offensive lineman, especially at the guard position, and he was one of the best pulling and run blocking offensive linemen the Buckeyes have ever produced. Parker was a two-time All-American at OSU and went on to become an eight-time All-Pro with the Baltimore Colts. He is a member of both the college and pro football halls of fame.

4. JIM HOUSTON

Houston first made an impact as a sophomore for the 1957 national championship team. He became a two-way starter at tight end and defensive end on a Buckeye team that had everything—an offense ranked eleventh in the nation and a swarming defense that allowed an average of just 9.2 points per game. Houston went on to win All-America honors in 1958 and 1959 and was also named team MVP both of those years. He went on to a thirteen-year career in the NFL with Cleveland and earned enshrinement in the College Football Hall of Fame in 2005.

5. AURELIUS THOMAS

One of the unsung stars of the 1957 national championship team, Thomas starred as both a guard and linebacker for the Buckeyes. Head coach Woody Hayes thought him so valuable that Thomas averaged fifty-two minutes per game during that 1957 season. He earned All-America honors as a senior and was elected to the College Football Hall of Fame in 1989.

6. LOREN "BOB" WHITE

One of the stars of the 1957 national championship team, White began that season as a little-used linebacker. But early that year, Woody Hayes started to use

White as a fullback and he turned in several outstanding performances. His best game came against Iowa when he carried on nearly every play of the game-winning touchdown drive. When White finished his career, he was third on OSU's career rushing list with 1,816 yards.

7. FRED BRUNEY

A ball hawk that played for Wes Fesler and Woody Hayes in the early 1950s, Bruney smashed all of the Ohio State records for interceptions during his career. His seventeen career picks rank second all-time only to Mike Sensibaugh's twenty-two, and Bruney is the only Buckeye ever to twice record three interceptions in a single game. He did it in 1951 during a 0–0 tie with Illinois, and again in 1952 during a 27–7 victory over Michigan, OSU's first win over its archrivals in eight years.

8. JIM MARSHALL

A rough, tough player who instilled fear in his opponents (as well as more than a few of his teammates), Marshall earned All-America honors as a junior in 1958. He was also a record-setting shot put and discus thrower for the OSU track team. Marshall left the Buckeyes after his junior season to play in the Canadian Football League and later became a star in the NFL as a member of the Minnesota Vikings' famed "Purple People Eaters" defense.

9. DEAN DUGGER

Dugger was a three-year starter on offense and defense during the early 1950s. He earned All-America honors as an end in 1954, helping the Buckeyes to the national championship. When he earned induction into the OSU Athletic Hall of Fame in 1995, Dean joined his brother as only the second pair of siblings so honored. Jim (1979) and Lindell Houston (1991) were the first.

10. GEORGE JACOBY

Jacoby was a three-year letterman from 1951–53, who anchored the OSU offensive and defensive lines from his tackle position. He earned back-to-back All-Big Ten honors in 1952 and 1953, served a co-captain of the 1953 squad, and was voted team MVP that season.

AURELIUS THOMAS was an unsung hero in 1957. He played line-backer and of-fensive guard, while averaging an astonishing 52 minutes per game.

Photo courtesy of OSU Sports Information

1960–69

1. REX KERN

He was never the biggest or the fastest or the one with the best arm. In fact, measured by statistics alone, Kern's career at Ohio State wouldn't stand out much at all. But when you measure him with the ultimate statistic—winning—Kern comes out as one of the best quarterbacks the Buckeyes have ever produced. He reigned over one of the most prosperous three-year periods in OSU history when the team won the 1968 national championship and boasted a record of 27–2, a winning percentage of better than 93.1. Kern wound up his career with 2,444 yards passing and 19 TDs to go along with 1,714 yards rushing and 16 scores, and was elected to the College Football Hall of Fame in 2007.

2. JACK TATUM

Threatening. Dominating. Intimidating. Menacing. Frightening. Every defensive player who ever strapped on the pads would like to be known by any of those descriptions. But when Ohio State football players are discussed, there's usually only one who fits every one of them. Tatum terrorized opposing ball-carriers from the middle of the OSU defense from 1968–70, earning two All-America honors and being named national college defensive player of the year in 1970. In addition to his bone-crushing tackles, Tatum was a complete athlete. He was typically the strongest of the defensive backs and usually the fastest player on the entire squad. Head coach Woody Hayes often said that he would have excelled at any number of positions on the field. Tatum was elected to the College Football Hall of Fame in 2004.

3. JIM STILLWAGON

One of the quietest, most efficient players on the 1968 national championship team at Ohio State played at a dirty, thankless position. Thanks to Stillwagon, however, middle guard will forever be known as a position of strength for the Buckeyes. He earned two All-America honors and then received the ultimate honor from his teammates in 1970 when they voted him team MVP. After that season, Stillwagon became the first-ever winner of the Lombardi Award and later added the Outland Trophy, becoming only the second Buckeye to win that honor (Jim Parker was the first in 1956). Stillwagon was elected to the Ohio State Athletic Hall of Fame in 1979 and the College Football Hall of Fame in 1991.

4. BOB FERGUSON

Beginning in 1959, Ferguson started chewing up chunks of yardage for the Buckeyes and didn't stop until the team had bludgeoned Michigan and earned a share of the national championship during his senior year. Ferguson led his team to the Football Writers Association of America's version of the national championship in 1961, capped by a four-touchdown performance in a 50–20 rout over Michigan. Ferguson finished second in the 1961 Heisman Trophy voting and capped his career with 2,162 yards and 26 touchdowns. He was also extremely reliable, carrying 423 times and losing yardage on only one of those carries.

5. PAUL WARFIELD

Warfield was one of the most valuable players for the Buckeyes during the early part of the 1960s, excelling on offense, defense, and special teams. On offense, he would line up at a variety of spots out of his halfback position, and he ran and caught the ball with equal proficiency. On defense, he played in the secondary and was assigned to shut down the opposing team's best receiver. On special teams, he was one of the team's top punt returners. Warfield went on to a Pro Football Hall of Fame career as a receiver with the Cleveland Browns and Miami Dolphins.

6. JOHN BROCKINGTON

A big, bruising running back who spent the first part of his OSU career as a blocker, Brockington came into his own as a senior in 1970 when he became only the second Buckeye in history to top the 1,000-yard mark. His record of 261 carries that year still ranks ninth in school history nearly four decades after his final game. Green Bay made Brockington the ninth overall pick in the 1971 NFL draft, and he repaid them with 1,105 yards and by winning NFC Offensive Rookie of the Year honors.

7. ARNIE CHONKO

One of those rare talents who succeeds in whatever they try, Chonko was a three-year starter in the defensive backfield from 1962–64 and earned All-America status in 1964—becoming the first OSU defensive back to be so honored. He was also a standout baseball player for the Buckeyes, earning All-America status in that sport as well and playing first base on the school's 1965 College World Series runners-up. Chonko later became a doctor, specializing in internal medicine and nephrology at the University of Kansas School of Medicine.

8. DWIGHT "IKE" KELLEY

Intensity has long been a trademark of Ohio State linebackers, and perhaps one of the most intense of all was Kelley. A two-time All-American, Kelley played for the Buckeyes from 1963–65 during a turbulent time for the program. OSU lost at least two games in each of those seasons as some Buckeye boosters began to wonder if Woody Hayes's mastery of the game had passed him by. But Hayes continued to recruit a vast array of talent, and Kelley was one of the best during that era. He earned All-America honors in 1964 and 1965, making him the first Ohio State linebacker in history to earn two such honors.

9. MIKE SENSIBAUGH

Sensibaugh was a vital member of the Super Sophs who helped lead the Buckeyes to the 1968 national championship, three straight Big Ten championships, and a 27–2 record from 1968–70. He excelled at the cornerback spot, setting a new school record with twenty-two interceptions in the process, and also served as the team's punter. In fact, Sensibaugh still holds the Ohio State bowl record for punting yardage with 319 yards against Southern California in the 1969 Rose Bowl.

10. DON UNVERFERTH

This strong-arm quarterback's legacy has largely been forgotten, and that's too bad. As a sophomore, Unverferth ran for the winning touchdown in OSU's 14–10 victory at Michigan in 1963, and then he engineered a 9–7 win at Ann Arbor two years later. When he finished his career, he had set the school career record with 2,518 passing yards. The mark stayed on the books for sixteen years, until Art

JACK TATUM. Big and mean, Tatum literally ran over the competition.

Photo courtesy of Brockway Sports Photos

Schlichter broke it midway through the 1979 season. After his football career ended, Unverferth went on to graduate number one in his class from the OSU Medical School and became a world-renowned cardiologist at University Medical Center.

1970-79

1. ARCHIE GRIFFIN

He was never the biggest football player on the field, nor was he the strongest or fastest. But Archie Griffin outworked, outhustled, and outplayed every competitor on his way to becoming the first player in history to start four consecutive Rose Bowls, and the only college player to own two Heisman Trophies. He was a three-time All-American, still holds the school's career rushing record with 5,589 yards, and holds membership in the OSU Athletic, College Football, Rose Bowl, and National High School halls of fame. In 1999, he became the first Ohio State football player to have his jersey number retired.

2. RANDY GRADISHAR

Woody Hayes called Gradishar the finest linebacker he ever had the pleasure to coach, and a look at the 1973 season tells why. That year, Gradishar led one of the best defensive units in OSU history. While the Buckeyes were piling up 413 points on offense, the stop troops were yielding only 64, giving up an average of just 5.8 per game. Gradishar led the Buckeyes with 134 tackles that season, as the team rolled to a 10–0–1 record that included a 42–21 revenge victory over USC in the Rose Bowl. In addition to earning his second consecutive first-team All-America honor that year, he finished sixth in the Heisman Trophy balloting—almost unheard of for a linebacker.

3. JOHN HICKS

Hicks was 6'3" and 258 pounds but had the mobility of a much smaller player. He was a rare blend of size, strength, speed, attitude, and coachability that comes along only once every so often. In fact, Woody Hayes made a highlight reel of

DWIGHT "IKE" KELLEY

Photo courtesy of Brockway Sports Photos

Hicks's blocking technique and used it as a teaching tool for the remainder of his coaching career. Hicks topped off his college career in 1973 with a second All-America honor as well as the Outland Trophy and Lombardi Award. He was finished runner-up in the Heisman Trophy balloting to Penn State running back John Cappelletti, the highest finish ever for a lineman in the Heisman voting.

4. CORNELIUS GREENE

Perhaps no other Ohio State player in history—and maybe all of college football for that matter—ever lived up to his nickname more than Greene. Called "Flam" by his teammates because of his flamboyant nature on and off the field, Greene was the touchstone for the star-studded Buckeye backfields of the mid-1970s. With Greene at the controls, Archie Griffin piling up record yardage totals, and Pete Johnson scoring touchdowns by the bunches, Ohio State averaged 35.3 points per game over a three-year span from 1973–75. Greene is the only Buckeye ever to finish his career with more than 2,000 yards passing and 2,000 yards rushing.

5. PETE JOHNSON

Playing the same backfield with Griffin and Greene sometimes overshadows what Johnson was able to accomplish as a Buckeye. But it shouldn't. Johnson not only paved the way for Griffin to win his second Heisman Trophy in 1975, he was also a 1,000-yard rusher and led the nation in scoring, setting an OSU record with 26 touchdowns that has never been equaled. By the time he played his final game in Scarlet and Gray, Johnson had established scoring records for the most points in a game (30), season (156), and career (348). Each of those marks still stands, with the exception of the career scoring mark. Johnson held onto that for twenty-eight years until kicker Mike Nugent broke it in the final game of his career in 2004.

6. TOM COUSINEAU

Cousineau was a rough-and-tumble linebacker who seemingly was in on every tackle of every play. He started for three seasons in the middle of the OSU defense and finished his career with a then-school record 569 career tackles. Although that mark has since been broken, Cousineau holds just about every other tackles record in school history, including most solos in a game (sixteen against SMU in 1978). He also owns six games, with at least 21 tackles or more. No other Ohio State defender ever had more than two.

7. CHRIS WARD

Ward began a three-year run as the starting left tackle for the Buckeyes in 1975 and paved the way for Archie Griffin to win his second Heisman Trophy before blocking for the likes of Jeff Logan in 1976 and Ron Springs in 1977, both of whom became 1,000-yard rushers. Ward was a two-time All-American who started thirty-six consecutive games and was part of an offense that piled up 1,469 points over four seasons—an average of 30.6 per game. He was also part of a team that won or shared the Big Ten championship every year he was a Buckeye.

8. TOM SKLADANY

Skladany is one of only eight Buckeyes in history to earn All-America honors three times, and the only kicker to achieve that honor. He helped his teams to three consecutive Rose Bowl appearances and is acknowledged as the first kicking specialist ever to earn a football scholarship from Woody Hayes. Among Skladany's school records is the best single-game punting average—52.3 yards against Michigan in 1976.

9. VAN NESS DECREE

A two-time All-American and three-year starter at defensive end, DeCree played in three Rose Bowls during his OSU career. Teams on which he played from 1972–74 posted a combined record of 29–4–1 and never finished lower than eighth in either of the major polls. DeCree was named to the university's athletic hall of fame in 1990.

10. BOB BRUDZINSKI

A two-time all-conference selection and an All-American in 1976, Brudzinski racked up 209 career tackles from his defensive end position. He played in three Rose Bowls and was named team MVP his senior year. Brudzinski was a first-round NFL draft choice in 1977 and spent thirteen years in the league with the Rams and Dolphins.

1980–89

1. CHRIS SPIELMAN

If there could be only one player from the modern Ohio State era that was the perfect embodiment of a football player from the top of his head to the soles of his feet, it would have to be Spielman. The guy woke up every morning and went to bed every night thinking about football, and probably still does. During his standout career, Spielman earned three first-team All-Big Ten and two All-America honors, and was the recipient of the 1987 Lombardi Award. He finished his college career with a school-record 283 solo tackles and then made four Pro Bowl appearances in six years with the Detroit Lions. In 2009, Spielman is scheduled to receive an honor richly deserved and long overdue—induction into the College Football Hall of Fame.

2. KEITH BYARS

Byars used size and speed to become one of the most explosive running backs of his era. Despite missing most of his senior season because of an injury, his 3,200 career yards still make him the fifth all-time rusher in OSU history, and he remains one of only four Buckeyes ever to score 300 or more career points. He will be forever remembered for his performance during a 45–38 win over Illinois in 1985. After the Buckeyes had fallen behind 24–0, Byars ignited a frenzied comeback that included a 67-yard touchdown sprint down the sideline during which he completely reversed field, lost one shoe, and still outraced the Illinois secondary to the end zone. He scored five touchdowns in that contest, including the game-winner with just thirty-six seconds to play, and totaled 274 yards to establish a new single-game OSU record.

3. CRIS CARTER

Carter was one of the top receivers Ohio State has ever produced, finishing a three-year career with 164 catches for 2,725 yards and 27 touchdowns. He made a huge splash as a freshman in 1984, catching nine passes for 172 yards and a TD in the Rose Bowl loss to USC. The 172 yards broke a long-standing Rose Bowl

TOM SKLADANY. One of the best kickers to ever play the game, Skladany earned All-American honors three times.

PHoto courtesy of Brockway Sports Photos

CRIS CARTER

His 1986 season of 69 catches for 1,127 yards and 11 TDs is one of the best ever.

record set by the legendary Don Hutson of Alabama in 1935. Two years later, Carter shattered all of OSU's single-season receiving records with 69 receptions for 1,127 yards and 11 TDs. He went on to a 16-year NFL career, retiring following the 2002 season with 1,101 career catches for 13,899 yards and 130 TDs.

4. ART SCHLICHTER

Despite well-chronicled off-the-field problems, Schlichter remains one of the iconic figures of Ohio State football history. He started more games at quarterback than any other player who wore the Scarlet and Gray, and his 36 career victories are more than any other OSU signal-caller. In a Buckeye uniform, he completed 497 of 951 passes for 7,547 yards and 50 touchdowns, and more than a quarter-century after his career ended, the attempts and yardage remain tops in school history, while the completions are second and the touchdown total remains fourth.

5. JOHN FRANK

Frank is likely the finest pass-catching tight end ever to play for the Buckeyes. He earned All-Big Ten honors in his junior and senior seasons and was named co-captain, team most valuable player, and most inspirational player during his senior year in 1983. Frank finished his college career as the second all-time leading receiver in Buckeye history (and first among tight ends), with 121 catches for 1,481 yards. His 45 receptions in both 1981 and 1983 still stand as single-season highs for OSU tight ends. He also excelled in the classroom as a two-time Academic All-American and a Rhodes Scholar nominee following his senior season.

6. THOMAS "PEPPER" JOHNSON

Nicknamed "Pepper" by an aunt who observed him regularly sprinkling pepper on his breakfast cereal, Johnson teamed with Chris Spielman in 1984 and 1985 to give the Buckeyes one of the most awesome one-two linebacker punches in college football history. Johnson topped 140 tackles in each of those seasons and was voted the team's defensive most valuable player both years. Earning All-

America honors as a senior, he was also voted one of the team captains in both his junior and senior years.

7. WILLIAM WHITE

A four-year starter at cornerback for the Buckeyes from 1984–87, White was a leader on some excellent Ohio State defenses. He also had a nose for the ball. He is one of eight players in school history to grab three interceptions in a single game (vs. West Virginia in 1987) and he finished his OSU career with sixteen picks, tying him for third place on the all-time list.

8. MARCUS MAREK

Marek led the Buckeyes in tackles for three straight seasons, earning second-team All-America honors in 1980 and 1981 and getting a first-team nod as a senior in 1982. His 178 total stops as a senior is the third highest single-season total in school history, and he finished his career with 572 total tackles, more than any other player in Ohio State history. His 316 assists is also a school record.

9. TIM SPENCER

Spencer began his OSU career as a fullback before turning into a prolific tailback. He paved the way for Calvin Murray to rush for more than 1,200 yards in 1980, and then led the team in rushing as both a junior and senior. Spencer totaled 1,217 yards in 1981 and then exploded for 1,538 yards the following year. As a senior, he set a new school record with 273 carries and earned his second straight first-team All-Big Ten honor. Spencer remains third on the Buckeyes' all-time career rushing list with 3,553 yards.

10. JIM LACHEY

Most Buckeye fans believe Lachey was a dominant offensive lineman during his OSU career. The truth is that he was a starter for only one season—but that season was tremendous. He anchored the line in 1984, paving the way for Keith Byars to rush for 1,764 yards and 22 TDs. Lachey earned All-America honors that year and went on to an all-pro career in the NFL.

1990–99

1. ORLANDO PACE

Some may question placing a lineman at the top of this list, but no less an authority than 1995 Heisman Trophy winner Eddie George sums it up nicely: "If it wasn't for Orlando Pace," George once said, "you'd have never heard of me." Pace was the most decorated offensive lineman ever to play at Ohio State, and he was a star from the first time he set foot on campus during his freshman season of 1994. Had he not left early for the NFL and returned for his senior year in 1997, he could have been the first lineman ever to win the Heisman Trophy. Simply put, he was just that good. As it was, Pace filled his trophy case with two All-America honors, back-to-back Lombardi Awards, and the Outland Trophy. He was also named the 1995 Big Ten player of the year, making him the only offensive lineman in the last forty-five years to have been named conference MVP.

2. EDDIE GEORGE

George had a storybook season for the Buckeyes in 1995, rolling to the Heisman Trophy as he set record after record. He rushed for 207 yards during an emotional 45–26 win over Notre Dame, one of 12 straight performances of 100 yards or more which included 314 yards against Illinois, establishing a new OSU single-game record. By the time George was through that season, he had smashed the school's single-season rushing record with 1,927 yards. Finishing his career with 3,768 yards and 44 touchdowns, George finished second only to two-time Heisman winner Archie Griffin (5,589, 1972–75) in yardage, and third in touchdowns to Pete Johnson (56, 1973–76) and Keith Byars (46, 1982–85).

3. ANTOINE WINFIELD

Winfield was an almost unbelievable star at cornerback, because he stood only 5'9" and weighed 180 pounds. But he more than held his own against bigger and stronger wide receivers, earning the 1998 Thorpe Award as college

ORLANDO PACE.
Simply one of the best
college offensive line-
men to play the game.
Pace has gone on to
have an illustrious NFL
career as well.

Photo courtesy of Buckeye Sports Bulletin

football's most outstanding defensive back. He was named All-American twice, and as he finished his career, he had become the first non-linebacker to record more than 200 career solo tackles and the first cornerback ever to lead the team in tackles, when he did so with 100 stops as a junior in 1997.

4. JOE GERMAINE

Germaine came from virtually nowhere to become one of the most prolific quarterbacks in school history. The 6'0", 202-pounder was a junior college transfer who constantly had to prove he had a big-time arm worthy of a big-time program. By the time he left Ohio State, Germaine had nothing left to prove. He started only 13 games in his three seasons as a Buckeye but finished with 439 completions in 741 attempts for 6,370 yards and 56 touchdowns. His career completion percentage of 59.2 is the second-best in school history, while his yardage total is third best. Germaine was named the Big Ten's offensive player of the year in 1998 as well as the conference MVP after throwing for a school-record 3,330 yards.

5. KOREY STRINGER

Overshadowed somewhat by fellow offensive tackle Orlando Pace, Stringer was one of the reasons why Ohio State fielded such offensive powerhouses in the mid-1990s. The big, burly Warren, Ohio, native cleared opposing tacklers like a hot knife through butter and finished second in 1994 in both the Outland Trophy and Lombardi Award voting. Nevertheless, Stringer was a consensus first-team All-American that season and then was selected in the first round of the 1995 NFL draft by the Minnesota Vikings. Before his tragic death in 2001, Stringer played six seasons in Minnesota, during which the Vikings made the playoffs five times, including the NFC championship game twice.

6. ANDY KATZENMOYER

Few defensive players have made as big a splash during their freshman seasons as "The Big Kat." He chalked up 23 tackles for loss in 1996, including five in the Rose Bowl victory over Arizona State, and finished his OSU career with 50

TFLs, fourth in school history and the most for any Buckeye who played only three seasons.

7. DAVID BOSTON

In just three years of action, Boston rewrote the Ohio State receiving record books as a big, agile football magnet. He set or tied twelve different school records and left with career marks for receptions (191), yardage (2,855), and touchdown catches (34). His junior season in 1998 featured 85 receptions for 1,435 yards and 14 TDs, and was topped off by 10 catches for 231 yards and 2 touchdowns in a 31–16 victory over Michigan.

8. STEVE TOVAR

A quiet, unassuming workhorse, Tovar was one of the few defensive stars for Ohio State during the early part of the John Cooper era. The two-time All-American led the Buckeyes in tackles for three consecutive seasons, one of only four players to accomplish that feat since 1970 (Marcus Marek, A. J. Hawk, and James Laurinaitis are the others).

9. RAYMONT HARRIS

"The Quiet Storm" is one of the most underrated tailbacks in the modern era of Ohio State football. His 1,344 yards in 1993 ranks as the tenth best single-season total in program history, and his 2,649 career yards are ninth on the all-time list. He was also MVP of the 1993 Holiday Bowl win over BYU with 235 yards and 3 TDs. The yardage and touchdown totals are OSU bowl records.

10. TERRY GLENN

The 1995 Biletnikoff Award winner as college football's top receiver, Glenn went from walk-on to star. In 1995, he had 61 receptions for 1,411 yards, smashing the old single-season mark of 1,127 set in 1986 by Cris Carter. Glenn's average yardage per catch that season was 22.0, which is the second-best mark in school history.

STEVE TOVAR. A reserved man off the field, Tovar was a menace on it, leading OSU in tackles three seasons in a row.

Photo courtesy of OSU Sports Information

2000–08

1. TROY SMITH

Smith was a rags-to-riches story who went from occasional kickoff returner to Heisman-winning quarterback. He got the starting job only when Justin Zwick got hurt midway through the 2004 season, but Smith made the most of his opportunity. He sported a 25–3 record as a starter and set the school single-season record for touchdown passes in 2006 with 30, the same year he captured the Heisman Trophy. But Smith's legacy will be how he performed against archrival Michigan. He became only the second quarterback in OSU history to beat the Wolverines three times as a starter, and in those three games against Michigan, Smith completed 69 of 101 pass attempts (68.3 percent) for 857 yards, 7 touchdowns, and just 1 interception, and tacked on another 194 yards and 2 TDs rushing.

2. A. J. HAWK

Hawk was the epitome of the hard-nosed Buckeye linebackers of the past. He led the team in tackles three consecutive seasons and earned three straight All-Big Ten honors to go along with a pair of All-America accolades. After his senior season in 2005, Hawk was voted the Big Ten's defensive player of the year and captured the Lombardi Award, given annually to the top defensive lineman or linebacker in college football. He finished his Ohio State career with 394 tackles, good for fifth on the school's all-time list, and the Green Bay Packers made Hawk the fifth overall selection in the 2006 NFL draft.

3. MIKE NUGENT

Nugent was the unsung hero of the 2002 national championship run as the kicker set nine school records that year, including more field goals in a season (25) and most points scored by a kicker in a single season (120). He also kicked at least one field goal in each of the team's first twelve games that year, and in thirteen of the fourteen games overall. Nugent finished his career after the 2004 season with a first-team All-America honor and the Groza Award as college football's top kicker. He also broke the all-time career scoring record and became the first kicker ever voted Ohio State MVP by his teammates since the award began in 1930.

4. MIKE DOSS

In addition to being one of only eight three-time All-Americans in program history, Doss was also a three-time All-Big Ten selection and was named the conference's defensive player of the year as a senior in 2002. He started forty games in a row for the Buckeyes and finished his career with 331 total tackles, including 221 solos. The tackle figure is tops among defensive backs in school history.

5. JAMES LAURINAITIS

Laurinaitis finished his Ohio State career as one of the most decorated linebackers in school history. As a sophomore in 2006, he won the Nagurski Award as college football's top defensive player as a sophomore in 2006 and followed with the Butkus Award as the top college linebacker in 2007. He then took home the Lott Trophy following his senior season as the top defensive impact player. Additionally, he was named All-American three times, was a two-time winner of Jack Lambert Trophy as college football's best linebacker, and earned first-team All-Big Ten honors three times. He also led the Buckeyes in tackles for three consecutive seasons and wound up with 375 career tackles, seventh on the school's all-time list.

6. TED GINN JR.

Ginn was one of those rare talents who could single-handedly change the momentum of a football game—usually in the blink of an eye. He raced across the landscape at Ohio State and in three short years returned more kicks for touchdowns than any other player in the long and storied history of the Big Ten. When he completed his three-year career after the 2006 season, Ginn had returned six punts for touchdowns—twice as many as anyone else in school history and one more than any other Big Ten player. He was also a prolific receiver with career totals of 135 receptions, 1,943 yards, and 15 TDs.

7. WILL SMITH

Smith helped to redefine the defensive end position for Ohio State, and in the process he helped the Buckeyes win their first national championship in more than three decades. He totaled eight tackles and a sack as the Buckeyes took a 31–24 double overtime victory over Miami (Florida) to capture the 2002 national championship, then used that performance as a springboard to win Big Ten defensive player of the year honors as a senior in 2003. He finished a brilliant career with 167 total tackles (111 solos), 46 1/2 of which were for loss.

8. LECHARLES BENTLEY

A four-year letterman for the Buckeyes from 1998–2001, Bentley was a two-year starter at center in 2000–01 and won the 2001 Rimington Award as the nation's top college center. New Orleans made him a second-round pick in the 2002 NFL draft, and he went to two Pro Bowls with the Saints.

9. SANTONIO HOLMES

Never the biggest or fastest receiver on the team, Holmes simply got open, made catches, and scored touchdowns. He led the Buckeyes in receiving in 2004 and 2005 and finished his three-year career with 140 receptions for 2,295 yards and 25 TDs. All-time, Holmes ranks fifth in catches and yardage and third in touchdowns. His 224 yards against Marshall in 2005 also stands as the second-best day for an OSU receiver.

10. VERNON GHOLSTON

Gholston had a superlative junior season in 2007, establishing new school records for sacks in a single season (14.0) and sack yardage (111), as well as tying the single-game sack mark with four against Wisconsin. He finished fifth on the career sacks list with 22 1/2 and became the sixth overall pick in the 2008 NFL draft.

SANTONIO HOLMES. One of the all-time Buckeye receiving leaders, Holmes has won a Super Bowl ring with the Pittsburgh Steelers.

Photo courtesy of Susan Zeier

Chapter 8

THE BEST DAMN FANS IN THE LAND

To be an Ohio State football fan is to belong to one of the largest extended families in the world. And like family, Buckeye fans can argue among themselves all day long about which player is the greatest of all time, which coach is the best, and whether or not the 1996 offense could have scored on the 1973 defense. Let some interloper start criticizing the Scarlet and Gray, though, and they've got a fight on their hands.

Who better to explain the love affair between die-hards and their favorite team than the head Buckeye himself?

"It isn't just about us or the people that went here. Ohio State football means an awful lot to an awful lot of people," head coach Jim Tressel said. "I think the more you're around it, the more you get it. If you'd see some of my mail—pictures of people's wedding cakes in Scarlet and Gray, they're naming their dog Brutus or Griffin or Woody, they're naming their kids Eddie or Troy or Orlando—and these people didn't even go to Ohio State. You see and hear about that kind of stuff and I don't know how you could help but get it.

"What we do is important to so many people's lives, and I think you have to be aware of that. You're not only playing for yourselves and your school, you're playing for all of those people out there who support you in their everyday lives. Maybe they're not donating a million dollars or maybe they don't have enough money to come to one of our games. But they support us in their own ways, whether that's watching us on TV or talking about us with their friends, and you can't put a price on that kind of support."

Imagine trying to explain to someone who had never experienced Ohio State football exactly what it was like to be a die-hard Buckeye fan. It would be like trying to explain life itself, because being a Buckeye fan is a way of life. We watch our Scarlet and Gray-clad heroes on the television, line up for hours to get an autograph, and hang around outside the Woody Hayes Athletic Center just to catch a glimpse of them. Our love for the Buckeyes is why closets are filled with OSU jerseys, caps, and sweater vests. Our love for the Buckeyes is why a company manufactures a toilet that plays "Buckeye Battle Cry" every time the seat is lifted. Our love for the Buckeyes is why the university gets hundreds of requests each year from fans who wish to scatter the ashes of a deceased loved one on the hallowed ground inside Ohio Stadium.

Pure love and camaraderie are what bind die-hard Buckeye fans. There are no membership drives, no annual dues, no fund-raising activities. Most of the time, we grow up as Buckeye fans. My father was an Ohio State alum, and on Saturday afternoons in the fall we listed to Marv Homan calling OSU football games on the radio. I didn't have much of a choice when it came to becoming a Buckeye fan. But that's OK. I'm glad I didn't. Anything that interested my dad was more than good enough for me.

One of the best parts of being a Buckeye fan is that you can immerse yourself in your fandom from any spot on the globe. Thanks to the Internet and overseas radio, soldiers in Afghanistan and Iraq can stay as close to their favorite team as those of us lucky to live just a stone's throw from the Horseshoe.

We are all a part of the Buckeye Nation, and that nation is a melting pot of nationalities, colors, creeds, political persuasions, ages, and occupations. We are the CEO of the Fortune 500 company who wears his OSU tie to work and the

Photo courtesy of Jeff Brehm/Buckeye Sports Bulletin

JAMES LAURINAITIS at Media Day. One of the best things about OSU football is the availability of the Buckeye players. On the field, they play their hearts out, but off the field they're always available for an autograph or a handshake.

construction worker with a Brutus decal on his hardhat. We are the middle-aged guy pulling the authentic Troy Smith jersey over his head and the toddler dressed up in the mini-Ohio State cheerleader outfit. We are Buckeye Guy and the Woody impersonators.

For this chapter, we solicited the help of die-hard Buckeye fans who were gracious enough to share their memories of what Ohio State football has meant to them. Their stories give new meaning to the group known as "The Best Damn Fans In The Land."

PUTTING A STOP TO BADGERING

By Susan Zeier

My husband, David, is a bona fide Cheesehead. He was born and raised in Wisconsin, is a certified shareholder in the Green Bay Packers, and graduated from the University of Wisconsin.

Some of his longtime friends are extremely passionate, die-hard Badger fans, and one is just as emotional about his hatred for my Ohio State Buckeyes. Chris is his name, and beginning from the time Dave and I married, Chris never hesitated to call our house every time Ohio State would suffer a football loss.

One day in July 2002, there arrived in the mail an autographed picture of then Wisconsin quarterback Brooks Bollinger. The signature was personalized in my husband's nickname and read, "To Diz, The Horseshoe. They built it. We OWN it!! Brooks Bollinger #5."

Upon opening the envelope and revealing the contents inside, Dave was a little bit irritated because he knew the gesture was directed at me. He offered to tear up the picture, but I insisted it was finally an opportunity for me to turn the tables on Chris.

First, I urged Dave to call Chris and verify that the words were absolutely written by Bollinger. Chris explained how, after the Badgers' spring scrimmage, he met some players, and having a spring media guide, ripped out the page featuring a photograph of Bollinger. Chris claimed that he told Brooks he wanted to obtain the autograph for a good friend who was married to a die-hard Buckeye

10 18 '02

TRESSEL and Dave "Diz" Zeier. The two meet after Diz's Brooks Bollinger photo became bulletin board material for the Buckeyes.

fan and the both of them discussed what would be best written that would really stick it to said Buckeye fan. Since Wisconsin had won its previous two games at Ohio Stadium, the two of them came up with the message that Bollinger wrote before signing his name.

About a month later, I scanned the picture with the intention of e-mailing it to a couple of people, including then Ohio State running back Lydell Ross. Another fellow I sent it to is an acquaintance of OSU assistant coach Luke Fickell, who offered to forward it on to Luke. From there, it seemed news of Bollinger's bold statement grew like wildfire on several Ohio State website fan forums.

It finally found its way to Kirk Herbstreit, who in August 2002 showed a copy of the photo to Mike Doss. Mike confirmed that he had seen it before and that copies of it were hanging up all over the locker room and other areas of Ohio State's football practice facility.

After hearing about the Doss–Herbstreit interview, Dave e-mailed Chris and told him about the publicity the autograph was generating in Columbus. Chris was outraged, exclaiming that the picture was meant for Dave's eyes only (yeah, right!), and how could he permit his wife to send it on to Ohio State football players.

That's when I decided to take the original picture with me to media/photo day. Back then, fans were allowed to attend the event, take pictures, and get autographs. The first person I showed it to was Fickell, who asked to borrow it for a little while. Luke showed the photograph to every potential starting defensive player and to all the assistant coaches on defense. Several even added their signatures to the photo.

As the event was winding down, I figured I would show it to Coach Tressel. He said he was already aware of the photo and thanked me for bringing it to the team's attention. Then, after seeing all the other Buckeye signatures, Coach Tressel asked if he could autograph it. He then proceeded to write, "Diz. Be a Buckeye!!! Jim Tressel."

Several weeks later, when Coach Tressel was talking about his team's upcoming game at Camp Randall Stadium, he told reporters that his team had that date

THIS PHOTO of Wisconsin QB Brooks Bollinger caused a national stir.

Photo courtesy of Dave Zeier

circled since fall camp began. When he was asked why, the coach talked about the Bollinger photo. Later, linebacker Matt Wilhelm confirmed that Fickell had made copies and plastered them all over the practice facility as a motivational tool for the football team.

Within the next few days, the story of the photo spread from the Internet to local Ohio newspapers to such national outlets as ESPN, the *Chicago Sun Times*, and the *Los Angeles Times*. Of course, most of the Wisconsin newspapers ran the story, too, and it was all over Madison's sports talk radio programs.

It was more than Chris could take. He was furious with Dave—so much so that we were un-invited to his annual Wisconsin homecoming tailgate party.

The rest is history. Bollinger was forced to leave the 2002 game against Ohio State after suffering a concussion at the hands of some hard-hitting Buckeyes. OSU went on to win a 19–14 decision, putting another check in the win column on the road to an undefeated season and eventual national title.

I was told later by a couple of Ohio State football players that I had a hand in that national championship, because the Bollinger picture was a factor in forming an outline for the team's goals for the year.

For me, I was just happy my longtime Wisconsin nemesis had finally quit "badgering" me.

LONG-DISTANCE SHARING

By John Sharp

Sometimes I feel sorry for my dad. He lives in a horrible place—central Florida—where the only football he hears, sees or reads about is either Florida, Florida State, or Miami. The only place worse would be Ann Arbor, and he would rather chew off his right arm than live there. ESPN provides highlights of his Buckeyes, but rarely does a whole game grace his picture tube. I suppose that's the price he pays for wearing shorts year round and not having to own a snow shovel.

This isolation doesn't sit well. Every time I talk to him in the fall, he's crabbing and moaning about the Florida teams getting all the attention. He always vows that next year he'll spend the extra money to see the games on premium cable, but he never does. It's a pretty hard cost to justify.

Still the worst thing is that he hasn't been to a game since he moved. We're both President's Club members, and before he moved we'd been going to games together since the 1970s. He still buys tickets that he sells to me. But I doubt he'll ever again sit in the Horseshoe, because to do so would require walking and climbing that his knees no longer allow. The *prospect* of the exertion is tiring to him, let alone the exertion itself. He is rightfully happy in his Florida life, though I feel a twinge of sadness for him during football season.

It was this sadness I carried to the 1998 Michigan game. I sat through 3 1/2 quarters waiting for the bottom to drop out as it had in so many Michigan games in those years. But it didn't. And as the last of the doubters began to realize that we could win, the fervor in the stadium swelled. We were on the verge of something wonderful. Everyone was standing. You could feel Michigan losing hope, feel the Buckeyes salting one away for the ages. The noise grew deafening as our hearts filled to bursting with the joy that came with finally beating Michigan. Everything was perfect; everything except Dad.

With a couple of minutes left, I looked down the row to where he would have sat—where my friends were sitting then. My only wish was that he could be there

GAMEDAY HAUNTS

Out-R-Inn Pretty it's not, but the Out-R-Inn has been one of the primo pre-game gathering places for Buckeye fans for a long, long time. The outside Bloody Mary bar is a killer!

The Thirsty Scholar One of the prime game day spots since it was the Black Forest Inn back in the day. Located right around the corner from the Horseshoe, it's perfect for before the game, after the game...even a quick halftime shot.

Bernie's Bagels & Deli Great breakfast sandwiches, cheap drinks and a quick walk to the stadium from its 15th and High location in the heart of the OSU campus.

to celebrate his Buckeyes with us. And then I realized he could. I pulled out the cell phone and called. I could barely hear for the noise, but I could tell he answered.

"Hi, Dad!" I shouted. "I can't hear you so don't talk. Just listen."

And as I held up the phone so he could hear the joy, I managed to squeeze one more body into that sold-out stadium. I closed my eyes and imagined him amid the sea of Scarlet and Gray, smiling in understated contentment. I could feel the bonds that united us crackling across airwave and wire. I could fully rejoice because Dad was finally there.

As the final seconds were counted down, we were together for that most cherished of moments. We would talk later, but now I just let him hear (and I hoped feel) what 95,000 of us were experiencing. And as I held that phone high above my head, it occurred to me: Though Dad and I had sat together before for victories over Michigan, I don't think I'd ever felt so close.

I wrote this sometime after the 1998 Michigan game, when Ohio State posted a rare victory amid a string of disappointments. During those years, the expectations of winning diminished with each loss, and it sometimes felt as though the Buckeyes would never win again. So when the final gun sounded, not only was the celebration for this one game, it was for the rekindling of The Rivalry and the restoration of our pride. My dad passed in 2003, and this was one perfect moment and memory during less than perfect times. It was a thing to be cherished and shared with those we cared about.

A FAN BEHIND ENEMY LINES

By Paul L. Fine, M.D.

I had just returned from my first visit to Ohio Stadium in October 2001 and wrote down a few observations and thoughts.

I have an unusual Buckeye background. I never attended Ohio State. I am a graduate of the (cue the scary music!) University of Michigan Medical School and am currently on the faculty there. I was raised in the Toledo area and started rooting for the Bucks in the early 1970s.

Toledo at that time was the hotbed of the Ohio State–Michigan rivalry—within Ohio, but closer to U of M geographically. It really seemed to be split 50–50, and that made the atmosphere surrounding the game particularly exciting. At any rate, the OSU allegiance that I forged in my younger days remained strong, and I'm known around the medical school and hospital as a passionate (and misguided, in the view of most) Buckeye fan.

With this background as something of an "outsider," I traveled with my 9-year-old son (also an avid OSU fan, despite being brought up near Ann Arbor) for my first game at Ohio Stadium. It was wonderful.

We got to the stadium at 8 a.m. and walked around, enjoying being in the presence of other Buckeye fans. We attended the Skull Session and thought it was one of the highlights of our trip. I must admit that I found myself with tears in my eyes many times during the band's performance.

At 11:30 or so, we walked over to the stadium where we discovered that there was a problem with our tickets (a long story), and that we couldn't enter the stadium. I knew we didn't have enough time to take a shuttle bus back to our car to get what we needed, so I was standing outside the Stadium gates wondering if I had enough cash left to buy two tickets from one of the many people who were wandering about selling them.

At that point, a man and his father came up to me and said that they could tell that something was wrong and asked if I'd like two tickets. I said that I would, told them a little of what had happened, and asked the price. "Oh nothing," the man replied. "They weren't going to be used anyway, and my father and I would like you and your son to have them." We gratefully accepted and found that the seats were better than those we had originally.

Inside the stadium, we reveled in being part of the Buckeye crowd, chatting enthusiastically with the friendly people sitting around us and eagerly taking in the sights and sounds of Ohio Stadium during a game. Did the Bucks play their best game? Certainly not, but we loved every minute of it anyway. In fact, we kept hoping for clock stoppages, not for strategic purposes generally, but so that it would take longer for the game to end.

When I got home Saturday, I thought immediately of perusing the Buckeye-Sports.com message board. Though I post rarely, I check in during the season many times each day to read what others (usually much more knowledgeable about football than me) have to say. It's my way, you see, of immersing myself in a Buckeye community from here in Michigan.

That Saturday, though, I didn't look at the message board, because I knew it would spoil the experience. I knew that the Buckeyes had played lethargically at times, that their defense was unimpressive in the first half, that the quarterback had suffered through his usual inconsistency, and that the kicking game had been poor. I knew what the tone on the board would be. Because I wanted to enjoy the victory, I avoided it.

That realization made me rather sad and reminded me of something I learned about myself. Though I mentioned that I am a sort of Buckeye outsider, I still care passionately about the team and its success. I have OSU memorabilia all over my office, band CDs in my CD auto-changer, and videotapes of all Buckeye victories since 1995. I have been carried to the heights with big victories and driven to new depths with crushing defeats (you can imagine how much fun it was to see the newspaper or come to work after the OSU–Michigan games in 1995 and 1996). I even had to get rid of an electric razor because I had purchased it on the morning of the Saturday that MSU ruined our perfect season in 1998, and I couldn't use it without having that horrible memory brought back to me.

I finally realized with great embarrassment that I had been taking the joy out of the games with critical comments, worrying, and outbursts of temper. In short, though considered an easygoing person otherwise, I wasn't much fun to be around during the games, even in victory. When I stopped to contemplate the situation further, I realized that I was taking the joy out of the games for myself, too. I recognized that I enjoyed watching other teams' games more, because I was able to view them without the anxiety, palpitations and draining emotional roller-coaster ride that I attached to Buckeye games.

I have since made a conscious effort to have more fun with the games, to care about them, but not to let my passion ruin what is supposed to be an enjoyable experience. I have tried to adopt more of my son's perspective—be realistic about how they are doing, but also fundamentally supportive and always looking for reasons to be optimistic instead of reasons to be pessimistic. I have not always succeeded in toning down the anxious passion and dialing up the enjoyment, but I am making progress.

I know the Buckeyes aren't going to win every game, but they're my and my son's team. I look forward to each autumn, because it gives me a new opportunity to root for my team and not lose that perspective. I've become willing to trade a little critical realism for some idealistic enthusiasm.

That's why I now associate Buckeye football with the Woody–Bo contests of my youth, the excitement of my children, TBDBITL's energetic renditions of "Across the Field" and "Buckeye Battle Cry," and the kindness of the generous stranger who helped out a fellow Buckeye fan outside the Horseshoe on a Saturday afternoon in 2001.

Thanks for reading and GO BUCKS!

A HEALTHY RESPECT FOR THE RIVALRY

By Rob Halkides

I have always loved Ohio State football. Unfortunately those around me never really felt the same way.

See, I grew up in Southeast Michigan, and everyone around me was a Wolverine. Michigan State might have been mentioned come basketball season, but for the majority I got to hear how great the University of Michigan was.

Growing up under these conditions was anything but easy to say the least. Much the same way today, I was a stubborn kid who would wear OSU shirts and hats almost daily in wholehearted support.

Heck, on some days I would specifically don the apparel just to get a rise out of those around me. I've had people come right up to me in restaurants with their middle finger extended, school chums spray-paint my locker maize and blue, and even barbers pass me off to other staff members. Some of these actions were good-natured razzings, but many others were done with no humor intended. I always just looked at it as a part of being a sports fan.

Fast forward to today, and I realize it's not just about being a sports fan, but about being a part of the most passionate rivalry in all of sports. I have driven down to the Horseshoe from my address in Ann Arbor to home games on all but two occasions over the past five years, and also have been lucky enough to travel to several away and bowl games as well. While I hate consistently going over on my leased mileage, I absolutely love the atmosphere on game day and always get the chilled feeling that people describe when they see a celebrity.

I have also developed a huge respect for my dad, who has one of the smartest recruiting minds and is one of the most knowledgeable Michigan football fans I have ever been around. My respect for him doesn't center on that knowledge, however. Time after time, he supported and backed me when others asked him, in all sincerity, "What happened to your son?"

Now that I have a wife of my own and kids coming in the near future, I can't imagine how tough that was for him at times. The thought of my future son being a Michigan fan just absolutely eats at me already. Regardless, I have learned over these many years that these two rivals do indeed hate each other, but they also hold each other to the highest regard and truly respect each other.

Knowing this all now, no matter what the score is in any given year, I genuinely feel lucky to be part of something so great. So, if my boy wants to someday play or root for Michigan, I will proudly tell him, "No!"

GAME DAY TRADITIONS LIVE ON

By Pete Anthony

I wasn't much of a sports fan for any team until I became a student at Ohio State. There, you became a Buckeye fan if you wanted to fit in. Looking back, I can't believe I didn't embrace my Scarlet and Gray-ness at an earlier age.

When I was a student, one of my favorite traditions on game days was to wake up early, put on my Buckeye necklace, and find my lucky Scarlet and Gray wool cap. I would then head over to my friend Charlie's house where there were always frosty, cold beverages.

Just walking across campus early in the morning and seeing other students clad in Ohio State hats and shirts, grilling food, playing games, and having a good time was one of the best memories of my life. I loved walking through the streets hearing everyone yelling, "O-H!" and yelling back at the top of my lungs, "I-O!" This yelling got even louder as we headed to the stadium from Charlie's.

Now that I have graduated and do not have the privilege of going to every home game like I used to, I am following new traditions. On game days, I still wake up early and start the morning popping in the Ohio State Marching Band CD. I crank it up loud (much to delight of my neighbors, I'm sure) and I get to hear all of my favorite game day songs.

I still put on my Buckeye necklace and my Scarlet and Gray cap and park myself in front of the TV to watch College Gameday on ESPN. Then, as game time approaches, with the CD still playing, my family and I gather to watch the game. We have the grill going with brats, burgers, and hot dogs, and there are plenty of frosty, cold beverages. The smells take me back to campus as I walk over to Charlie's and then to the stadium.

Whenever I come back to campus for a game, I always park off-campus so I can make that old, familiar walk. I can still hear the people yelling "O-H!" and I shout back "I-O!" That sound makes me smile, laugh, and remember the great times I had at school.

MEETING 'THE MAN'

By Ed Tober

My family and I moved from Columbus to Virginia in the late 1970s. We were and still are die-hard Buckeyes.

Several years after Woody was fired, we returned to Columbus for the big game with "That Team Up North." Woody was becoming more public and re-emerging as the program's icon, and I was determined to meet him and personally thank him for what he had done as a role model for the state of Ohio, OSU football, and me. Additionally, I wanted my family to meet him.

I stopped by his office in the old ROTC Building several times on Thursday before the big game, but with no luck. I decided to take my family to the Horseshoe. If we couldn't meet Woody, they could at least see the stadium.

The gates were open in those days, and we were able to easily get in. There were several hundred people (mostly students) playing around on the turf, and my oldest son (then 8 years old) and I began throwing a football in the stadium. That was an awesome memory in itself.

My wife and other two children sat in the field seats watching us and taking in the atmosphere. Suddenly, my wife excitedly gestured for me to look up in the stands. There was Woody being interviewed by Brent Musberger. We watched for at least forty-five minutes until the interview was completed. The cameraman packed up while Woody kept talking to Brent, and that went on for another thirty minutes.

I gathered my family and began moving closer to Woody and Brent. Woody was doing all of the talking. He was talking about World War II. Honestly, Brent seemed like he wanted to move on, but Woody kept talking. After another twenty minutes, I mustered enough nerve to interrupt Woody. I thanked him and shook his hand and introduced my family. He was very gracious. He said he had seen my son throwing the football and told him to keep throwing. Then he looked to Brent and asked him to tell me and my son why John Elway was such a great quarterback. Woody inserted me and my son into the conversation. Brent dutifully complied and told us that what made Elway great was his running ability.

What an awesome experience.

WHAT A SEASON TO BECOME A DIE-HARD

By Joshua Neukam

I've been a huge college football fan since Charlie Ward won the Heisman Trophy in 1993, but I never really had a team.

When I was eighteen years old, I had an apartment in Louisville, and on the first day of the 2002 season, I decided to watch the Ohio State–Texas Tech game.

As it turned out, I witnessed the debut of Maurice Clarett. Regardless of what has happened since, Clarett was an animal that day, rushing for 175 yards and three touchdowns.

It was that game that made me a Buckeye fan. There was something about the way they played, the heart of the players, the play calls, whatever it may have been, that made me fall in love with the Buckeyes that day. I ended up watching every Ohio State game that the local station covered that season, and I fell in love, a love that has grown to me checking several Internet message boards every day since.

When we played Miami (Florida) in the title game that year—an unbeatable team or so I thought at the time—I remember being happy just for playing in the national championship game. But what I'll never forget is jumping up and down on the couch after Miami quarterback Ken Dorsey missed a pass in double overtime.

As much as I love the Buckeyes, for me nothing will beat watching an entire season and falling in love with a team, so much so that I'm now a die-hard fan. I've made a point of watching every Buckeye game since and will continue to do so 'til the day I die.

ME AND MY HELMET

By John Matthew

I have a tradition that I have done for the last twenty years or so that my friends have teased me about repeatedly. You see, I am quite superstitious when it comes to my beloved Buckeyes. I still wear the same lucky twenty-year-old jersey like lots of fans do to the games, but my superstition involves my favorite piece of sports memorabilia—my autographed Chris Spielman helmet.

I have been going to every home football game since I was a teenager. However, where my superstition comes into play is during my "pregame ritual." Before I leave for campus at around 7 a.m. on game days, I will bring my helmet (appropriately named "Chris") out to the living room and have a little pregame pep rally with him. I sit there and tell him what to look for in the game, and tell him what his "role" is to be for the day. I then turn him toward the turned-on TV, and as I walk out the door, I yell "Go Bucks!" and tell Chris to root our Buckeyes on.

So, while I am down on campus watching the games and drinking a few cold ones, my Spielman autographed helmet is sitting there all alone in front of my TV set as the game blares on!

Some of us are truly crazy! GO BUCKS!!

THE LAST MAN IN THE GATE

By David Weintraub

I flew out from Jersey by myself to the 2002 Michigan game. I had no game ticket, airfare was expensive, and I had nowhere to stay, but I didn't care. I made the plunge. I knew we were going to win this one like we had all the rest that year.

My decision between going to the national championship game or the Michigan game was easy. I knew we would play in both, but one clearly meant more to me at the time. I had experienced too many heartbreaks, like Michigan in '93 and '97 and Michigan State in '98. But the Cooper Era had passed, and I needed things to be different. I chose the Horseshoe.

Since I had nowhere to stay, but had a lot of friends in town, I figured I would just wing it—spend the weekend doing my own thing, finding a place to crash, having no allegiance to any group of people or tailgate. Just the way I liked it. It seems everyone else was trying that move, too, and there was very little room to stay anywhere. Luckily I managed floor space downtown at the Hyatt on Capitol Square.

Game tickets were going from anywhere between $200 and $700, but I was firm that I would not pay more than $200.

On game day, I headed down to the stadium with my buddies Alan and Cory, who had let me crash on the floor of their hotel room. They had tickets, but I was still coming up empty. I had been looking the night before, and the day of the game in the hotel, but no one had any. It looked grim, that's for sure, and I figured it was a lost cause.

About forty-five minutes before game time, we decided to head from the Varsity Club to the stadium. I realized I was the only guy who did not have a ticket, but I decided to walk over with them anyway.

O-H-I-O in Iraq. The reach of Ohio State fandom is far and wide.

On my way out of the VC, I ran into three guys I had known years earlier. I had been friends with these guys years before at school, and it seemed I always ran into them at road games. So there we were in the Varsity Club when all of a sudden, the game came on the TV. The four of us looked at each other and knew we couldn't be watching on TV when the game was going on just across the street. Finally, Brian spoke for all of us when he said, "We have to get in there somehow."

All four of us ran out of the Varsity Club and headed over to the stadium. Quickly Brian found a ticket and said, "I got one! I'm going in!" Dave, Kevin and I stood there, knowing full well we were not getting in, when out of nowhere

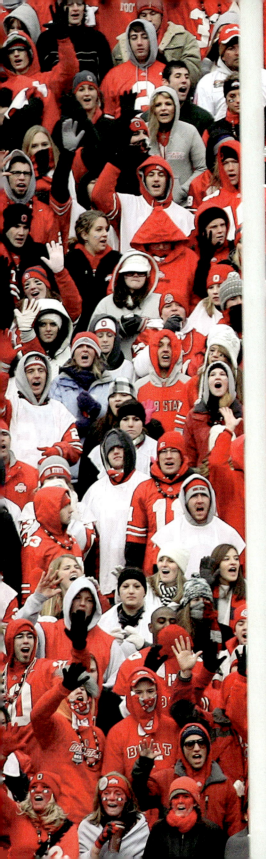

BUCKEYE FANS in action vs. the Michigan Wolverines on November 22, 2008. Ohio State beat the Wolverines 42–7.

Newscom

some kid came riding down the street toward us with his backpack on, somewhat bundled up. Dave approached him as the kid waved him over as if he had tickets. Kevin and I followed. The kid had only one ticket, but it was a student ticket. He said, "I have a huge test Monday and I can't go. You want the ticket?"

He not only gave Dave the ticket for face value, but added, "Here, you'll need my student ID. I can get another one."

Dave held the ticket, looked at Kevin and then said to me, "Hey, man, you take it. We have friends back at the bar. And you look like this kid a lot more than we do."

I didn't argue. I hugged him, took the ticket and ID and ran in. I missed only the first four minutes. The seat was in C deck, but I didn't care. Coincidentally, the guys I used to watch the games with back in the day were all there! None of us ever had seats there, but we just made it happen, and there we were again.

It was a great game, capped off with Maurice Clarett catching the game winning TD pass right in front of us.

The next day I was in the airport, and I noticed Chris Fowler from ESPN at my gate. I went over, introduced myself and said, "Great game yesterday, huh?"

Barely looking up at me, Fowler said, "Yeah, it was pretty good. But you guys are going to get killed by Miami."

Noticing he did not seem interested, and realizing he felt the need to burst my bubble, I replied, "And to think, they actually pay you to be wrong."

Chapter 9

OHIO STATE VS. MICHIGAN

THE GREATEST NORTH AMERICAN SPORTS RIVALRY

There are rivalry games throughout college football. Pittsburgh and West Virginia square off in the Backyard Brawl, Oklahoma and Oklahoma State take on one another in the Bedlam Series, and Oregon and Oregon State wage an annual civil war.

And then there is Ohio State vs. Michigan. No pretense, no catchy nickname. When the Buckeyes and Wolverines meet every fall, their contest is known simply as The Game.

The archrivals have been doing battle for 105 years in what has become one of college football's greatest rivalries. In 2000, the game was ranked by ESPN as the greatest North American rivalry in all of sports.

Michigan dominated the early part of the series that began in 1897 before the Buckeyes finally broke through in 1919 behind All-America halfback Chic Harley. Since that time, the teams have faced one another boasting some of the greatest college players of all time, including Tom Harmon, Howard

"Hopalong" Cassady, Ron Kramer, Jack Tatum, George Webster, Archie Griffin, Anthony Carter, and Eddie George.

Since the game was moved to the final Saturday of the Big Ten season in 1935, the game has had the potential for major impact in the conference standings forty-five times. That includes twenty-three contests in which the two schools have decided the championship between themselves, including a streak between 1972–81 when the Ohio State–Michigan game determined the conference's Rose Bowl representative each year.

The rivalry was already a hotly contested one when a brash young coach named Bo Schembechler took over at Michigan prior to the 1969 season. Schembechler was an Ohio native and a former member of Ohio State head coach Woody Hayes's staff, and he knew what the rivalry meant to so many people in both states.

On November 22, 1969, Hayes led his top-ranked team into Michigan Stadium, riding the crest of a 22-game winning streak, and with sights firmly set on a second consecutive national championship. But behind a stifling defensive effort that intercepted Ohio State six times, Schembechler and his team engineered a stunning 24–12 upset win.

That game touched off "The Ten-Year War" between Hayes and Schembechler, and it raised the frenzy of the OSU–Michigan rivalry to a fever pitch.

During the decade between 1969 and 1978, the two grizzled coaches pitted some of their strongest teams ever against one another. Four times between 1970 and 1975, each team was ranked in the top five heading into their traditional season-ending matchup. In every one of those years, Michigan entered the game undefeated and won only once.

During "The Ten-Year War," either Ohio State or Michigan won the Big Ten championship every year, and the two rivals shared the title six times during the decade.

The "War" ended after Hayes's final season in 1978, but the battles continue. Because of its early dominance, Michigan continued to lead the overall series heading into the 2009 season, owning a 57–42–6 advantage over the Buckeyes. But over the past eighty-two games, things couldn't be more even. Since 1927, each school has thirty-nine victories, and there have been four ties.

Since the Ohio Stadium dedication game in 1922, nearly eight million fans have witnessed The Game in person, more than any other college rivalry in history. Fifty-eight of those eighty-six games have been sold out, including the last forty in a row.

Here are some of the most memorable moments in the history of The Game.

STADIUM DEDICATION (1922)

Michigan served as the opponent as Ohio State dedicated its new Ohio Stadium on October 21, 1922. The largest crowd ever to witness a football game in the Midwest was officially announced at 72,500 although there have been thousands more than that inside the Horseshoe. Many fans unable to secure tickets for the sold-out game forced their way through a fence at the south end of the stadium.

The dedication game festivities were wonderful; both the Ohio State and Michigan marching bands performed at halftime and more than thirty former OSU team captains were seated together on the sideline. The only disappointment was the final score as the Buckeyes dropped a 19–0 decision, breaking their three-game win streak in the series.

Future Michigan head coach Harry Kipke was the star for the Wolverines, scoring a touchdown at halfback and keeping the Buckeyes pinned deep in their own territory most of the afternoon with his pinpoint punting.

SEESAW BATTLE (1944)

Before a homecoming crowd of 71,958 in Ohio Stadium, the third-ranked Buckeyes won an 18–14 classic over the No. 6 Wolverines.

The lead changed hands four times in the back-and-forth contest that started with Ollie Cline's 1-yard touchdown plunge to give Ohio State a 6–0 lead late in the first quarter. Michigan grabbed its first lead at 7–6 just 22 seconds before halftime on a short TD run by Dick Culligan and the subsequent extra point.

Gordon Appleby recovered a Michigan fumble midway through the third period, setting up a touchdown run by Heisman Trophy winner Les Horvath to give the

ARCHIE GRIFFIN VS.
Michigan (1975)

Photo courtesy of Brockway Sports Photos

Buckeyes a 12–7 advantage. But the Wolverines came back with an 83-yard march in the fourth quarter topped by another Culligan TD to regain the lead at 14–12.

Michigan couldn't hold the advantage, however, and Horvath capped a 14-play, 52-yard drive with a 1-yard touchdown at the 3:16 mark of the fourth quarter. OSU defensive halfback Dick Flanagan ended the Wolverines' hopes for another comeback when he intercepted a pass from Culligan in the waning seconds, preserving the 18–14 victory for the Buckeyes.

Horvath rushed for 106 yards and helped keep Ohio State undefeated for the season, and the Buckeyes were declared the National Civilian Champions for 1944. They finished second to Army in the final Associated Press poll.

GOAL-LINE STAND (1954)

Another Big Ten championship was on the line when the undefeated Buckeyes took on the once-beaten Wolverines.

The teams played to a 7–7 tie after three quarters before Michigan opened fourth-quarter play with a first-and-goal at the OSU 4-yard line. Spearheaded by 6' 3", 275-pound lineman Jim Parker clogging the middle, the Buckeyes made one of the classic goal-line stands in school history.

Michigan pounded the ball to the 1-yard line on its first two plays, but the Buckeyes would not budge after that. Parker, along with teammates Jim Reichenbach, Frank "Moose" Machinsky, and Hubert Bobo, stopped the Wolverines on third down and again on fourth down inside the 1.

After taking over on downs, the Ohio State offense took the ball and marched more than 99 yards for the go-ahead touchdown. They added one more score to put the finishing touches on a 21–7 victory, a win that helped propel the team into the Rose Bowl and an eventual national championship.

SO LONG, HOP (1955)

All-America halfback Howard "Hopalong" Cassady completed his college career with a thrilling final performance on his archrival's home turf.

Cassady rushed for 146 yards and scored his final collegiate TD early in the fourth quarter as the Buckeyes shut out the Wolverines, 17–0. The performance helped solidify Cassady as college football's best player in 1955, and a month later he captured the Heisman Trophy by a wide margin over runner-up Jim Swink of TCU.

Michigan crossed midfield only once in the game as Ohio State's stifling defense denied the Wolverines a Rose Bowl bid. Instead, OSU picked up the conference championship with its first win in Ann Arbor since 1937.

The Buckeyes were barred from playing in Pasadena due to the Big Ten's no-repeat rule, and Michigan State was the conference's representative to the Rose Bowl. There, they defeated UCLA with a thrilling 17–14 win.

'BECAUSE I COULDN'T GO FOR THREE' (1961)

The Buckeyes erupted for 512 yards of total offense and rolled to a 50–20 victory over the Wolverines, sewing up the Big Ten championship as well as the national championship from the Football Writers Association of America.

Senior fullback Bob Ferguson rushed for 152 yards and became the first OSU player to score four touchdowns in a game against Michigan. The Buckeyes also scored on an 80-yard pass from Joe Sparma to Bob Klein, the longest scoring pass play in The Game's history.

Ohio State blew open the game with a 29-point explosion in the fourth quarter, including a late two-point conversion after the final touchdown. When asked after the game if he was trying to run up the score, Woody Hayes replied that he was simply wanted the point total to equal 70 in honor of longtime assistant coach Ernie Godfrey's 70th birthday.

Several years later, Hayes changed his story. When asked why he went for two points in that situation, he simply replied, "Because I couldn't go for three."

THE LUCKY CHINSTRAP (1968)

National championship implications were on the line as the No. 2 Buckeyes hosted the fourth-ranked Wolverines. After spotting the visitors an early 7–0 lead, Ohio State rolled to a 50–14 victory, clinching the Big Ten championship and a Rose Bowl berth against USC and Heisman Trophy winner O. J. Simpson.

On the night before the game, during a huge on-campus pep rally, fullback Jim Otis was approached by a Buckeye fan. The fan said that Bob Ferguson had given him his chinstrap as a souvenir following the 1961 OSU–Michigan game, a contest during which Ferguson had scored four touchdowns against the Wolverines. The fan, who referred to himself only as "Scooter," said he wanted Otis to have the strap for good luck the next day.

Otis carefully taped the chinstrap inside his shoulder pads the next morning and proceeded to rush for 143 yards and four touchdowns against Michigan.

THE 'WAR' BEGINS (1969)

Ohio State was poised for a second consecutive national championship when the Wolverines pulled off one of the greatest upsets in college football history. Michigan entered the game as 17-point underdogs and came away with a 24–12 shocker.

Michigan's first-year head coach Bo Schembechler was well-schooled in the tendencies of a Woody Hayes team after spending five years on Hayes's staff at Ohio State from 1958–62. As a result, the Wolverines virtually shut off the Buckeyes' vaunted option play, forcing OSU to throw the ball. That played right into Schembechler's hands, and his team picked off six interceptions to aid in the victory.

The game was a nip-and-tuck affair with the lead changing hands three times in the first half as the Wolverines clung to a 14–12 advantage. But after Barry Pierson returned a punt 60 yards for Michigan to set up another touchdown, the Wolverines never looked back. The Buckeyes moved past midfield only once in the second half as the Michigan defense was stifling. In addition to his big punt return, Pierson was also defensive star of the game, grabbing three of his team's six interceptions.

The contest was the opening salvo in what became known as "The Ten-Year War" between Schembechler and Hayes.

REVENGE IS SWEET (1970)

To say Woody Hayes was obsessed with beating Michigan in 1970 would be like saying the Grand Canyon is a hole in the ground. Hayes had a huge rug made with the 1969 score woven into it, and had it installed just outside the Buckeyes' locker room. Every day, Ohio State players and coaches had "Michigan 24, Ohio State 12" staring them in the face.

By the time the two teams met on November 21, 1970, the Buckeyes were at a fever pitch and responded with a stifling 20–9 victory.

The teams traded field goals for a 3–3 tie early in the second quarter before OSU quarterback Rex Kern hit split end Bruce Jankowski for a 26-yard touchdown, giving the Buckeyes a 10–3 advantage at the half.

Michigan threatened to tie the game on a third-quarter touchdown pass from Don Moorhead to Paul Staroba, but Ohio State defender Tim Anderson blocked the extra point, and that was as close as the Wolverines got.

Kicker Fred Schram booted a 27-yard field goal early in the fourth quarter to widen Ohio State's lead to 13–9, and then linebacker Stan White intercepted Moorhead deep in Michigan territory, setting up a 4-yard touchdown run by tailback Leo Hayden.

Hayden rushed for 117 yards in the game, leading the Buckeyes' offensive attack that ground out 329 total yards. The Wolverines committed three turnovers and were limited to 155 yards.

The victory put the finishing touches on a perfect 9–0 regular season for Ohio State and served as the final home game for the "Super Sophs," who finished their careers with an unblemished 16–0 record in Ohio Stadium.

THE 'OTHER' GRIFFIN (1975)

The Buckeyes and Wolverines were meeting for the seventh time in eight seasons to determine the Big Ten's Rose Bowl representative, and an NCAA-record crowd of 105,543 squeezed into Michigan Stadium, where the Wolverines were working on a 41-game unbeaten streak.

Ohio State was trailing 14–7 with 7:11 remaining in the game and hadn't registered a first down since early in the second quarter. But quarterback Cornelius Greene drove the team 80 yards for the game-tying score with 3:18 left to play.

With the score knotted at 14—and the Wolverines knowing a tie would send the Buckeyes to Pasadena—Michigan head coach Bo Schembechler was forced to try and create something on offense. On third-and-19 at his own 11, quarterback Rick Leach tried to find a receiver past the first-down marker down the middle but threw too far and in the vicinity of OSU sophomore safety Ray Griffin.

The younger brother of two-time Heisman Trophy winner Archie Griffin snagged Leach's pass at the Michigan 32 and streaked his way back down the sideline to the 3-yard line. On the next play, fullback Pete Johnson thundered into the end zone and the Buckeyes had secured a 21–14 victory.

Photo courtesy of Brockway Sports Photos

ART SCHLICHTER vs. Michigan 1979. Schlichter and his OSU teammates defeated the hated Wolverines to go onto the Rose Bowl.

In the game, Archie Griffin had his NCAA-record streak of consecutive 100-yard rushing games snapped at 31. But his brother Ray had a coming-out party with 14 tackles, including 10 solo stops and 2 sacks, along with the all-important interception.

After the game, Woody Hayes told reporters, "I'd have to say this is our greatest comeback, so this has got to be the greatest game I've ever coached."

BUCKEYE BLOCK PARTY (1979)

There was a lot riding on Earle Bruce's first Michigan game as Ohio State head coach. The Buckeyes, unranked at the beginning of the season, had rattled off ten straight victories and invaded Ann Arbor as the nation's No. 2 ranked team.

Thanks to a fourth-quarter blocked punt by linebacker Jim Laughlin, OSU squeezed out an 18–15 victory and earned the right to play for the national championship in the Rose Bowl.

The game was a seesaw battle with Ohio State grabbing a 3–0 lead in the second quarter before Michigan seized a 7–3 advantage. The Buckeyes cut the deficit to 7–6 by halftime, and then went back in front when sophomore quarterback Art Schlichter threw an 18-yard touchdown to Chuck Hunter. The two-point conversion try failed, leaving OSU with a 12–7 lead.

Michigan quickly responded, thanks in part to a 66-yard pass play from QB John Wangler to fleet receiver Anthony Carter, and running back Roosevelt Smith scored on a 1-yard run to put the Wolverines back in front at 13–12. Smith also ran for the two-point conversion, pushing his team's lead to 15–12 with 3:50 left in the third quarter.

That was the way things stayed until just over four minutes left to play in the game. With Michigan protecting its three-point lead and forced to punt, Bruce called for an all-out attempt to block the kick. The Wolverines got everyone blocked except for Laughlin, who ran through untouched to smother punter Bryan Virgil at the Michigan 23-yard line. Ohio State teammate Todd Bell scooped up the loose football and scampered 18 yards to paydirt, sending the Buckeyes to Pasadena for the first time in four years.

VAUGHN'S BIG BLOCK (1981)

Ohio State ruined Michigan's planned trip to Pasadena with a 14–9 victory in Ann Arbor.

The Buckeyes entered the game with a pass defense that ranked among the worst in the nation, but they picked off Michigan quarterback Steve Smith three times.

In all, the Wolverines got inside the OSU 10-yard line four times but only managed a single touchdown. Meanwhile, the Buckeyes got a 1-yard touchdown drive from quarterback Art Schlichter for a 7–3 halftime lead. Michigan got two field goals in the third quarter from kicker Ali Haji-Sheikh to take a 9–7 lead, but that simply set the stage for one of the most famous blocks in Ohio State history.

With 2:50 to play and facing third-and-goal on the Michigan 6, Schlichter rolled out on an option play. As he moved toward the sideline, fullback Vaughn Broadnax locked on a linebacker then pushed him backward into the safety, paving the way for Schlichter to dance into the corner of the end zone, preventing Michigan from claiming the Big Ten championship.

Ohio State wound up in the Liberty Bowl, where it defeated Navy 31–28, while Michigan fell all the way to the Bluebonnet Bowl, where it took a 33–14 win over UCLA.

THE EARLE GAME (1987)

Fired after nine seasons as head coach, Earle Bruce received a final tribute from his players with a come-from-behind 23–20 victory in Michigan Stadium.

Wearing headbands emblazoned with "EARLE" across the front, the Buckeyes overcame a 13–7 halftime deficit thanks to some inspired play in the second half.

On the team's first possession of the third quarter, quarterback Tom Tupa connected on a short pass to tailback Carlos Snow, who made one fake and then outraced the rest of the Wolverines to the end zone for a 70-yard touchdown.

OSU pushed the lead to 20–13 on Tupa's 1-yard plunge midway through the third period, but kicker Matt Frantz missed the PAT. That extra point loomed large when Michigan running back Leroy Hoard burst up the middle for a 10-yard touchdown to tie the score.

EARLE BRUCE'S Final Game. Bruce was carried off the field by his players (many wearing headbands with "EARLE" printed on the front) after beating Michigan in his final game as head coach.

But Frantz got a chance at redemption and made the most of it, booting a 26-yard field goal with 5:18 to play in the game.

OSU's defense held for the remainder of the game, and Bruce triumphantly pumped his fist into the air as he was carried off the field on the shoulders of his team.

TUNNEL OF PRIDE (1994)

Cooper was 0–5–1 against the Wolverines but got a little help to secure his first victory in the series—some of it from an unwanted source.

Early in the week, Michigan receiver Walter Smith boasted, "We want to get Cooper fired. That's what I want to do. We want to keep on beating them and beating them until he's not there."

The comments so incensed OSU alumni that several hundred former players lined up on the Ohio Stadium field during pregame festivities to show their support of the program, forming the first-ever "Tunnel of Pride."

In Cooper's six previous games against Michigan, the football always seemed to bounce the Wolverines' way. This time, it was the Buckeyes who got all the breaks.

OSU took a 12–3 halftime lead on a safety, a 4-yard touchdown scramble by quarterback Bobby Hoying, and a 26-yard field goal by Josh Jackson.

In the second half, OSU defensive back Marlon Kerner blocked a field goal and defensive lineman Luke Fickell grabbed a fourth-quarter interception at the Michigan 16-yard line.

Five plays later, tailback Eddie George ran into the end zone from 2 yards out, and the monkey was finally off Cooper's back.

TITLE HOPES FALL DOWN (1996)

This game was supposed to mark a turn in the series in Ohio State's favor, but will likely forever be remembered as the contest during which All-America cornerback Shawn Springs fell down.

NOVEMBER 25, 1995. Ohio State and Michigan go head to head in Ann Arbor, Michigan.

Getty Images/Jonathan Daniel/Stringer

The Buckeyes had already sewed up the Big Ten championship and their first Rose Bowl berth in a dozen seasons. They simply needed to beat Michigan at home to preserve an undefeated regular season and a shot at the national championship.

It appeared that OSU would accomplish that feat, getting three Josh Jackson field goals in the first half for a 9–0 lead.

But Michigan struck quickly in the third quarter when quarterback Brian Griese connected with split end Tai Streets on a 69-yard touchdown pass on the second play of the second half. Springs slipped down on the play, enabling Streets to run untouched into the end zone.

The Wolverines later took the lead at the end of the third quarter on a Remy Hamilton field goal, then tacked on another three points with 1:19 to go. Ohio State had one final possession, but quarterback Joe Germaine's desperation heave on a fourth-and-23 play was intercepted, ending any hopes of a miracle comeback.

The Buckeyes went on to beat No. 2 Arizona State, 20–17, in the Rose Bowl, scoring the winning touchdown on a 5-yard pass from Germaine to David Boston with just 19 seconds left in the game. But OSU had to settle for finishing second in the final polls, watching Florida take the national championship.

> **I can assure you that you will be proud of our young people in the classroom, in the community, and most especially in 310 days in Ann Arbor, Michigan, on the football field.**
>
> Jim Tressel, shortly after being hired

MOST SATISFYING WIN (1998)

Cooper had arguably his best team in 1998, but the Buckeyes had suffered an upset loss to Michigan State two weeks earlier to knock them out of the national championship picture. The team desperately wanted to salvage its season with a win over Michigan and it did with a convincing 31–16 win that really wasn't that close.

The contest featured more passing yardage that any other game in the series. Joe Germaine threw for 330 yards for Ohio State while Michigan quarterback completed 31 of 56 attempts for 375 yards. Both totals represented series highs for the respective teams.

OSU broke out on top early when Michael Wiley ran 53 yards for a touchdown on his team's second possession of the game. The Buckeyes set up their next two scores with special teams play, forcing a minus-yardage punt on one play and blocking a punt on another. Germaine later hooked up with receiver David Boston for a 43-yard touchdown following an interception by OSU linebacker Jerry Rudzinski.

The Buckeyes completely shut down the Michigan rushing attack, limiting the Wolverines to a net of 4 yards on the ground.

Especially gratifying for Ohio State was the fact the victory broke Michigan's Big Ten winning streak at 16 games.

310 DAYS LATER (2001)

When Jim Tressel was hired to replace John Cooper in January 2001, one of his stated objectives was to reverse Cooper's 2–10–1 record against Michigan. But no one expected Tressel to say what he did in front of a basketball crowd at Value City Arena just a few hours after being introduced as the new coach.

"I can assure you that you'll be proud of our young people in the classroom, in the community, and most especially, in 310 days in Ann Arbor, Michigan," the new coach said.

The crowd erupted, but after the initial frenzy died down, many wondered if the Buckeyes could back up Tressel's assertion.

As things turned out, they needn't have worried. The Buckeyes scored a 26–20 victory, their first in Ann Arbor since Bruce's final game in 1987.

Senior tailback Jonathan Wells continued his breakout season, rushing 23 times for 122 yards and three touchdowns. All three scores came in the first half as Ohio State jumped out to a 23–0 lead over the 11th-ranked Wolverines.

Not that there weren't some anxious moments in the second half. Michigan scored on an 11-yard pass from Navarre to receiver Marquise Walker with 2:26 left in the game to get the home team within six points of the Buckeyes.

But OSU receiver Chris Vance recovered the ensuing onside kick, effectively ending Michigan's hopes of coming all the way back. Navarre did get a few seconds at the end of the game, but his Hail Mary pass was intercepted by freshman cornerback Dustin Fox to cement Ohio State's victory.

ON TO THE TITLE (2002)

Before an Ohio Stadium-record crowd of 105,539, the Buckeyes overcame a fourth-quarter deficit to beat Michigan and secure the Big Ten's first-ever spot in the Bowl Championship Series national title game.

Freshman tailback Maurice Clarett energized the crowd when he shook off a shoulder injury to run for 119 yards, breaking the school's single-season rushing record for freshmen.

But it was a 26-yard pass reception in the fourth quarter that could have been Clarett's biggest play. It helped set up a 4-yard touchdown run by sophomore tailback Maurice Hall, giving the Buckeyes a 14–9 lead with 4:55 remaining in the game.

Michigan had two more chances to pull the game out of the fire. QB John Navarre drove his team to the OSU 30-yard line, but he fumbled after a hard sack by defensive tackle Darrion Scott, and defensive end Will Smith pounced on the loose football.

Then in the final minute, the Wolverines got the ball back and got all the way to the OSU 20 before safety Will Allen picked off Navarre near the end zone to end the threat.

The victory gave the Buckeyes a share of the Big Ten championship with Iowa, preserved their undefeated season and put them into the BCS championship game against defending national champion Miami (FL). Then, on January 3, 2003, at the Fiesta Bowl in Tempe, AZ, Ohio State defeated the Hurricanes 31–24 in double overtime to capture the school's first consensus national title since 1968.

TROY STORY (2004)

Troy Smith had the best statistical day an Ohio State quarterback has ever had against Michigan, rushing and passing for 386 yards and three touchdowns in a relatively easy 37–21 victory for the Buckeyes.

The Wolverines entered the November 20 contest on an eight-game winning streak, boasting a 9–1 record and ranked No. 7 in the country. They were already on their way to a Rose Bowl date against Texas and installed as a 41/2-point favorite to beat the unranked Buckeyes.

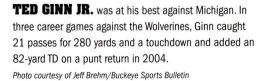

TED GINN JR. was at his best against Michigan. In three career games against the Wolverines, Ginn caught 21 passes for 280 yards and a touchdown and added an 82-yard TD on a punt return in 2004.

Photo courtesy of Jeff Brehm/Buckeye Sports Bulletin

But Michigan had no answer for Smith. He directed one touchdown drive of 99 yards and another measuring 97 yards and turned in the finest running and passing day ever for an Ohio State quarterback against the Wolverines.

The sophomore QB rushed for 145 yards and one touchdown and threw for 241 yards and a pair of scores. The Buckeyes had never had a quarterback rush for more than 100 yards and throw for more than 200 in the same game in program history.

Smith's game overshadowed several other fine individual performances, including freshman sensation Ted Ginn Jr. His 82-yard punt return for a touchdown in the third quarter was his fourth of the 2004 season, tying the all-time NCAA record for the most in a single season and establishing new single-season and career records at Ohio State.

CHIC LEADS BUCKEYES TO FIRST WIN OVER MICHIGAN

Ohio State and Michigan have had a long and storied rivalry that has experienced tremendous ups and downs for both schools. During the early history of the series, however, there were precious few ups for the Buckeyes.

Over the first fifteen games the two teams played, OSU never tasted victory. The closest the Buckeyes had come to beating their rivals were a pair of ties—0–0 in 1900 at Michigan and 3–3 in 1910 in Columbus.

In 1919, the Scarlet and Gray was hopeful things were about to change. John W. Wilce was in his seventh season as head coach of the Buckeyes and was fielding one of his strongest teams. OSU went into the October 25 contest against the Wolverines with a full head of steam, having won its first three games of the season. Not only were the Buckeyes on a winning streak, they had been dominant against opponents Ohio Wesleyan, Cincinnati, and Kentucky. OSU had outscored that trio by a 133–0 margin.

Wilce's team was bolstered by the return from World War I of many stars, including two-time All-America halfback Chic Harley. The 5'8", 165-pound senior had never lost a game while wearing an Ohio State uniform, but he also had never faced Michigan.

Patrolling the sideline for the Wolverines was longtime head coach Fielding Yost, who was in his 19th season in Ann Arbor. Michigan had won five championships under Yost in eight years as a member of the Western Conference, and the Wolverines again fielded a powerful team in 1919. Like their counterparts from Ohio, Michigan entered the contest undefeated and unscored upon.

The Wolverines had the added advantage of history on their side. They entered the contest with a 13–0–2 record against the Buckeyes, having outscored the Buckeyes by a 369–21 margin that included an 86–0 loss in 1902, still the worst loss in Ohio State history.

Things got off to a rather inopportune start for Ohio State as sophomore Pete Stinchcomb fumbled the opening kickoff, and Archie Weston recovered for Michigan at the OSU 10-yard line. Still, the play was costly for the Wolverines as senior end Harold Rye was lost for the rest of the game with a broken leg.

Still, the hosts were eager to seize the early momentum and nearly did so when Weston made what looked like a sure touchdown reception. But the Michigan senior somehow muffed the catch and the football dropped harmlessly to the ground.

Midway through the first quarter, the Buckeyes finally got a couple of breaks. After Michigan had pushed the ball to midfield, the Wolverines were penalized 15 yards. On the next play, quarterback Cliff Sparks lost 3 yards and then had a punt go off the side of his foot, giving OSU possession at its own 49-yard line.

Harley immediately went to work, slicing through the line over right tackle for a 22-yard gain. The Buckeyes eventually got to the 6-yard line before the drive stalled and Harley was asked to try for a 20-yard field goal. His drop kick went just wide of the goal post and Michigan took over possession.

The Wolverines had dodged a bullet—but not for long. Sparks fumbled the snap on the first play and teammate Robert "Duke" Dunne managed to recover. Sparks lost 5 more yards on the next play before fullback Ernie Vick got 2 back on third down. Faced with a fourth-and-15 situation, Yost had no choice but to call for Sparks to punt.

This time, though, the Buckeyes swarmed on the Michigan punter, and sophomore linemen Iolas Huffman and Cyril "Truck" Myers—a pair of future All-Americans—blocked the kick. Right end Jim Flowers recovered in the end zone for the Buckeyes as most of the 25,000 fans on hand at Ann Arbor's Ferry Field fell silent. Not so for the approximately 5,000 rooters who had taken the train north from Columbus. They made a thunderous roar that got the attention of everyone wearing maize and blue.

Then as today, teams that scored a touchdown had the opportunity to kick an extra point, but the practice was much harder and more complicated in 1919. The scoring team had to drop-kick or punt the ball from behind the goal line from the point where the ball-carrier entered the end zone. A member of his team then had to field the ball cleanly on the field of play, and then from that spot the kicker was given a chance to try for the extra point. If the receiver of the "kick-out" dropped the ball or missed catching it entirely, there would be no PAT try.

After the touchdown against Michigan, Harley executed the kick-out and then added the extra point to give Ohio State a 7–0 lead with about two minutes remaining in the opening period. It marked the first time in the history of the series that the Buckeyes had ever enjoyed a lead over the Wolverines.

They threatened to build on that advantage later in the first quarter after backing up Michigan and forcing a quick punt. OSU took over on the Wolverines' 31-yard line and quickly moved to the 20 on back-to-back pass completions from Stinchcomb to Harley. The Buckeyes inched closer to the goal line when, on third-and-2 from the 12, Flowers gathered in a pass from Harley at the 3. But as he was being tackled, Flowers fumbled the ball, and Weston recovered for the Wolverines just short of the goal line.

Michigan got back into things by playing field position in the second quarter. A 50-yard punt by Sparks rolled dead on the Ohio State 5-yard line, and Wilce decided to play it safe. After a 2-yard run by Stinchcomb, Harley was instructed to punt the ball away on second down.

The strategy caught the Wolverines by surprise, but Harley's short kick trickled out of bounds at the OSU 38. The Buckeyes held on defense, but then Sparks—with the aid of a gusting wind—drop-kicked a beautiful 43-yard field goal and brought his team within four points of the lead at 7–3.

That's the way things stayed until early in the third quarter when Michigan threatened again. The Wolverines pushed their way to the 33-yard line and seemed poised to take control of the game. But Yost may have outthought himself. Despite the fact his team was having success running the ball, the veteran coach called for a pass on a fourth-and-1 play. Luckily for the Buckeyes, Vick threw incomplete to Dunne, and Ohio State took over on downs.

Michigan's failure on the fourth-down play proved to be a turning point in the game. Stinchcomb took the snap on the first play of the OSU drive and darted quickly ahead, gaining 25 yards before being stopped. That pushed the ball out to the Michigan 42, and Harley took over from there.

The Ohio State senior took a pitch from Stinchcomb, eluded right end Willard Peach in the backfield, and then zigzagged his way down the field, side-stepping Weston and Sparks about the 15-yard line before cruising into the end zone. The 42-yard touchdown play gave the Buckeyes a 13–3 advantage midway through the third period. OSU missed an opportunity to increase their lead when Harley's kickout hit the ground and the Buckeyes lost their chance to try for the extra point.

Later in the third quarter, Michigan threatened again. Facing second-and-8 at the Ohio State 32, Vick pulled off an excellent fake handoff and rolled out of the backfield, spying Dunne breaking free near the goal line. The Michigan quarterback heaved the ball toward his teammate when Stinchcomb came flashing in from his defensive halfback spot. The OSU junior flicked the ball away at the last possible second, thwarting the touchdown.

Two plays later, still at the OSU 32, the Wolverines tried to throw the ball again when Harley picked off Sparks at the 15-yard line to end the threat.

Each team had other chances to score late in the game.

The Buckeyes blocked another Michigan punt early in the fourth quarter and managed to take the ball to the 4-yard line. But Tom Davies fumbled just short of the goal line and Sparks recovered for the Wolverines.

Later, Michigan tried to play catch-up through the air and was stopped by Harley on three different occasions. The Ohio State All-American intercepted a long pass near midfield halfway through the final period, and then picked off the Wolverines two more times on successive plays down the stretch.

Harley intercepted Sparks again at the OSU 26-yard line, and then when the Wolverines got the ball back, the senior star picked off Vick on the first play of that possession. It was Harley's fourth interception of the afternoon, a single-game Ohio State record that has never been equaled.

After that final interception, the Buckeyes managed to play keep-away from Michigan for much of the final few minutes and finally closed out a 13–3 victory, their first ever in the rivalry that had begun with a 34–0 loss to the Wolverines in 1897.

The final statistics showed a lopsided advantage for Ohio State with the Buckeyes rolling up 176 yards of total offense to just 85 for the Wolverines. In the second half, Yost had gone to the air to try and narrow the gap, but his team threw 16 times and failed to complete a single pass.

Meanwhile, Harley was a one-man wrecking crew. He had rushed for 17 times for 90 yards and a touchdown, completed 5 of 9 passes for 37 yards, and punted 11 times for an average of 42.5 yards to go along with his four interceptions.

Following the game, Yost did something he had never done in his previous 18 seasons as Michigan head coach. He had never before visited the opposing locker room after a loss, and after a congratulatory handshake with Wilce, he asked to address the Buckeyes.

"You deserve your victory," he said. "You fought brilliantly. You boys gave a grand exhibition of football strategy, and while I am sorry—dreadfully sorry—that we lost, I want to congratulate you."

Then, seeing Harley wearily removing his jersey in a corner of the locker room, the Michigan coach said, "And you, Mr. Harley, I believe, are one of the finest little machines I have ever seen. Again, I want to congratulate Ohio State."

The Harley-led victory signaled a sea change in the Ohio State-Michigan rivalry. Heading into the 2009 season, the previous 82 games in the series were dead even—39 wins for the Buckeyes, 39 wins for the Wolverines, and 4 ties.

GOLD PANTS CLUB

Francis Albert Schmidt was successful in nearly everything he ever tried.

He won a varsity letter at Nebraska during the only season he played college football. He served in the U.S. Army during World War I and rose to the rank of captain. And he won championships at nearly every stop during a 24-year College Football Hall of Fame coaching career, including two each at Tulsa, TCU, and Ohio State.

Why then would Schmidt, in his first season as head coach of the Buckeyes, have been the least bit intimidated on the eve of his initial encounter with archrival Michigan?

That task would have given most men pause. Ohio State had tasted victory over the Wolverines only six times in the thirty times the teams had played over the years and were working on back-to-back shutout losses in 1932 and 1933, defeats that had helped to cause the dismissal of Sam Willaman, Schmidt's predecessor as head coach.

But Schmidt had already given an indication of how he felt about going against Michigan when he met with Columbus newspaper reporters eight months earlier. The day the coach was formally hired by the university, he sat through a battery of questions from interviewers until the inevitable was asked.

"Michigan is pretty tough," a reporter offered. "How concerned are you about them?"

"How concerned should I be?" Schmidt replied with a wry smile. "Don't forget they put their trousers on one leg at a time, just the same as anyone else."

No one knew it at the time, especially since the coach was simply repeating an old Texas aphorism, and somewhere along the line "trousers" were substituted for "pants." But it was the genesis of one of Ohio State's oldest and most cherished traditions—the Gold Pants Club, with membership exclusive only to those team members who beat Michigan.

There wasn't much need for such a club in the early part of the rivalry. The best the Buckeyes could do during the first fifteen games in the series was two ties, and things hadn't gotten much better by the time Schmidt arrived in Columbus. The Wolverines had taken three of the previous four in the series, and nine of the previous twelve.

Making Schmidt's task even more daunting was the fact Michigan entered the 1934 season as defending national champions. The Wolverines had run

DID YOU KNOW?

Heading into the 2009 season, the **Ohio State-Michigan rivalry** has been a dead heat over the past half-century. Since 1959, the Buckeyes and Wolverines have each been victorious 24 times and there have been two ties.

roughshod over the college football landscape in 1933, rolling to an undefeated 7–0–1 record while outscoring the opposition by a 131–18 margin, including a 13–0 win over the Buckeyes.

But head coach Harry Kipke didn't have much left over in his cupboard for the 1934 campaign. By the time the Wolverines invaded Columbus in mid-November, they had won only once in six games, and they had been held scoreless in four of their five losses.

That didn't matter much to Schmidt, however, who wanted to guard against his team taking the Wolverines lightly. Before each of the previous six games, the first-year coach allowed senior members to address the team in the locker room prior to kickoff. This time, he decided to speak, and according to a former Ohio State player in the room, it was a most unusual pep talk.

"He spoke in a very low voice with practically no inflection, the way a father would talk to his son," the ex-Buckeye reported. "He did not lift his voice once. But it was all so simple, so understandable, so human. He finished by saying simply, 'Now go out there and do your best. This is your day of days.' That was all. How I would have liked to play under that guy."

The talk had the desired effect. The Buckeyes proceeded to give Michigan its worst pounding in the rivalry to that time, rolling to a 34–0 victory.

In front of an Ohio Stadium record crowd of 68,678, Ohio State scored two first-half touchdowns behind a ferocious running attack before a defensive score opened the second half. The Buckeyes then switched to the air in the final minutes to cross the goal line twice more.

OSU got on the board in the first quarter after a nine-play, 50-yard drive was capped by a 2-yard touchdown burst by junior halfback Dick Heekin. The score was set up on a trick play during which quarterback William "Tippy" Dye stood up as if to pass before halfback Damon "Buzz" Wetzel snatched the ball out of Dye's hand. The so-called "Statue of Liberty" play netted 12 yards and served to poke a finger in the eye of the Wolverines, since the trick formation was first designed and used by legendary Michigan head coach Fielding Yost.

Wetzel added a 5-yard touchdown romp in the second quarter to give the Buckeyes a 13–0 halftime lead, and the game remained that way until Ohio State broke things open in the fourth quarter.

Halfback Jack Smith fumbled on the 1-yard line, but OSU teammate Frank Antenucci pounced on the loose football and stretched over the goal line for the Buckeyes' third score of the afternoon. Later, All-America end Merle Wendt scored on a 68-yard touchdown reception from backup quarterback Frank Fisch, and then Frank Cumisky put the exclamation point on the win with a 33-yard touchdown pass from Dye.

The final score was barely indicative of just how lopsided the game really was. Ohio State piled up 24 first downs to only three for Michigan, and the Buckeyes amassed 460 yards of total offense. The Wolverines had just 40.

The next day, a banner headline in *The Columbus Sunday Dispatch* proudly proclaimed, "OHIO STATE SMOTHERS MICHIGAN 34 TO 0" while sportswriter Irven C. Schelbeck pulled no punches in his account of the game: "A cloak of invincibility, worn by Michigan football teams since the turn of the century, was ripped away by an unsentimental Ohio State eleven Saturday, leaving the Wolverines nude and shivering under the cold blast of a 34-to-0 defeat."

After the game, the crowd poured onto the field and tore down the goal posts in triumph. It was believed to be the first time in Ohio Stadium that the posts had come down after a big victory. Not completely satisfied with simply tearing down the posts, several students hoisted them on their shoulders and carried them away as souvenirs.

Ohio State finished its first year under Schmidt the following week with a 40–7 victory over Iowa, putting the finishing touches on a 7–1 campaign with the only loss a 14–13 defeat at Illinois in the season's second week.

Even though the victory over the Wolverines was billed as "The Battle of How Michigan Puts On Its Pants," the comment was largely forgotten until the following season when the two rivals played for the first time in the regular season finale for both. This time, Schmidt's Buckeyes doled out an even bigger beating to their arch nemesis, rolling to a 38–0 victory.

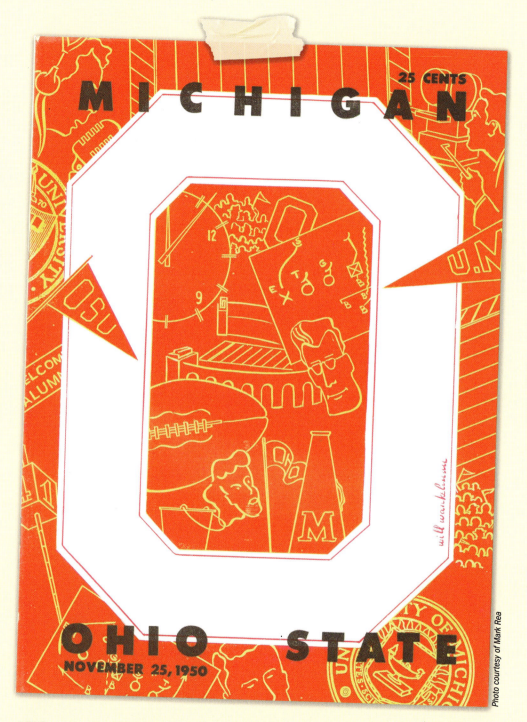

1950 OSU-Michigan Program (Snow Bowl). Conditions for the game have been described as the worst in Ohio Stadium history. OSU lost the game 9–3.

That win sewed up the Western Conference championship for Ohio State, the program's first title since 1920. And when it came time for the traditional awards banquet, Schmidt surprised his players by issuing each a small golden charm to be worn on their watch chains. The charm was molded into the form of gold pants—the pants Michigan players wore then and continue to wear to this day—and was engraved with the winning score and the players' names.

Schmidt beat Michigan again in 1936 and 1937—shutting the Maize and Blue out again both times—and became the first and only OSU head coach ever to notch victories against the Wolverines in each of his first four tries.

He remained at Ohio State through the 1940 season, winning another conference championship in 1939 and finishing with a record of 39–16–1.

And although Schmidt died in 1944 at the age of 58, the exclusive Gold Pants Club lives on as one of the greatest traditions in Ohio State football history.

THE SNOW BOWL—1950

Saturday, November 25, 1950, was supposed to be a cool, crisp late autumn day in Columbus with no precipitation in the forecast.

When OSU coach Wes Fesler awoke the next morning and looked out his window, he couldn't believe his eyes. It would be an understatement to say that the weather had taken a turn for the worse.

By 10 a.m.—four hours before the scheduled kickoff—the Ohio Stadium field was already covered with ice and snow. The bottom had dropped out of the thermometer and 40 mph winds whipped through the Horseshoe, sending the mercury plummeting to near zero.

Ohio State athletic director Richard Larkins huddled with his Michigan counterpart, Herbert O. "Fritz" Crisler, to debate whether to cancel the game, postpone it, or go ahead and play. Larkins tried to reach Big Ten commissioner Kenneth L. "Tug" Wilson for a recommendation but was unable to get a message through to Wilson.

Larkins immediately wanted to postpone the contest, but Crisler was steadfast. Either play the game or cancel it completely. Had the game been canceled and not made up at a later date, Ohio State could have won the conference championship outright.

Canceling the game would have benefited the Buckeyes, but they didn't want to take the easier path.

"When we heard the choices, there was no question in our minds," remembered former OSU All-American tackle Bob Momsen years later. "We didn't want any favors from Michigan. We wanted to play."

Janowicz told *Buckeye Sports Bulletin* in a 1989 interview that Fesler originally sided with those in favor of canceling the game.

"Our coach didn't want to play," Janowicz said, "but ultimately, he left the decision up to us. We wanted to play and Fesler took that message back to the athletic directors."

Armed with that knowledge, the decision was made to go ahead with the game. Larkins was sure he had made the correct choice when he learned the Illinois-Northwestern game had continued despite blizzard conditions in Evanston, but the decision became infamous as the 1950 Ohio State-Michigan game became forever after known as the Snow Bowl.

More than a half-century later, controversy and debate still hovers over the decision to play the contest in what could be described as the worst game-day conditions ever experienced at Ohio Stadium.

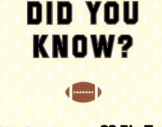

DID YOU KNOW?

Ohio State has won **33 Big Ten titles**, including a remarkable six straight from 1972–77.

"In my opinion, that was a game that should never have been played," said Ohio State football historian Jack Park. "Many of the people I have talked to over the years who were actually at that game went home at halftime. Even so, many of the people who drove to the game from outside Columbus couldn't get to their cars. I've been told they couldn't get them out of the stadium parking lot until the following Tuesday or Wednesday."

As the snowfall mounted, Columbus officials declared a snow emergency and instructed all citizens to stay home if they could.

The game was delayed 20 minutes past its scheduled 2 p.m. start while grounds crew members and volunteers from the stands tried to remove the $3,000 protective tarpaulin that had covered the field but was now frozen to it.

They were only partially successful.

"One thing that has been lost down through the years is that they actually played the game with half the tarp still on the field," said former Ohio State sports information director Marv Homan.

Then in his first year as the play-by-play announcer on football broadcasts for university station WOSU, Homan remembered the fruitless efforts to remove the tarp.

"They tried to roll it away, but of course, that wasn't going to happen," he said. "And they tried cutting it away, but that didn't work either. After a while, they just decided to leave it. Not that it really mattered anyway. There was so much snow and ice that you had no traction of any kind, so I doubt that it had any impact on the game whatsoever."

Grounds crew workers drafted fans into action and passed out shovels and brooms to try to clear the field. A road grader even was pressed into service to clear the snow from the playing surface.

None of the efforts had much effect.

"It wasn't just the snow," Momsen said. "It was cold. And when I say cold, I mean cold. Our ears were cold, our feet were cold, our hands were cold. When we took our showers after the game, we actually had to sit down in the showers because we'd pretty much lost all feeling in our legs and feet."

The conditions were so bad to start the game that the opening coin toss was held inside the stadium tower. Inside the press box, heat pipes had frozen and all of the windows were covered with frost. Four spotters on the field used telephones to relay plays to public address announcer Tom Johnson.

Homan was perched inside the press box and called the game through chattering teeth.

"You couldn't see a thing, so we had to open the windows and leave them open," he said. "I'd venture to say it was at least as cold inside that press box as it was outside. It was like doing a game while sitting inside a refrigerator."

Nevertheless, the game went on and the Buckeyes took an early 3–0 lead after Momsen blocked a punt.

"I remember I was able to get in and block that punt and Joe Campanella recovered it on the 3-yard line," Momsen said. "But on the first play after that,

Janowicz tried to pass and threw the ball out of bounds in the end zone. In those days, that was a 15-yard penalty and it backed us up."

As a result, the Buckeyes' drive stalled, and Fesler instructed Janowicz to try a field goal. The OSU all-purpose star powered the football through the uprights despite the swirling, gale-force wind for a 38-yard field goal and a 3–0 Ohio State lead.

"That was a pretty good kick," Janowicz remembered several years later with a smile. "But I had been practicing my kicking so much that I treated it just like any other kick."

Writers who witnessed the kick into the wind had a little different take on Janowicz's humble memory. They wrote that it was the single biggest achievement of the entire 1950 college football season.

"I'd even go that one better," Homan said. "I truly believe had the Buckeyes won that game, that kick would have gone down as the single most important kick in Ohio State history."

Shortly after the field goal, however, Janowicz was attempting to punt out of his own end zone. Michigan captain Allen Wahl blocked the punt and it rolled out of the end zone for a safety to make the score 3–2.

Then, with 47 seconds left in the first half, Janowicz attempted another punt. This one was blocked by Michigan's Tony Momsen—Bob's brother—who also recovered the ball in the end zone for a Michigan touchdown.

"I'll never forget that one," Homan said. "The ball was blocked behind Janowicz, but the question was where it had been recovered. The officials had to call timeout and use shovels and brooms to determine if the ball had gone over the end line of the end zone.

"I recall it was several minutes before they had determined the ball had actually been recovered by Michigan in the end zone."

Fesler took a great deal of criticism for the play since he had instructed Janowicz to attempt the punt on third down.

"We had two plays left," Fesler later explained, "but there was too much time to close out the end of the period. So rather than take a chance of anything happening, I wanted to get the ball out of there."

The decision was questioned again and again over the years and continues to be debated today.

"I've often wondered why Fesler wouldn't have run another play and let the clock wind down some more before punting," Park said. "He had plenty of time to just run it up the middle and then kick on fourth down. I really don't know why he didn't do that."

A little-known Ohio State redshirt freshman halfback sat huddled in the stands with some other fans when Fesler ordered the third-down punt. That little-known Buckeye? Earle Bruce.

"I was sitting in the west stands on the 40-yard line right behind a little old lady who was covered in a blanket," the former OSU head coach remembered. "When it became apparent that Janowicz was going to punt on third down, this lady threw off that blanket and yelled at the top of her lungs, 'Don't punt the ball, Fesler! Please don't punt the ball!'

"I guess she knew a pending disaster when she saw it."

After the officials had determined the play was a touchdown, Michigan kicker Harry Allis booted his extra point through the uprights for a 9–3 Wolverine lead.

Weather conditions got even worse in the second half. The driving snowstorm was so blinding that players standing on one sideline could not see their opponents on the other sideline. Grounds crew members with brooms had to sweep snow from the field just to place the ball for each play.

"It was without a doubt the most bizarre football game I was ever a part of," Bob Momsen said. "We couldn't see across the field. All kinds of people came out of the stands to help try and keep the field cleared and snow piled up a foot or two on the edge of the field."

Michigan eventually won the game 9–3, and when Northwestern upset Illinois in their "Blizzard Bowl," the Wolverines captured the Western Conference championship and a trip to the Rose Bowl. The Buckeyes, who had been ranked eighth nationally prior to the game, had to settle for a second-place tie with Wisconsin while Illinois fell to fourth.

Less than three weeks after the game, Fesler resigned under mounting pressure from the fans and alumni.

In his defense, the Ohio State coach told many friends he was on the verge of a nervous breakdown during the entire 1950 season and had cited "poor health" in his official letter of resignation to the university.

Coincidentally, it was Fesler's 0–3–1 record against Michigan—he was 21–10–2 against all other opponents in his OSU tenure—that had many fans and alumni calling for OSU president Howard L. Bevis to fire him.

A three-time All-America player at Ohio State, Fesler was mentally drained from his four-year tenure as head coach in the pressure-cooker atmosphere of Columbus. However, even before the Buckeyes hired a little-known coach named Woody Hayes to be his successor, Fesler became head coach at Big Ten rival Minnesota for the 1951 season.

"I don't have any proof of this," Park said, "but it's always been hearsay that because Larkins felt so badly about the turn of events, he helped Fesler get the job in Minnesota. Those two were very close friends and I've always heard Larkins went to bat for Fesler in Minnesota."

The statistics in the Snow Bowl were almost unbelievable.

Michigan won the game without the benefit of a single first down or pass completion. The Wolverines gained a total of 27 yards and fumbled six times. Backup fullback Ralph Straffon was the team's top ground-gainer with 14 yards on 12 carries.

"Can you imagine a team winning without gaining a single first down?" Momsen said. "To this day, that still boggles the mind."

Homan remembered Michigan coach Bennie Oosterbaan had instructed his team to let Ohio State make the mistakes.

"He had an interesting strategy," Homan said. "Oosterbaan didn't want the ball, so he started punting on first down. They had fumbled several times in the game, so he didn't want to take a chance on his team making any more mistakes in the second half. It was just another weird aspect of a very weird game. Absolutely bizarre from start to finish."

The Buckeyes had only three first downs and fumbled four times. They managed 16 yards on the ground and 25 more through the air, completing three of a remarkable 18 pass attempts considering the playing conditions. Chuck Gandee was the Buckeyes' top rusher with 15 yards on 11 carries.

There were a Big Ten-record 45 punts in the game. Michigan's Chuck Ortmann punted 24 times, a conference record which still stands, while Janowicz had 21 punts, an OSU single-game record which remains on the books.

Although 82,300 tickets were sold for the game—which would have made for the third-largest crowd in stadium history at that time—the official attendance was counted at 50,503 who braved the elements. Before the game, the few ticket-takers who had been able to man their posts were told to go home, and the stadium gates were opened for anyone who wanted to attend the game.

"I know what the estimated crowd was," Homan said, "and, believe me, that was an estimate. I'm not saying it wasn't accurate. There could have been 50,000 in the stands when the game began, but I'd venture to say there were only about 5,000 when it ended."

Copies of the game program are extremely rare. Most were either water-damaged by the snow or burned by fans in the stands for a small bit of heat.

"In the years since, I think the game has kind of been embellished a little bit," Momsen said. "To us at the time, it was just another Michigan game that we wanted to win for the conference title. But as I said before, it turned out to be a truly bizarre game."

DID YOU KNOW?

Although the Buckeyes' first home game was against Wooster, on November 1, 1890, the school unveiled **Ohio Stadium** in 1922. It was built entirely from donations, and superstar All-American Chic Harley appeared several times for fundraisers.

BATTLE OF THE UNBEATENS ENDS IN CONTROVERSY—1973

When Ohio State and Michigan squared off against one another in 1973, it marked a milestone in the rivalry that had already witnessed more than its share. For the first time in seventy meetings between the two hated rivals, the Buckeyes and Wolverines each entered the traditional season finale with an unblemished record.

The Scarlet and Gray were the No. 1-ranked team in the nation as they headed to Ann Arbor, and their ranking was unquestioned on the strength of nine straight victories by an average of 36.4 points. Behind sophomore running back Archie Griffin and an offensive line that featured All-America tackle John Hicks,

Ohio State punished opponents with a running attack that averaged a school-record 355.3 yards per game.

On the other side of the ball, the Buckeyes were just as strong with a bevy of All-Americans, including defensive end Van Ness DeCree and linebacker Randy Gradishar. While the offense was steamrolling opponents, the OSU defense had already recorded four shutouts and was allowing an average of only 3.7 points per game heading into the Michigan contest.

Meanwhile, the Wolverines weren't too shabby themselves. They had been ranked in the top five all season and entered into the game against the Buckeyes as the No. 4 team in the nation.

Former OSU assistant Glenn E. "Bo" Schembechler was in his fifth season in Ann Arbor and already had become a thorn in his former mentor's side. Schembechler's 1969 team had pulled off a huge upset over Woody Hayes's top-ranked team, preventing them from playing for a second straight national championship, and the Buckeyes were 0–2 in Michigan Stadium since Schembechler had taken over.

In 1973, the Wolverines had also played in their share of blowouts. Their average margin of victory was 26.2 points per game heading into the season finale, and their defense had shut out three opponents and held four others to a touchdown or less.

They were led by All-Americans such as defensive tackle Dave Gallagher (Piqua) and safety Dave Brown, as well as shifty quarterback Dennis Franklin and hard-nosed fullback Ed Shuttlesworth. Upping the ante even more was the fact that all four of those players were native Ohioans, a fact not lost on the Wolverines leading up to the game.

"Yes, we're from Ohio," Franklin told a reporter, "but all the good ones go to Michigan."

When asked during his weekly press luncheon why so many Ohio natives had chosen to play their college football at Michigan, Hayes glared at the questioner and shook his head.

"Does anyone else have anything?" the coach finally said after several awkward seconds.

A handful of Ohio natives wearing maize and blue weren't the only Michigan team members with ties to the Buckeye State. Schembechler, of course, was also an Ohio native, had been on Hayes's staff in Columbus from 1958–62 and had been head coach at his alma mater Miami (Ohio) from 1963–68. Members of his staff in 1973 included Gary Moeller, who played for Hayes and was OSU team co-captain in 1962, as well as Chuck Stobart and Elliot Uzelac, who would later become assistant coaches under John Cooper at Ohio State.

"That game was right in the middle of what they call 'The Ten-Year War' between Woody and Bo," said Ohio State football historian Jack Park. "There was a lot of mutual respect between the two coaches, but no love lost when it came to playing one another.

"Just like this year, that game was huge. Both teams were undefeated, tickets were going for outrageous prices and the game was for the Rose Bowl and a chance to win the national championship. There was just so much buzz and electricity leading up to it."

OSU quarterback Cornelius Greene recalled that the week leading up to the game seemed endless.

"We had beaten Iowa pretty good the week before (55–13) and a lot of the starters didn't play much in the second half," Greene said. "That just made the wait seem longer. It was like time stood still that week. Saturday took forever to get there."

While the buzz reached a fever pitch at midweek, everyone started to don a game face in the hours leading up to the contest.

"The campus got real quiet as the game got closer," Gradishar said. "You could sense there was something different. You could feel the intensity building. Not just the players and students—the faculty, the whole city of Columbus. It was the perfect record, the polls, the conference championship and the Rose Bowl trip, and of course the whole Bo and Woody thing."

The same was true in Ann Arbor.

"I remember this one German professor," Franklin said. "She taught calculus and she couldn't stand athletes. If you were an athlete, she wouldn't even talk to you, and if you came into her class unprepared, you were going to suffer. That particular week, though, she smiled at us. That was about it, but we considered it a major victory."

DID YOU KNOW?

Ohio State and Michigan have combined to win **75 Big Ten championships** or co-championships. All of the other conference members, both past and present, have combined for only 88. The last time neither the Buckeyes nor the Wolverines won or shared the Big Ten championship was in 2001 when Illinois won the outright title.

The day after Thanksgiving, the Buckeyes made the 200-mile trip north to Ann Arbor, ate their traditional meal, watched the movie *Billy Jack* for the third time that season, and turned in for the night.

They awoke the next morning to a chilly rain mixed with occasional sleet and an atmosphere that had reached a fever pitch. By the time the team made it from the hotel to the stadium, pulses were racing and emotions were off the charts. When it came time for the teams to leave the cramped tunnel that leads from the locker rooms to the Michigan Stadium field, the tension overflowed.

As players streamed onto the field in front of an NCAA-record crowd of 105,233, several collided in a mass near midfield, and in the confusion, the blue banner that stretches across the field for Michigan players to run under went tumbling to the ground. Legendary Michigan radio announcer Bob Ufer, known for his unbridled love for anything maize or blue, went absolutely apoplectic, accusing the Ohio State players of tearing the banner down and imploring the Wolverines to "make them pay."

Hicks was always blamed for the incident, but he swears he had nothing to do with it.

"I was unjustly accused of tearing the banner down," he said. "That got torn down when we started coming out, but I wasn't the one who did it. But nobody wants to claim it, so they just blame it on me."

Once the game began, the defenses took over. Despite its powerful offense, Ohio State was forced to punt away each of its first three possessions, and even squandered away an opportunity when defensive back Neal Colzie recovered a Michigan fumble at the OSU 40-yard line.

Things began to change, however, near the end of the first quarter as the Buckeyes finally mounted a charge. With Griffin leading the way, Ohio State finally got moving. The tailback broke a 38-yard run to the Michigan 34, giving his team its best field position of the game.

But the drive bogged down, and the Buckeyes had to settle for a 31-yard field goal from kicker Blair Conway, making it 3–0 with 11:04 remaining in the second quarter.

On the ensuing kickoff, Ohio State lost freshman kicker Tom Skladany to a frightening injury. Unlike most kickers, Skladany was a good enough athlete to find a seam and sneak downfield to assist on tackles. He tried to do just that moments after the Buckeyes' first score, but on the play a Wolverine player flew into the back of his left leg, breaking it and severely dislocating his left ankle.

"The bone was almost protruding and the ankle was almost completely out of its socket," Skladany said. "It was one of those injuries that was so gruesome that I didn't feel any pain. My body just shut off. I remember (head trainer) Billy Hill and (team physician) Dr. Bob (Murphy) telling me not to look."

Just before the end of the half, Hayes walked to the bench to check on his kicker.

"He came over and asked if I could still kick off," Skladany remembered. "The doctors said, 'No, he's in pretty bad shape.' So Woody said, 'Well, at least tape him up so we can use him for punting.'"

The clip on Skladany wiped out a long return by Michigan, sent the Wolverines back to their own 12-yard line and helped set the tempo for the remainder of the first half.

The Buckeyes completely shut down Michigan while the offense was picking up steam. Ohio State played the field-position game until taking possession at its own 45 with under four minutes left until intermission. From there, the Buckeyes marched 55 yards in eight plays—mostly runs by Griffin—before freshman fullback Pete Johnson bulled his way into the end zone from 5 yards out with only 53 seconds left.

Conway added the extra point, giving Ohio State a 10–0 halftime lead and what appeared to be an insurmountable lead. But all was not well in the OSU locker room at halftime. Greene, who had entered the game with a sore thumb on his throwing hand, had tweaked the injury, and the thumb was beginning to swell.

After that, Hayes made the decision that his team would stay strictly on the ground in the second half. Unfortunately, that strategy backfired as Michigan began to stack the line of scrimmage with eight and nine defenders in the second half.

Behind the running of Shuttlesworth, the Wolverines gained the early second-half momentum and got their first scoring opportunity of the game. But Colzie created another turnover, intercepting a Franklin pass in the end zone to end the threat.

Michigan was revitalized by the resurgence of its offense, however, and got into scoring position again before the third quarter ended. Shuttlesworth pounded away time after time, and the Wolverines were able to get a 30-yard field goal from kicker Mike Lantry before the third quarter ended.

As the fourth period began, Michigan was on the move again. After a short punt by Skladany's replacement, Tom Bartozek, gave the Wolverines possession at their own 49, Franklin connected with tight end Paul Seal for a 27-yard gain. A few plays later, faced with third-and-three at the 10, Franklin faked a handoff to Shuttlesworth and rolled around right end to the end zone. Lantry tacked on the PAT to tie the game at 10–10 with 9:32 remaining.

Ohio State's last best chance to win the game came on its next possession. Taking the ball from their own 20, the Buckeyes marched to the Michigan 38. But on third-and-six, Griffin managed only three yards and Hayes elected to punt.

With the clock winding down under five minutes, the Wolverines took over at their own 11-yard line and Franklin quickly moved them out, completing passes of 15 and 14 yards to wingback Clint Haslerig, another Ohio product. On the next play, the Michigan quarterback completed a short pass to Shuttlesworth, but was thrown hard to the turf. The result was a shoulder separation, knocking Franklin out of the game.

The drive stalled quickly, but with time running out and no overtime rule in those days, Schembechler asked Lantry to try a 58-yard field goal into the swirling wind. The left-footed kicker, a 25-year-old Vietnam War veteran who had returned to school after his military service, appeared to have enough leg for the attempt, but it sailed just outside the left upright.

With 1:01 remaining, Hayes finally decided to substitute at quarterback, sending senior co-captain Greg Hare into the game in relief of Greene. But after running an ultraconservative offense through the second half, Hayes suddenly went to the air with disastrous results. Hare's first-down pass was intercepted by Michigan defensive back Tom Drake, giving the Wolverines one last chance to win the game.

This time, Lantry lined up from 44 yards away. Reminding himself the previous kick had gone slightly left, he compensated—but too much. His attempt sailed just outside the right upright.

Ohio State took over on their own 20 and used up the final 24 seconds with three unsuccessful passes from Hare.

The final stats showed big days for Griffin and Shuttlesworth. Griffin rushed for 163 of the Buckeyes' 247 total yards during the game while Shuttlesworth gained 116 yards. It was the passing yardage that separated the two teams, however. Before his injury, Franklin completed 7 of 11 attempts for 99 yards while the Buckeyes failed to gain a single yard through the air.

Buttoning up his offense and sitting on the lead was a move by Hayes that has been debated to this day. A former player, who did not want to give his name, said that was the only time he remembered the legendary coach's strategy being second-guessed.

"I don't want to disrespect Coach Hayes, but we could have won that game," the player said. "We should have won that game."

Greene later added, "Woody only called two passes when I was in, and I ended up running on both of those plays. Hare came in late and threw an interception, but they missed the field goal.

"That was real tough for me because when the game was on national TV and the season was on the line, I always felt like it was my time to shine. I never missed a game and never missed a practice, so it wasn't fun standing there."

As the teams left the field, Michigan was in a much more upbeat mood. The band started playing "California Dreamin'." Meanwhile, a jubilant Schembechler was telling reporters, "In my opinion, we're No. 1. (Ohio State) was No. 1 and we outplayed them in the second half."

Because the two teams finished the season with identical 7-0-1 records, and played to a tie in head-to-head competition, the Big Ten athletic directors would have to be called upon to break the tie and decide which team would be the league's Rose Bowl representative.

TIMELINE

» **1890**
Buckeyes play first game, a 20–14 win over Ohio Wesleyan, on May 3.

» **1892**
Ohio State completes first winning season, 5–3, under Jack Ryder. Only Dayton YMCA and Western Reserve score points.

» **1897**
Buckeyes play first game against Michigan, a 34–0 loss.

» **1899**
Ohio State completes its first un-beaten season. Of ten opponents, only one, Case, scores points.

» **February 14, 1913**
Wayne Woodrow "Woody" Hayes is born in Clifton, Ohio.

» **1913**
John W. Wilce begins a 16-year run as the Buckeye head coach.

» **1916**
Buckeyes complete first unbeaten conference season, at 4–0.

» **1919**
Ohio State scores first win over Michigan, 13–3, on October 25.

» **1919**
Charles "Chic" Harley becomes the school's first three-time All-Ameri-can.

» **1921**
Ohio State plays in its first Rose Bowl game on January 1.

» **1934**
The Francis Schmidt era begins with a 33–0 win over Indiana on October 6.

» **1942**
Ohio State wins its first national championship.

» **1944**
Les Horvath becomes the school's first Heisman Trophy winner.

» **1950**
Buckeyes win their first Rose Bowl game, 17–14 over California, on January 2.

» **1951**
The Woody Hayes era begins with a 7–0 win over Southern Methodist on September 29.

» **1954**
Ohio State wins its second na-tional championship.

» **1957**
Ohio State wins its third national championship.

» **1961**
Ohio State wins its fourth national championship.

» **1968**
Ohio State wins its fifth national championship.

» **1970**
Ohio State wins its sixth national championship.

» **1974**
Archie Griffin wins the first of his two Heisman trophies.

» **1978**
The Woody Hayes era ends.

» **1987**
Woody Hayes dies on March 12, at the age of 74.

» **2001**
The Jim Tressel era begins with a 28–14 win over Akron on Septem-ber 8.

» **2002**
Buckeyes win school's seventh national championship with a classic, 31–24 win over previously No. 1 Miami, on January 3.

» **2006**
Troy Smith wins the school's seventh Heisman Trophy.

RUNNING BACK CHRIS WELLS breaks away for a
59-yard thouchdown in the first quarter vs. the Michigan Wolverines on November 22, 2008. Ohio State beat Michigan 42–7.
Newscom

A meeting was called for the following day in Chicago to poll the ADs, and as the stadium emptied, Schembechler figured his team had done everything it could to sway the vote.

"We did everything we could to win, including gambling in our territory and going for the victory," he said. "If they vote us to go, then we deserve it. Frankly, I'll be disappointed if the vote goes the other way."

Less than 24 hours later, the word "disappointed" would not come close to describing Schembechler's mood.

By the time all ten conference athletic directors arrived in Chicago, the assumption was that Michigan would win the vote. Although the Big Ten had done away with its self-imposed rule not to allow teams to go to successive Rose Bowls, the prevailing thought remained that because Ohio State had been to Pasadena the previous year, it was the Wolverines' "turn."

Also in Michigan's favor was the fact that four of the conference's athletic directors—William Orwig of Indiana, Chalmers "Bump" Elliott of Iowa, Burt Smith of Michigan State and Elroy "Crazy Legs" Hirsch of Wisconsin—were all either former Michigan athletes or coaches.

With Michigan athletic director Don Canham obviously voting for his school, conventional wisdom gave the Wolverines at least five votes. In case of a tie between the ADs, the team that had been to Pasadena more recently would be eliminated, giving Michigan the Rose Bowl trip.

Hayes had spent a difficult morning back in Columbus. He woke up to the news that OSU's head athletic trainer Alan Hart had died at the age of 37 after a bout with cancer. Later, he visited Skladany in the hospital before going to his St. John Arena office.

About 1:30 p.m., the telephone rang in Hayes's office. He answered, mumbled a couple of words and then hung up. The coach picked up the phone again, dialed his wife and hummed the first few bars of "California, Here We Come."

The conference athletic directors had voted 6–4 to send the Buckeyes back to Pasadena.

"I was shocked," Hare admitted. "I didn't think we'd go, but it would have been terrible to watch Michigan go out there and play Southern Cal."

Meanwhile, Schembechler was fit to be tied.

"I'm very bitter," he told reporters. "It's a tragic thing for Big Ten football. This is the darkest day in my athletic career."

The Michigan coach's outlook did not improve any when he discovered the outcome of which athletic directors voted for Ohio State. They included Hirsch and Smith, both of whom indicated they leaned toward the Buckeyes because Franklin's injury would likely have sidelined him for the Rose Bowl.

"I did what I felt was best for the conference," Smith said later. "Naturally, Franklin's injury would have something to do with the decision. That's only natural. I agree with the decision because it's a conference decision."

That did not sit well with Schembechler.

He stated that if Clarence "Biggie" Munn was still athletic director at Michigan State and Hugh "Duffy" Daugherty was still head coach of the Spartans, MSU would have voted for the Wolverines "because they're class guys and would have done what's right."

Park is not so sure.

"I have always had a theory about that vote," the OSU football historian said. "I can't prove this, of course, but from following the story and from interviews I have done over the years, I think that vote might have been a little payback from Michigan State.

"When Michigan State joined the Big Ten in 1953, Ohio State supported their membership, but Michigan wanted the University of Pittsburgh. It wasn't that Michigan loved Pitt, but I think they just didn't want another Michigan team in the conference because of recruiting and revenue and things of that nature.

"I certainly don't have any evidence of that, but when you look at who voted for who, what happened in 1953 when Michigan State wanted to join the Big Ten may have impacted that vote."

There is another theory, first floated in the 1974 book *Buckeye: A Study of Coach Woody Hayes and the Ohio State Football Machine*. Author Robert Vare surmised that many of the Big Ten's athletic directors were known to resent Canham, a self-made millionaire whose business savvy and talent for selling and promotion were the talk of the college football world.

DID YOU KNOW?

The top six coaches in all-time winning percentage for Big Ten games (with at least 10 years of service in the league) are all from Ohio State or Michigan. **Woody Hayes** and **John Cooper** of the Buckeyes are joined at the top of the list by former Michigan coaches Bo Schembechler, Fielding Yost, Lloyd Carr and Fritz Crisler.

"In five years, Canham has transformed Michigan's floundering sports programs into one of the nation's money-making showcases, and he was being widely hailed as the prototype of the new breed athletic director," Vare wrote. "Next to Canham, most of the directors looked like candy store operators and they knew it.

"Besides being envious, several directors were said to be nursing grudges against Canham. A man with a habit of stepping on toes and speaking plainly, Canham had more than once publicly referred to his Big ten counterparts as a 'bunch of donkeys.' One of them, Northwestern's Tippy Dye, has something more specific to be mad about.

"Several years earlier, Northwestern had been on the verge of closing a deal to rent its stadium to the Chicago Bears. Canham, thinking that it would set a dangerous business precedent, had led the drive to quash the play, cost the Big Ten's only private school much-needed revenue. It certainly seemed hard to believe that Dye's vote was not influenced by a desire to get even."

Vare added that it didn't seem likely that someone like Smith would have voted for Ohio State just because he believed it was the stronger team, believing it only natural that the Michigan State athletic director would want to deny his sister school the recruiting clout a Rose Bowl appearance would bring.

Furthering the "conspiracy theory" was the fact that although many of the ADs brought up Franklin's injury as a reason for their vote, none of them contacted the Michigan team doctors to ask about the quarterback's prognosis for playing in the Rose Bowl. In addition, eight of the ten men had not seen the OSU–Michigan game.

"The Rose Bowl is supposed to be a reward, and an educational experience, and our kids earned it," Schembechler fumed. "But the directors and (Big Ten commissioner Wayne) Duke were running scared. After losing four straight Rose Bowls, they needed a winner to help their prestige.

"Well, the Big Ten has lost any prestige it ever had. I'm disillusioned with the administration of college football. This is why kids are losing respect for America. You wonder why kids go wrong? I wouldn't trust the older generation either. They're just out for themselves."

Those comments incensed the Big Ten athletic directors, although none would say so publicly. Even so, that did not prevent them from expressing their opinions. Former Ohio State athletic director Jim Jones, who was an assistant AD under J. Edward Weaver in 1973, remembered a phone call Weaver took after the Buckeyes had rolled to a 42–21 victory over USC in the Rose Bowl.

"It was Hirsch," Jones said. "He had been vacationing in Hawaii and had been, shall we say, celebrating a bit. His first words were, 'Well, I guess we showed 'em that the ADs do know a little something about football after all.'"

CLASH OF THE TITANS—NO. 1 VS. NO. 2

Troy Smith flashed a brilliant smile and said he probably would be wearing it for quite some time.

Doug Datish, who had been playing football almost as long as he could walk, said it was the most fun he had ever had on the football field. David Patterson called it the happiest moment of his life.

Top-ranked Ohio State had just claimed a heart-thumping 42–39 victory over No. 2 Michigan, a win that finished off a perfect 2006 regular season for the Buckeyes and propelled them into the Bowl Championship Series national title game.

But while Buckeye upperclassmen basked in the afterglow of the victory at Ohio Stadium, no one's happiness seemed more ebullient than a beaming Kirk Barton, who showed up to the postgame press conference sporting a victory cigar.

"Red Auerbach, baby," the junior offensive tackle shouted in reference to the late Boston Celtics head coach who was legendary for lighting a stogie as soon as his team had clinched a championship.

"This is about as good as it gets," Barton said as he sat in a chair, puffing away. "T.J. Downing is one of my best friends in the whole world, and we just got through drinking a bottle of Dom Pérignon in the locker room. It was 350 bucks, and that took about all of the money I had to my name, but it was worth it. This is as good as it could be."

As the blue smoke from the cigar circled Barton's head, he sat back with a contented look on his face, almost as if he were remembering the big plays during the Buckeyes' victory.

There were plenty of them to remember, from long touchdown romps by Chris Wells and Antonio Pittman to four touchdown passes from Smith, the last of which came at the 5:38 mark of the fourth quarter and provided what were the eventual winning points.

"This was a great game, a great game to be a part of," Barton said. "You have to give credit to Michigan for the way they played because we felt like we had to score a touchdown on every drive. Michigan is a great team, but I felt like the better team won today. I really do. We took their best shot and kept coming right back at them."

The Wolverines scored a touchdown on the game's first possession, blowing right through the OSU defense for 80 yards in just under 2 1/2 minutes. But the Buckeyes roared back to match that score then tacked on two more touchdowns to take a 21–7 lead.

The rest of the game resembled a heavyweight boxing match with two old rivals pummeling one another, looking for the knockout blow, as Ohio State withstood Michigan's late assault to preserve the three-point win.

"I don't know where to start," OSU head coach Jim Tressel said at his postgame press conference, where he was joined by the team's captains. "Michigan is a great football team. Everyone saw that. They weren't going to give up because that's the way they're built, and I can't say enough about them. But these guys up front right here—Troy Smith and Quinn Pitcock and David Patterson and Doug Datish—they're extraordinary at what they do. It's really amazing."

The Wolverines entered the game with the nation's No. 3 unit in total defense but were gashed for 503 yards by the power-laden Ohio State attack. Minnesota had the previous highest total yardage figure against Michigan this season, gaining 323 yards in a 28–14 losing effort. The Buckeyes had already piled up 320 by halftime.

"Everyone talked all week about their defense," OSU offensive lineman Steve Rehring said. "That's all we heard—how good their defensive line was and how we were going to have a tough time moving the ball against them. And I will say this: They are good. They're very good.

"But I like to say that we go against one of the best defensive lines in college football every day in practice. Once you go up against guys like Dave Patterson,

Quinn, Vern Gholston and Jay Richardson, you've already seen the best. So if you're asking if I'm surprised we got that many yards, the answer is no. Not really."

Barton chipped in, "We knew they had a good defense, but we also knew they hadn't gone against a team that blocked like us."

In addition to being stingy in total yardage, the Wolverines had all but outlawed the run by their opponents this season. Michigan entered the game as the nation's top-rated defense against the rush, giving up an average of only 29.9 yards per game.

That average was shattered by the Buckeyes, who jumped on Michigan for 187 yards on the ground and an average of 6.4 yards on 29 carries. Pittman carried most of the load, totaling 139 yards and a touchdown on 18 carries, while Wells added 56 yards on just five totes.

But while Ohio State was softening up the Wolverines with the run, it was Smith who was the catalyst for the offense. He completed 29 of 41 passes—both career highs—and threw for 316 yards and four touchdowns.

"What a pleasure it is to block for a guy like Troy," Barton said. "I don't know if I can describe it—he just makes everybody else look good. I hope he wins the Heisman because I think he truly deserves it."

While the Buckeyes were charging out to their 28–14 halftime lead, it was Smith leading the charge, carving up the Michigan defense like a Thanksgiving turkey. By the time the teams headed to the locker rooms for halftime, the Ohio State quarterback had already completed 21 of 26 passes for 241 yards and three touchdowns.

He experienced some problems in the second half, having a deflected pass wind up as his fifth interception of the year and mishandling a couple of errant shotgun snaps from Datish—both of which the center later blamed on himself—that wound up as fumble recoveries for Michigan.

But when his team needed him most, it was Smith who moved the Buckeyes 83 yards in eleven plays to turn what was becoming a game that was too close for comfort back into an 11-point lead with 5 1/2 minutes to play.

"We made some mistakes there in the second half and let them back in it," the OSU quarterback said. "But the important thing was that we didn't quit on each other. We don't do that. After they scored there to make it 35–31 or whatever it was, we knew we needed to go right back down the field and score a touchdown.

"When they scored, the best thing we could do was answer with a score of our own. That's what we did at the beginning of the game and that's what we did there in the fourth quarter. You have to give Michigan credit because they kept coming back. But so did we."

Each of Smith's touchdown throws was to a different receiver as eight Buckeyes caught at least one of his passes. Junior receiver Ted Ginn Jr. had a game-high eight receptions for 104 yards and a score while sophomore Brian Robiskie chipped in with seven catches for 89 yards and a touchdown.

The other two touchdown receptions went to junior flanker Anthony Gonzalez, who added four catches for 50 yards, and senior Roy Hall, who stepped up with three receptions for 38 yards.

"We've got some guys who can catch the ball," Hall said. "I was just thankful I could get in there and help out."

On the other side of the field, the Wolverines were doing their best to keep up with the Buckeyes. Junior tailback Mike Hart rushed for 142 yards and three touchdowns, while quarterback Chad Henne connected on 21 of 35 passes for 267 yards and a pair of scores.

But after their initial score to go ahead 7–0, the Wolverines were constantly playing from behind.

"It's definitely hard to swallow, but you know, it's never fun losing to Ohio State," Henne said. "It's a great rivalry and great tradition goes with it. But we fought, and Ohio State—they just made a lot more bigger plays."

The Ohio Stadium-record crowd of 105,708 was getting settled for an expected low-scoring affair when Michigan exploded out of the blocks. On the second play from scrimmage, Henne connected with split end Mario Manningham on a simple slant pattern that picked up 24 yards.

Three plays later, the same combination on the same route clicked for another 25 yards to push to the Ohio State 1-yard line. Hart finished things off with a quick burst around right end, and when kicker Garrett Rivas added the extra point, the Wolverines had a 7–0 lead with only two minutes, 28 seconds gone from the game.

OHIO STATE RUNNING BACK Antonio Pittman carries the ball on a 56-yard touchdown run during the third quarter against Michigan on November 18, 2006. Ohio State won 42–39.

Newscom/UPI Photo/Brian Kersey

"They kind of came out and hit us right in the mouth," OSU linebacker James Laurinaitis said. "We made a couple of adjustments after that, but I guess you could say they got our attention early."

The seven-play, 80-yard drive sent murmurs through the stadium, but those quickly turned to cheers as Smith rallied the Buckeyes on their initial possession.

Ohio State's first eight offensive calls were passing plays, the last of which was a 27-yard completion down the middle to Hall on a third-and-16 that pushed the ball to the Michigan 24. Three plays later, on third-and-five, Smith connected with Hall again, this time for 10 yards and another first down.

Fittingly, the capper of the drive was a 1-yard toss from Smith to Hall in the corner of the end zone. Aaron Pettrey came on to add the PAT, tying the game at 7 with 6:08 remaining in the first quarter.

The teams traded punts on their ensuing possessions. Then when Michigan failed to move the ball again as the second quarter began, the Buckeyes took advantage of a short punt and took over at their own 42-yard line.

Smith scrambled for a 6-yard gain on the first play of the drive before he handed off to Wells on the next play. The OSU freshman broke through the line of scrimmage and outraced everyone to the end zone for a 52-yard touchdown romp. Pettrey added the extra point, giving the Buckeyes a 14–7 lead at the 12:29 mark of the second quarter.

And they were just getting warmed up.

Following another Michigan punt, Ohio State went back to work, this time striking with alarming speed. Smith completed a sideline pass to Robiskie, who got loose from Michigan cornerback Leon Hall and turned the play into a spectacular 39-yard gain.

Two plays later, Smith carried out a beautiful fake handoff and found Ginn, who had gotten past Hall on a post route, for a 39-yard touchdown. Pettrey's PAT made it 21–7 and finished off the 91-yard drive that encompassed only four plays and one minute, 44 seconds.

To their credit, the Wolverines did not fold. With the clock winding under six minutes to play in the half, Henne engineered a six-play, 80-yard march that included a 30-yard burst by Hart on a well-designed draw play and a 37-yard touchdown pass to Adrian Arrington along the OSU sideline.

Rivas added the extra point, getting Michigan back within seven at 21–14 with 2:33 left until halftime. But the way Smith was playing, that was too much time to leave on the clock.

The Ohio State quarterback immediately went back to the air, and in rapid succession he connected with Gonzalez for 12 yards, Ginn for seven and Robiskie for 17. That took the ball back into Michigan territory, and after an incompletion, Smith hit Gonzalez for 14 more, tight end Rory Nicol for two and Gonzalez again for 16.

With the ball at the Michigan 12-yard line and only 40 seconds remaining, Smith went back to Robiskie for a 4-yarder along the sideline before finding Gonzalez in the end zone for an 8-yard touchdown. Smith completed 8 of 9 passes during the march for 80 yards, and once Pettrey booted the extra point, the Buckeyes had what looked to be a comfortable 28–14 lead at the half.

As precise as the Ohio State offense was in the first half, it seemed to develop a distinctive sputter in the third quarter.

The Buckeyes had the ball to open the second half, but Michigan's defense forced a quick three-and-out. Meanwhile, the Michigan offense was gathering steam. Behind Hart, it moved 60 yards in less than two minutes to pull back within seven points at 28–21. Hart rushed four times for 59 of those yards, including the 2-yard touchdown.

Then the Wolverines got the ball right back when Smith was picked off by defensive tackle Alan Branch, who snagged the pass out of the air after it bounced off a Buckeye and a Wolverine defender.

The turnover gave Michigan the ball at the Ohio State 25-yard line, but the Buckeyes' defense rose to the occasion, forcing the Wolverines to settle for a 39-yard field goal from Rivas. Still, that tightened things to 28–24 in favor of OSU with 8:41 remaining in the third quarter.

This time, it was the Buckeyes' turn to respond. The Wolverines were called for a personal foul penalty on the ensuing kickoff, giving Ohio State possession at their 35-yard line instead of the 20. After a 9-yard hookup between Smith and

Ginn, Pittman broke through the left side of the Michigan line and outran safety Jamar Adams to the end zone for a 56-yard lightning bolt.

Pettrey added the PAT and re-established Ohio State's 11-point lead at 35–24 with 8:04 left in the third period.

Disaster struck the Buckeyes again at the end of the quarter, though, as Smith fumbled Datish's snap and Branch recovered the fumble at the OSU 9-yard line. Three plays later, Hart was in the end zone again off a 1-yard burst over right tackle, and the Wolverines were back within four points at the 14:41 mark of the fourth quarter.

Ohio State could not seem to get out of its own way, quickly moving back into Michigan territory but turning the ball over again on another bad exchange between Smith and Datish. This time, however, the Wolverines could not convert their opportunity and were forced to punt the ball away.

Undaunted, Smith went back to work and piloted an 83-yard drive that took 11 plays and, more importantly, shaved five important minutes off the clock.

"That was an important drive for us," the OSU quarterback said. "We'd been beating ourselves in the second half, and we knew we had to have a score right there. We knew that a touchdown in that situation would maybe help us put them away."

The march featured the Buckeyes' best blend of running and passing but was in danger of stalling on a third-and-15 at the Michigan 38 when Smith couldn't find Robiskie over the middle. But Wolverines linebacker Shawn Crable was called for a helmet-to-helmet hit on Smith as he released the ball near the sideline, and the penalty gave Ohio State a first down and new life.

Three plays later, Smith went back to Robiskie and this time the two connected with the sophomore running a stop pattern to leave Michigan cornerback Morgan Trent slipping on the turf while Robiskie got a toe inbounds for a 13-yard touchdown.

Pettrey added the PAT, giving the Buckeyes what appeared to be a comfortable 42–31 advantage with just 5:38 remaining in the game.

But Michigan had one last comeback up its sleeve. Henne moved his team 81 yards in just over three minutes, completing a 16-yard touchdown pass to tight

POSTGAME Michigan 2002.

end Tyler Ecker for the touchdown. His two-point conversion pass to Steve Breaston was also good, and the Wolverines had pulled to within a field goal at 42–39 with 2:16 left.

However, with just one timeout remaining and college football's new clock rules, Michigan head coach Lloyd Carr had no choice but to go for the onside kick. Ginn smothered the ball near midfield, and three Pittman runs were enough to finish things off as the crowd swarmed the field.

Defensively, the Buckeyes were led by Laurinaitis as the sophomore linebacker recorded nine tackles. Senior defensive back Antonio Smith was next with eight stops, including one of the four sacks on Henne. The others were credited to sophomore defensive end Lawrence Wilson, senior defensive tackle Joel Penton and Richardson.

Meanwhile, Smith became only the second Ohio State quarterback to beat Michigan three times. The other was William H. H. "Tippy" Dye, who played for the Buckeyes under head coach Francis A. Schmidt from 1934–36 and was in attendance at the game. The 94-year-old Dye later was head basketball coach at Ohio State from 1947–50 and athletic director at Northwestern.

Less than a month later, Smith was smiling again, this time holding the 2006 Heisman Trophy in downtown New York City.

  *Buckeye*

QUIZ

1. What are Ohio State's official colors?

2. What was Woody Hayes's favorite subject, besides football?

3. Who succeeded the iconic Hayes in 1979?

4. Who are the Buckeyes' two traditional rivals?

5. What was standout defensive back Jack Tatum's nickname?

6. What was the location of the first Ohio State games?

7. How many Buckeye players are in the College Football Hall of Fame?

8. Who cleared the way for tailback Archie Griffin, from the fullback position?

9. Legendary coach Paul Brown came to Ohio State from what high school?

10. What two incentives did Coach Carroll Widdoes offer Les Horvath in 1944?

11. Who became Ohio State's first African-American All-American?

12. Who did Woody Hayes consider to be his greatest offensive lineman?

13. Ohio State has retired the jersey numbers of seven players. Who are they?

14. Which former Buckeye head coach is in the Pro Football Hall of Fame?

15. Who was the program's first Lombardi Award winner?

16. What is the seating capacity of Ohio Stadium?

17. What exactly is…a buckeye?

18. In what year did the Ohio State—Michigan rivalry game become the season-ending game?

19. In 1926, Maudine Ormsby was named homecoming queen. Why is this significant?

20. Who chose the school's official colors in 1878?

21. When was Ohio Stadium built?

22. A recent walk-on became an All-American. Who is he?

23. Who owns the record for most 100-yard rushing games in a season?

24. What was Tom Skladany's punting average in 1975?

25. Which Ohio State player won two Super Bowl rings with the San Francisco 49ers?

26. How many passes did Cris Carter catch as a Buckeye?

27. Where did Earle Bruce play in college?

28. Who holds the single-game rushing record for Ohio State?

29. Which receiver holds the single-game record for most catches?

30. How many field goals did All-American Mike Nugent kick in his career?

31. Which two players hold the single-game record for most pass completions (31)?

32. Who was Ohio State's first head coach?

33. Who was the school's first Biletnikoff Award winner?

34. Who kicked a field goal in the famous 1950 "Snow Bowl" against Michigan?

35. Who holds the all-time record for average all-purpose yards per game?

36. Two players hold the single-game record for tackles, with an astounding 29. Who are they?

37. Which player has the most tackles for loss in his career?

38. Who has the most career interceptions?

39. What is the longest play from scrimmage in school history?

40. Which Buckeye team holds the season record for points scored with 475?

41. How many Buckeye passes did Chicago intercept in 1938?

42. Along with Ohio State, how many teams have won 800+ games?

43. How many All-Americans has Ohio State had?

44. How many undefeated seasons has Ohio State had?

45. When did Ohio State join the Big Ten Conference?

46. What was the school's first conference title?

47. Which high school did Chic Harley attend?

48. Who was the school's first rival?

49. What was Woody Hayes's last game?

50. What pre-game tradition do students take part in before the Michigan game?

ANSWERS

1. Scarlet and Gray
2. History
3. Earle Bruce (from Iowa State)
4. Michigan and Illinois
5. "Assassin"
6. Recreation Park, Columbus (1890–97)
7. 21
8. Pete Johnson
9. Massillon
10. Extra time to study for dental school, and flying him to games.
11. Bill Willis, 1943–44
12. Jim Parker, Outland Trophy winner, 1956
13. Charles "Chic" Harley (47); Les Horvath (22); Howard Cassady (40); Vic Janowicz (31); Bill Willis (99); Archie Griffin (45); Eddie George (27).
14. Paul Brown
15. Jim Stillwagon, 1970
16. 102,329
17. A small, brown nut found on the state tree.
18. 1935
19. Maudine was a cow.
20. Three students
21. 1922
22. Andy Groom, punter, 2002
23. Eddie George (12), 1995
24. An astounding 46.7
25. Dr. John Frank
26. 168
27. Ohio State, until a knee injury ended his career
28. Eddie George (314) versus Illinois, 1995
29. David Boston (14) versus Penn State, 1997
30. 72
31. Joe Germaine and Art Schlichter
32. Alexander S. Lilley
33. Terry Glenn, 1995
34. Vic Janowicz
35. Archie Griffin (145.8)
36. Chris Spielman (Michigan, 1986) and Tom Cousineau (Penn State, 1978)
37. Mike Vrabel (66 from 1993–96)
38. Mike Sensibaugh (22; 1968–70)
39. 89-yard run by Gene Fekete, versus Pitt in 1942
40. 1995
41. 8
42. Six—Michigan, Yale, Notre Dame, Nebraska, and Penn State are the others
43. 180
44. 9—1890s, 1916, 1917, 1944, 1954, 1961, 1968, 1973, and 2002
45. In the titanic year of 1912
46. The Ohio Athletic Conference of 1906
47. East High, Columbus
48. Kenyon College (Ohio State holds a 17–6 all-time record in this series)
49. The 1978 Gator Bowl
50. A leap into Mirror Lake

Acknowledgments

J ournalist, editor, and literary critic Burton Rascoe once wrote, "What no wife of a writer can ever understand is that a writer is working when he's staring out the window."

Not true in my case. My wife Lisa understands when I stare out the window. For that and countless other reasons she has my everlasting gratitude. She is my rock, my companion, my confidant, and the best friend I have ever had. We dated in high school and then went our separate ways for nearly fifteen years. By the time we got back together, I had nothing. Today, I have everything.

Many thanks are due Jim Fletcher, who created *The Die-Hard Fan's Guide* concept and brought me the opportunity to write the Ohio State version. Anyone who knows me knows I have been trying to get a book published for many years. Jim has allowed that dream to be realized, and I thank him very much.

I would also like to convey a debt of gratitude to Frank Moskowitz, publisher of *Buckeye Sports Bulletin* and BuckeyeSports.com. It was Frank who more than twenty years ago gave me my first chance to cover the Buckeyes on a daily basis. He shares with me a love and passion for the history and tradition of Ohio State football, and I am grateful for his tutelage and friendship over the years.

A huge thank you to everyone at the Ohio State Sports Information Department, past and present, most especially Shelly Poe and her staff, and to D.C. Koehl for his invaluable help over the years whenever I have sought historical information. Many thanks also to Michelle Drobak at OSU Photo Archives for being extremely helpful with this project.

It may sound cliché, but it has been an honor and a privilege to work with the experienced professionals at Regnery Publishing, most specifically editor Christian Tappe. Since I am a writer and editor by trade, it is sometimes difficult to allow another to put the editor's pencil to my work. Christian quickly put my mind at ease, and I appreciate his efforts as well as his fine work.

Also, thanks to Eagle Publishing art director Amanda Larsen and Amber Colleran for their help and friendly advice.

I would like to pay tribute to Sonny Brockway, who graciously allowed use of many of the action photos in this book. For the better part of the last 60 years, Sonny and his late father, Chance Sr., have been the photographers of record for Ohio State football. It has been my honor to know them and consider them friends.

Many of the fan photos are courtesy of Susan Zeier and her family—true die-hards and even better people who have become my good friends over the past few years.

It has been my pleasure to talk with countless Buckeye players and coaches over the years. Thanks to the many that provided insightful commentary and/or colorful background information for these pages as well as the hundreds more with whom I have come in contact. You guys *are* Ohio State football, and for that we are all grateful.

To Jess, my one and only—you have been an exceptional gift in my life. I can't say enough how much I admire you and how proud I am of your accomplishments.

Finally, I would like to pay tribute to my late parents for what they meant to me—what they still mean to me. Most would say that my overall character comes from my father and they would be correct. My creativity and storytelling, however—those were my mother. I like to think I got the best of both of their personalities, and for that I feel truly blessed.

My only regret about this project is that it was not able to be completed during their lifetimes. Still, I'm fairly certain they know about it and are somewhere nodding with approval. I only hope they are one-tenth as proud of me as I am to have been their son.

Index

A

"Across the Field," x, xv, 102, 221

All-Big Ten, 83, 127, 144, 150, 156, 175–77, 184, 194, 197–98, 204–5

Allen, Will, 122

Alpha Phi Omega, 109

Ameche, Alan, 134

American Football Coaches Association, 45–46, 150, 160

American Institute of Architects, 98

American Professional Football Association, 39

American Shipbuilding, 136

Ames, Knowlton Lymon "Snake," 5, 8

Andria, Ernie, 83

Ann Arbor, 27, 33, 38, 42, 72, 77, 95, 150, 165, 168, 188, 216, 219, 222

Antenucci, Frank, 114

Ariri, Obed, 84

Army, 20, 61, 128, 130

Atha, Bob, 84

Athletic Board, 51, 70, 96

Atlantic Coast Conference (ACC), 84

Auburn Training, 32, 38

Austin, Cliff, 84

B

Badgers, 38, 41, 116, 134, 212

Baldwin Wallace, 63

Baritone Cheers, 102

Bartholomew, Clyde, 66

baseball, 2, 18, 26, 34, 58, 66, 133–34, 171, 174, 176–77, 179, 182, 188

basketball, 18, 22, 26, 34, 37, 51, 58, 66, 72, 102–3, 170–72, 175–77, 179–81, 221

Battling Bishops, 7
Baugh, Sammy, 36
Bauman, Charlie, 82, 87
Bearcats, 50
Bedenk, Joe, 61
Bednarik, Chuck, 131
Bellisari, Greg, 121
Bellows, George, 26
Benton, Wayne, 65, 79
Berwanger, Jay, 75
Bevis, Howard L., 70, 259
Big Red, 66–67
"Big Six," the, 3, 168
Big Ten, 83, 111, 115–17, 133–34, 138–39, 144–45, 147,
    150–52, 154, 156–57, 169, 172, 179–82, 184, 188, 193,
    199, 201, 204–6, 223, 232, 235–36, 238, 241, 246–48,
    259, 264–65, 268, 271, 274–77
Bixler, Paul O., 58, 72
Blackwell Hotel, 102
Blanchard, Felix "Doc," 130–31
"Block O," 8, 106–8
Bloomington, 32, 144
Board of Trustees (OSU), 69–70, 98
Bobcats, 58, 122
Bolen, Charles "Shifty," 30, 32–33, 169
Boston Celtics, 277
Boston College, 139, 148
Boston, David, 202, 246–47,
Boucher, Frank, 114
Bradford, Joseph, 98
Brickels, Johnny, 67
Bricker, John W., 70
Brown, Dave, 266
Brown, Jim, 148
Brown, Leo, 148
Brown, Paul, xi, 56–58, 61, 67, 69–70, 75, 111, 128, 142,
    181
Broyles, Frank, 76

Bruce, Earle, xiv, 60–61, 82, 91, 240–41, 263
Brungart, John, 115
Brutus Buckeye, 102–4
Buckeye Battle Cry," 105, 210, 221
Buckeye Grove, 19, 24, 109, 111–12
Buckeye Hall of Fame Café, 36
Byars, Keith, 118–20, 157, 194, 198–99

C
Camp Randall Stadium, 32, 214
Camp Sheridan, 32
Camp Sherman, 32
Camp, Walter, 18, 29, 33, 43, 142, 167, 174
Canadian Football League, 148, 184
Canton Bulldogs, 53
captains' breakfasts, 39
Cardiff Road, 91
"Carmen Ohio," xiv, 109–10
Carnegie Tech, 114
Carpenter, Bobby, 126
Carter, Anthony, 232, 240
Carter, Cris, 118, 194, 196–97, 202
Case School of Applied Science, 13, 161, 168
Cassady, Howard "Hopalong," 34, 115, 134–36, 182, 232,
    235
Cato, Byron, 87
"Champions of Ohio," 16
Charles, Bert, xiv
Charles, Jamaal, 125
Cherry, Boyd, 17, 19, 29, 169–70
Chicago Bears, the, 39, 175, 276
Chicago Cardinals, 77
Chicago Staleys, 39
Chicago Sun Times, 216
Chicago Tribune, 18
Chicago White Sox, 34
"Chris" (German police dog), 103
Churchill, Winston, 92

Cincinnati Bengals, 138, 181

Cisco, Galen, 148

City League, 26

Clemson, 82, 84, 86–87, 89

Cleveland Browns, 56, 58, 69, 130, 134, 148, 179, 187

Cleveland Bulldogs, the, 52–53, 175

Cline, Ollie, 136, 180, 233

Cole, George N., 4–5, 9, 49

Colgate, 58

College Football Hall of Fame, 30, 36, 39, 44–45, 52, 75, 79, 92, 127, 131, 133, 136, 138, 148, 150, 172, 176–77, 180, 183, 186–87, 194

College of Wooster, 6, 50, 122, 165, 265

Collier's Weekly, 18

Colorado College, 18

Colosseum, 98

Columbus Chamber of Commerce, 96

Columbus Dispatch, The, 11, 21, 89, 151

Columbus Downtown Quarterback Club, 133

Coolidge, Charles, 21

Cooper, John, 61, 63, 202, 226, 243, 246–47, 267, 275

Cornell, 51

Cornell, Fred, 109, 165

Courtney, Harold, 30

Courtney, Howard "Hap," 30, 33, 169

Crisler, Herbert O. "Fritz," 151, 259, 275

Csuri, Chuck, 145, 180

D

Davey O'Brien Award, 142

Davis, Anthony, 138

Davis, Glenn, 130

Davis, Harry L., 99

Decatur Staleys, the, 34

Delaware Run, 8

Denison University, 6, 9, 21, 32, 50, 66–68, 81

Deshler Wallick Hotel, 114

Detroit Lions, the, 136, 148, 194

Devine, Dan, 76

"Dirty Thirty," 61

Doss, Mike, 115, 157, 205, 214

Drake University, 89, 114

Drake, Tom, 270

E

East High School, 26, 42

East–West Shrine Game, 77

Eckersall, Walter, 18

Eckstorm, John B., 11, 17, 51, 167

Edwards, David F., 50

Elliott, Chalmers "Bump," 150–51, 274

Enarson, Harold, 90–91

Engel, Rip, 61

Evashevski, Forest, 117

"Everybody Loves Raymond," 41

F

"Fanfare for a New Era," 102

Faurot Field, 76

Faurot, Don, 68, 73, 75–76

Fekete, Gene, 144–45

Fesler, Wes, xiv, 47, 58, 61, 68–75, 113, 115, 172, 173, 184, 259–64

Fickell, Luke, 121, 214, 216, 243

Fiesta Bowl, 68, 107, 141, 157, 158, 248

Fighting Irish, the (football), 46, 106

Fighting Muskies, 15

Florida Times-Union, the, 82

flying wedge, 9, 51

football eleven, the, 16

Football Writers Association of America, 150, 152, 187, 236

Fort Knox Armoraiders, the, 144

Foulk, Charles, 9–10

"Four Horsemen," 56

Frazier, Tommie, 139

French Fieldhouse, x
French, Edward, 162–63
French, Thomas E., 96–99
Fritz, Ken, 87
Fuller, Steve, 84, 86

G
Gaer, Warren, 69
"Game of the Century," 77, 114, 121
Gator Bowl, 82–83, 85, 89, 92
Gayman, Charles, 16
Geiger, Andy, 105
Gerald, Rod, 83–84
Gibbs, Alex, 86
Gillman, Sid, 47, 69, 176
Ginn, Dwight, 21
Gipp, George, 36
Glenn, Terry, 121, 202
Godfrey, Ernie, 70, 236
Gold Pants Club, the, 56, 254–55
Gold Pants, xiv, 177, 259
Gonzalez, Anthony, 124–25, 280, 283
Gordon, Sonny, 119
Graf, Campbell "Honus," 21, 171
Graham, Otto, 134
Grange, Red, 23, 25, 36, 144
Graves, Perry, 21
"Graveyard of Coaches, The," 68, 145
Great Depression, the, 66
Great Lakes Naval Base, 130
Grey Cup, 148
Griffin, Archie, xi, 23, 36, 111, 115, 136–38, 162, 180, 190,
    192–93, 199, 209, 232, 234, 238, 240, 265, 268–71
Griffin, Cedric, 125
Gross, Anne, 67

H
Hager, Bob, 13
Hale, Perry, 51

Hamby, Ryan, 123
Hardy, Paul, 13, 16, 162–64
Harley, Charles "Chic," 17–22, 23–39, 42–43, 53, 72,
    95–96, 99, 111, 115, 131, 164, 168–69, 171, 172, 231,
    250–54, 265
Harley Stadium, 36
Harlor, John, 26
Harmon, Ronnie, 119
Harmon, Tom, 23, 25, 75, 131, 231
Harvard Stadium, 98
Harvard, 2, 21, 45, 58, 72
Hawk, A. J., 122, 125, 126, 202, 204
Hawk, James, 15
Hayes, Effie Jane, 65, 79
Hayes, Isaac (Ike), 65, 79
Hayes, Mary, 65, 79
Hayes, Woody, xi, xiv, 8, 36, 41, 43, 61, 63, 65–93, 97, 102,
    106, 111, 117, 131, 134, 145, 147, 150–54, 156, 176,
    183–84, 186, 188, 190, 193, 210, 232, 236–37, 240, 264,
    266–71, 274–75
Heisman Trophy, xi, 7, 36, 75, 115–16, 118, 121, 124,
    127–60, 161, 179–80, 182, 187, 190, 192–93, 199, 204,
    224, 233, 235–36, 238, 279, 286
Heisman, John, 75
Herrnstein, A. E., 52
Hickey, Charles A., 50
Hill, George, 87, 89
Hillenbrand, Billy, 144
Hinchman, Lewis, 115, 176, 178
Hindman, Hugh, 82, 89–91
Hlay, John, 116
HMS Pinafore, 16
Holcomb, Stuart, 113
Holmes, Santonio, 125, 206–7
Holtz, Lou, 91, 121
Homan, Marv, xiv, 25, 37, 210, 261–65
Hooey, Bob, 25
Hope, Bob, 88, 106
Horn Cheers, 102

Hornung, Paul, 89–90

Horseshoe, the, ix, xiv, 6, 95–101, 111, 118, 123, 175, 210, 212, 217, 221–22, 224, 226, 233, 259

Horvath, Leslie, xi, 7, 111, 128–31, 144, 179, 180, 233–34

Howard, Frank, 84

Huston, Josh, 125–26

Hutson, Don, 197

I

"i"-dotters, 88, 106

Illibuck Trophy, the, 46

Indiana University Hoosiers, 21, 116, 134, 144

International News Service, 18, 169

Iowa State University Cyclones, 61, 63, 80

Iowa State University, 80–81, 91

Isaac, Clancy, 107

Ithaca Conservatory, 79

J

Jackson, Keith, 84

Janowicz, Vic, xi, 75, 111, 115, 131–33, 182, 260, 262–63, 265

Jessel, George, 79

Jobko, Bill, 148

John Carroll University, 77, 176

Jones, C. Rollins, 8

Jones, Gomer, 76–77, 79, 176

Jones, Howard, 52

Jones, Jesse, 9, 162

K

Kansas University Jayhawks, 114,

Karch, Robert, 30, 171

Karsatos, Jim, 118

Kennedy, Arthur, 9

Kenyon College, 6, 11, 15, 17, 50, 168

Kern, Rex, 63, 105, 153–55, 186, 237

Keyes, Leroy, 142

Kiefer, Arthur, 21

Kinnear Manufacturing Co., 22

Kittle, James "Boss," 13–14, 16, 164

Knight, Bobby, 66

Krause, Anne, 45

Kremblas, Frank, 148

Krenzel, Craig, xi, 121–22, 158

L

Large, Joseph H., 9

Larkins, Richard, 53, 69, 73, 75, 113, 259–60, 264

"Le Régiment de Sambre et Meuse," 108

LeBeau, Dick, 117, 148

Lilley, Alexander S., 5–9, 49–50

Lincoln, Paul M., 10, 168

Loew's Ohio Theatre, 106

Louis, Joe "The Brown Bomber," 56

Lucas, Jerry, 131

M

Mangold, Nick, 124

Marciano, Rocky, 134

Marietta College, 15–17, 162

Marquardt, Bill, 51, 165

Marshall, Jim, 148, 184

Mather, Chuck, 69

May Day, 8

McCoys, The, 108

McDonald, Clarence, 34

McLendon, T. J., 122

McMillin, Alvin Nugent "Bo," 144

Means, Dr. Jack, 19

Medics, the, 15, 17

Men's Glee Club (OSU), 16, 109

Miami University (OH), 68, 75, 90

Mid-American Conference, 58, 68

Miller, Jim, 116

Miller, Ryan, 121

Millner, Wayne, 114

Minnesota Vikings, 21, 28, 58, 73, 103, 146–48, 150–51, 154, 184, 201, 264, 278
Mitchell, Bobby, 148
Morrey, Charles, 9–10
Morrill Tower, 111
Morris, Clyde, 96
Mount Union College Purple Raiders, 113
Mount Union College, 58, 113
Muncie, Chuck, 138
Muskingum College, 15, 17, 164
Myers, Cyril "Truck," 38, 43, 175, 251

N

National Football League (NFL), 30, 58, 69, 77, 133, 138–39, 142, 148, 157, 175–76, 181, 183–84, 197–99
National Hospital for Diseases of the Heart, 45
National Register of Historic Places, 7
Navy, 114, 241
NCAA, 5, 39, 63, 97, 101, 118, 136, 138, 147, 157, 160, 180, 238, 240, 250, 268
New York Mets, 148
NFL draft, 136, 156, 177, 187, 193, 201, 204, 206
NFL Films, 223
Nicklaus, Jack, 108, 131
Nittany Lions, the, 61
Nixon, Richard, 92, 117, 156
North Carolina (UNC), 136
North Carolina State, 121
"North Dorm," 2
Northern Arizona University, 45
Northwestern University Wildcats, 21, 29–30, 38, 42, 114, 146, 154, 172, 260, 263
Northwestern University, 21, 29–30, 38, 42, 114, 146, 154, 172, 260, 163, 176, 286
Norton, Fred, 28

O

Oberlin College, 14–18, 21, 28, 38, 50, 122, 162, 164, 168

Ohio Agricultural and Mechanical College (Ohio A&M College), 2
Ohio Conference, 25, 27, 30
Ohio Field, 6, 13, 16, 19, 27–28, 30, 33–34, 95–96, 175
Ohio General Assembly, 108
Ohio High School Coaches Association, 69
Ohio legislature, 2
Ohio Medical. 15, 17, 50, 52
Ohio National Guard, 32
Ohio Stadium, 92, 97–98, 101–2, 107–9, 111, 117–18, 120–22, 131, 146, 156, 162, 169, 172, 175, 210, 214, 218–19, 233, 238, 243, 248, 256–58, 260, 265, 277, 280
Ohio State Alumni Association, 9, 138
Ohio State Athletics, 3
Ohio State Journal, 25, 32
Ohio State Marching Band, 102, 108, 223
Ohio State Monthly, 33
Ohio University, 13, 58, 122, 164
Ohio Wesleyan, 3–5, 7–9, 16, 19–20
Oklahoma State, 231
"Old Hickory," 8
Olentangy River, 2, 6–7, 34, 38, 97–98
Orange Bowl, the, 83
Oregon State University, 231
OSU Student Council, 39
Otis, Jim, xiv, 145, 153, 155, 236
Otterbein College, 11, 13, 18, 164
Oval, the, 96
Owen Stadium, 79
Owens, Jesse, 131
Oxley Hall, 2

P

Palau Islands, 61, 67
Pantheon, the, 98
Park, Jack, 28, 82, 146, 260, 267
Parseghian, Ara, 61
Paterno, Joe, 61

Pearl Harbor, 80
Penn State, 61, 101, 122, 192
Percussion Cheers, 102
Phi Gamma Delta (fraternity), 27
Pickerel, Lou, 21
Pino, David, 124–26
Pittman, Antonio, 125, 278–79, 281, 284, 286
Pittman, Billy, 124
Pittsburgh Panthers, the, 72, 115, 118
Pittsburgh Pirates, 133
Pittsburgh Steelers, 148, 207
Plank's Café, 119
Pollard, Dr. James E., 3
Princeton University, 2, 5, 8, 43, 50, 58, 72
Pro Football Hall of Fame, 30, 187
Provost, Ted, xiv, 153
Purdue University, 33, 142, 146, 153, 156

Q
Quinn, Brady, 142, 279

R
ramp cadences, 105
Reed, Kerry, 103
Richards, John R., 18, 53
Rivers, Philip, 121–22
Rockne, Knute, 36, 42, 45–47
Rogers, Tom, 67
Rose Bowl, the, x, xiv, 10, 39, 52–53, 68, 73, 81, 83, 111,
    127, 134, 136, 138, 146–52, 154, 156, 169, 172, 175,
    188, 190, 193–94, 201, 232, 235–36, 238–40, 246, 248,
    263, 267, 271, 272, 274–77
Rote, Kyle, 133
Rothgeb, Carl, 18
Rupp, N. G., 21
Rutgers, 2
Ryder, Jack, 6, 10–11, 50, 272

S
Saban, Lou, 144
Salad Bowl, the, 68
Salley, Nate, 126
Savoca, Jim, 86
Sawicki, Tom, 86
Sayers, D. B. "Del", 14–16, 161
Schafrath, Dick, 148
Schlegel, Anthony, 126
Schlichter, Art, 83–87, 91, 118, 190, 197, 239–41
Schmidt, Francis, 39, 56, 76–77, 177, 254–59, 272, 286
Schommer, John, 18
School of Architecture (OSU), 98
Script Ohio, 88, 92, 106–7, 114
Segrist, John, 6, 16
Shakespeare, Bill, 114
Simpson, O. J., xiv, 142, 154, 236
Sims, Rob, 123
Skladany, Tom, 23, 115, 193, 195, 269–70, 274
Skull Session, 102, 219
Sloopy, xiv, 108
Smith, Howard D., 98–99
Smith, Troy, xi, 111, 124, 141, 143, 176, 204, 212, 248,
    272, 277–78
Snow Bowl, the, 58, 68, 70, 73, 133, 258, 259–65
Snyder, Charles, 21
Soccer, 8
Sooners, 77
Sophocles, 92
Southern Methodist University (SMU), 133, 193
Spangler, Rich, 119
Spaulding Athletic Supply Co., 49
Spaulding, A. G., 5
Spielman, Chris, xi, 119, 194, 197, 225–26
Split T (formation), 75–77
Sporting News, 142
Springs, Ron, 84–87, 193
Springs, Shawn, 243, 246

Squier, George, 21
St. John Arena, 102, 274
St. John, Lynn W., 18–20, 46, 53, 75, 96, 99, 114
St. Louis Browns, 34
Stagg Award, 45
Stagg, Amos Alonzo, 18, 27, 36, 42, 45
Stebbins, Harold, 115
Stillwagon, Jim, xiv, 153–56, 186–87
Stinchcomb, Gaylord "Pete," 25–26, 30, 37–41, 43, 172, 251–53
Stuckey, Jim, 84
Sugar Bowl, the, 83
Super Bowl, the, 138, 148, 207
Super Sophs, 10, 188, 238
Sutherin, Don, 148
Sweed, Limas, 126
Sweetland, E. R., 51
Syzmanski, Dick, 70

T
Tarbill, John, 13
Tatgenhorst, John, 108
Tatum, Jack, xiv, 23, 96, 153–56, 186, 189, 232
Taylor, Fred, xi
Taylor, Ramonce, 123
Taylor, Sean, 157
Tennessee Titans, 139
Texas Christian University (TCU), 235, 255
Texas Christian University Horned Frogs, 147
Thanksgiving, 15–17, 32, 167, 268, 279
The Best Damn Band In The Land (TBDBITL), x, xiv, 105, 106, 108, 221
The Buckeyes, 26
The Florida Times-Union, 82
The House That Harley Built," 34, 95–126
"The Old Gray Lady of the Olentangy," 111
The War Song, 79
Thomas, Aurelius, 148, 150, 183, 185

Thompson, William Oxley, 2, 98, 113
Thorpe, Jim, 25, 53, 199
"three yards and a cloud of dust," 76–78
Thurber, James, 25–26
Tigers (Clemson), 82–89
Tigers (Princeton), 2, 5, 8, 43, 49, 50, 68, 72
Trapasso, A. J., 124, 126
Tressel, Jim, xiv, 17, 62–63, 102, 109, 123, 141, 160, 209, 213–14, 236, 247–48, 272, 278
Tressel, Lee, 63
Trojans (USC), xiv, 142, 154, 190, 194, 236, 277
Trombone Cheers, 102
Trumpet Cheers, 102
Tuba-Fours, 102
Tunnel of Pride, 105–6, 243

U
U.S. Marine Corps, 130
Union Cemetery, 36
United Press International, 18, 150, 156, 169
University of Chicago Maroons, 27
University of Chicago, 18, 27
University of Cincinnati, 16, 50
University of Illinois Fighting Illini, 20, 28, 32, 34, 38, 118, 139, 146
University of Iowa Hawkeyes, 52, 117, 119
University of Kansas School of Medicine, 188
University of Kentucky Wildcats, 30, 33, 114, 162, 250
University of Miami (FL) Hurricanes, 121, 157, 206, 225
University of Michigan Wolverines, 33, 42, 51–52, 56, 58, 63, 68, 70, 72–77, 83, 95, 99, 101, 105–6, 108–9, 116, 122, 133, 141–42, 144–47, 150–52, 154–57, 165–69, 174–75, 179, 181, 184, 187–88, 193, 202, 204, 217–22, 226, 231–86
University of Nebraska, 61, 122, 139, 156, 254,
University of Notre Dame, 46, 56, 70, 77, 101, 108, 114, 119, 121, 122, 139, 141–42, 199
University of Oklahoma, 63, 77–78, 131, 176, 230

Squier, George, 21
St. John Arena, 102, 274
St. John, Lynn W., 18–20, 46, 53, 75, 96, 99, 114
St. Louis Browns, 34
Stagg Award, 45
Stagg, Amos Alonzo, 18, 27, 36, 42, 45
Stebbins, Harold, 115
Stillwagon, Jim, xiv, 153–56, 186–87
Stinchcomb, Gaylord "Pete," 25–26, 30, 37–41, 43, 172, 251–53
Stuckey, Jim, 84
Sugar Bowl, the, 83
Super Bowl, the, 138, 148, 207
Super Sophs, 10, 188, 238
Sutherin, Don, 148
Sweed, Limas, 126
Sweetland, E. R., 51
Syzmanski, Dick, 70

T
Tarbill, John, 13
Tatgenhorst, John, 108
Tatum, Jack, xiv, 23, 96, 153–56, 186, 189, 232
Taylor, Fred, xi
Taylor, Ramonce, 123
Taylor, Sean, 157
Tennessee Titans, 139
Texas Christian University (TCU), 235, 255
Texas Christian University Horned Frogs, 147
Thanksgiving, 15–17, 32, 167, 268, 279
The Best Damn Band In The Land (TBDBITL), x, xiv, 105, 106, 108, 221
The Buckeyes, 26
The Florida Times-Union, 82
The House That Harley Built," 34, 95–126
"The Old Gray Lady of the Olentangy," 111
The War Song, 79
Thomas, Aurelius, 148, 150, 183, 185

Thompson, William Oxley, 2, 98, 113
Thorpe, Jim, 25, 53, 199
"three yards and a cloud of dust," 76–78
Thurber, James, 25–26
Tigers (Clemson), 82–89
Tigers (Princeton), 2, 5, 8, 43, 49, 50, 68, 72
Trapasso, A. J., 124, 126
Tressel, Jim, xiv, 17, 62–63, 102, 109, 123, 141, 160, 209, 213–14, 236, 247–48, 272, 278
Tressel, Lee, 63
Trojans (USC), xiv, 142, 154, 190, 194, 236, 277
Trombone Cheers, 102
Trumpet Cheers, 102
Tuba-Fours, 102
Tunnel of Pride, 105–6, 243

U
U.S. Marine Corps, 130
Union Cemetery, 36
United Press International, 18, 150, 156, 169
University of Chicago Maroons, 27
University of Chicago, 18, 27
University of Cincinnati, 16, 50
University of Illinois Fighting Illini, 20, 28, 32, 34, 38, 118, 139, 146
University of Iowa Hawkeyes, 52, 117, 119
University of Kansas School of Medicine, 188
University of Kentucky Wildcats, 30, 33, 114, 162, 250
University of Miami (FL) Hurricanes, 121, 157, 206, 225
University of Michigan Wolverines, 33, 42, 51–52, 56, 58, 63, 68, 70, 72–77, 83, 95, 99, 101, 105–6, 108–9, 116, 122, 133, 141–42, 144–47, 150–52, 154–57, 165–69, 174–75, 179, 181, 184, 187–88, 193, 202, 204, 217–22, 226, 231–86
University of Nebraska, 61, 122, 139, 156, 254,
University of Notre Dame, 46, 56, 70, 77, 101, 108, 114, 119, 121, 122, 139, 141–42, 199
University of Oklahoma, 63, 77–78, 131, 176, 230

Pearl Harbor, 80
Penn State, 61, 101, 122, 192
Percussion Cheers, 102
Phi Gamma Delta (fraternity), 27
Pickerel, Lou, 21
Pino, David, 124–26
Pittman, Antonio, 125, 278–79, 281, 284, 286
Pittman, Billy, 124
Pittsburgh Panthers, the, 72, 115, 118
Pittsburgh Pirates, 133
Pittsburgh Steelers, 148, 207
Plank's Café, 119
Pollard, Dr. James E., 3
Princeton University, 2, 5, 8, 43, 50, 58, 72
Pro Football Hall of Fame, 30, 187
Provost, Ted, xiv, 153
Purdue University, 33, 142, 146, 153, 156

Q

Quinn, Brady, 142, 279

R

ramp cadences, 105
Reed, Kerry, 103
Richards, John R., 18, 53
Rivers, Philip, 121–22
Rockne, Knute, 36, 42, 45–47
Rogers, Tom, 67
Rose Bowl, the, x, xiv, 10, 39, 52–53, 68, 73, 81, 83, 111,
    127, 134, 136, 138, 146–52, 154, 156, 169, 172, 175,
    188, 190, 193–94, 201, 232, 235–36, 238–40, 246, 248,
    263, 267, 271, 272, 274–77
Rote, Kyle, 133
Rothgeb, Carl, 18
Rupp, N. G., 21
Rutgers, 2
Ryder, Jack, 6, 10–11, 50, 272

S

Saban, Lou, 144
Salad Bowl, the, 68
Salley, Nate, 126
Savoca, Jim, 86
Sawicki, Tom, 86
Sayers, D. B. "Del", 14–16, 161
Schafrath, Dick, 148
Schlegel, Anthony, 126
Schlichter, Art, 83–87, 91, 118, 190, 197, 239–41
Schmidt, Francis, 39, 56, 76–77, 177, 254–59, 272, 286
Schommer, John, 18
School of Architecture (OSU), 98
Script Ohio, 88, 92, 106–7, 114
Segrist, John, 6, 16
Shakespeare, Bill, 114
Simpson, O. J., xiv, 142, 154, 236
Sims, Rob, 123
Skladany, Tom, 23, 115, 193, 195, 269–70, 274
Skull Session, 102, 219
Sloopy, xiv, 108
Smith, Howard D., 98–99
Smith, Troy, xi, 111, 124, 141, 143, 176, 204, 212, 248,
    272, 277–78
Snow Bowl, the, 58, 68, 70, 73, 133, 258, 259–65
Snyder, Charles, 21
Soccer, 8
Sooners, 77
Sophocles, 92
Southern Methodist University (SMU), 133, 193
Spangler, Rich, 119
Spaulding Athletic Supply Co., 49
Spaulding, A. G., 5
Spielman, Chris, xi, 119, 194, 197, 225–26
Split T (formation), 75–77
Sporting News, 142
Springs, Ron, 84–87, 193
Springs, Shawn, 243, 246

University of Oregon, 147–48, 231

University of Pittsburgh, 108, 114–15, 118, 120, 133, 144, 146, 182, 231, 275

University of Texas Longhorns, 20, 122, 123–26, 156, 248

University of Wisconsin, 18, 20, 28, 32–33, 38, 41, 43, 53, 92, 114, 116, 134, 144, 146, 150–51, 154, 206, 212, 214–16, 263, 274

USC (Southern California), xiv, 142, 154, 190, 194, 236, 277

USS Rinehart, 61, 67–68

V

Vanderbilt, 20, 167

VanDyne, Kelley, 30, 33

Vaughn, Harry, 52, 241

Veterans Administration Hospital, 36

Vibrations, The, 108

Victory Bell, 109

Vorys, John, 26

Vrabel, Mike, 121

W

Warner, Glenn "Pop," 36, 42, 113

Washington Redskins, 133

Weigel, Eugene L., 106, 115

Wendt, Merle, 115, 177, 257

Western Conference, 5–6, 17–18, 20–21, 26, 28–30, 38, 41–42, 56, 72, 76, 95–96, 169, 171, 174–75, 251, 257, 263

Western Reserve, 15–7, 47, 51, 168, 272

Westwater, James, 13–6, 164

White, Bob, 183–84

White, William, 198

Whitner, Donte, 126

Whittier Street, 6

Widdoes, Carroll C., 56–58, 128

Wilce Jr., Dr. James M., 45

Wilce, John W., 18, 21, 27, 36, 41–45, 46, 53, 171, 174, 250, 252, 254

Wilkinson, Bud, 76

Willaman, Sam, 46–47, 53, 58, 72, 76, 113, 171, 255

Williams College, 50

Wilson, C. R., 15

Wilson, Dave, 118

Wilson, Kenneth L. "Tug," 259

Wilson, Lawrence, 286

"Wipeout," 102

Withington, Paul, 28

Wittenberg University, 13, 66

WMCA, 79

Wolfpack, 121

Wooldridge, John, 119

Workman, Harry "Hoge," 38, 43, 174

World War I, 6, 38, 250

World War II, 58, 67–69, 223

Y

Yale Bowl, 98

Yale, 2, 18, 51–52, 98, 122

Yeomen, 14

Yerges, Howard, 30

Yost, B. F., 13–14, 164

Yost, Fielding, 27, 50, 251–56, 275

You Win With People, 86

Youboty, Ashton, 126

Young, Selvin, 125

Youngstown State, 63, 160

Z

Zuppke, Bob, 20, 27–28

Zwick, Justin, 124–26, 141, 204